The Neurobiology of Affect in Language

John H. Schumann
University of California, Los Angeles

©1997 Language Learning Research Club, University of Michigan

Blackwell Publishers, Inc.
350 Main Street
Malden, MA 02148 USA

Blackwell Publishers, Ltd.
108 Cowley Road
Oxford OX4 1JF
United Kingdom

0-63121-010-5
A CIP catalog record for this book is available
from the Library of Congress

To Beth

for the listening and the love

Contents

Series Editor's Foreword

One of the currently best-known theories of language acquisition—Universal Grammar—focuses on the similar processes that all learners use to acquire a language, whether it is their second or their first. In contrast, this is a book about differences. It is by now well established that individual second language learners learn at different rates, learn different aspects of the second language, ultimately attain different levels of proficiency, and do so by developing along a variety of different learning pathways. Indeed, there are far fewer similarities among second language learners than there are differences and universal properties of language acquisition are perhaps the rarest of phenomena. Why, then, has so much recent research set out to find the similarities among learners if there are so few and why has not more research focused on the differences, given that there are so many?

The answer to that question must be sought in the nature of theory construction. For decades, now, Universal Grammar has provided a well worked-out, explicitly stated set of propositions about human knowledge of certain syntactic and phonological phenomena. The propositions that together form the theory of Universal Grammar are explicit and the domain of applicability of the theory is all human language. For this reason, second language acquisition researchers have found it to be a powerful heuristic for understanding the phenomena of acquisition.

In contrast, theories that account for the differences among second language learners have been piecemeal. Research on affective variables in language acquisition has not been widely undertaken because of a lack of a consensus among researchers about their research methodology. Research on motivation has resulted in stable findings for learners in some communities that do not hold up when the same methods are applied to learners in a different cultural milieu. Research on variation in second language learners' interlanguage has identified a wide range of factors that contribute to interlanguage variation but, so far, researchers have been unable to integrate those disparate factors into an overarching theory.

Clearly, those researchers who fixate on similarities have until now had a better theory than those who are distracted by differences. But does this mean that our investigations of learner differences should be abandoned? If we did so, we would be like the drunk who, having dropped his house keys in the street one night, insisted on searching for them only in a small area illuminated by a street lamp, not because he had lost his keys there but because it was there that he could see better.

For decades, John Schumann has been exploring in those areas where the light of orthodox linguistics does not shine. And he has been doing so by going outside the accepted "feeder" disciplines of second language acquisition and bringing new theoretical perspectives to bear on the second language acquisition process. His early work comparing SLA with pidginization drew upon pidgin and creole studies; his work on acculturation drew on social identity theory; his work on affective variables developed new methodologies of introspection and narrative self-report to investigate phenomena which many other researchers refused to countenance because they lacked the tools to investigate them.

In his present book, Schumann expands yet again the boundaries of second language acquisition research to bring to bear the rapidly developing body of knowledge of how the brain works in processing, evaluating, recording, and responding to stimuli. For many of us who are untrained in functional neurobiology, such a disciplinary leap will be hard to make, especially given the highly technical nature of the new field. But it repays the effort because it is from the findings of neurobiology that Schumann derives his theory of differences. We now know enough about the brain—in particular about how emotions are inseparably bound up with perception and cognition—that differences in learning trajectories can be accounted for by different patterns of stimulus appraisals throughout the life of the learner.

Every theory needs to be tested. In this book, Schumann tests his theory of stimulus appraisals as an *explanation* for different language learning trajectories by examining learner's biographies, narratives, and learning diaries. According to those learners who have reexamined their language learning experiences from within the stimulus-appraisal framework, the theory passes the test. A much more difficult test awaits us—how to test the theory as a *prediction* of language learning behavior.

This book is the first volume in the *Language Learning Monograph Series*. The object of this series is to advance knowledge in the language sciences by making explicit the connections between language sciences such as SLA and other disciplines. Each volume in the series will be an authoritative statement by a scholar who has led in the development of a particular line of interdisciplinary research and is intended to serve as a benchmark for interdisciplinary research in the years following publication. Schumann's "The Neurobiology of Affect in Language" is in itself a benchmark for the interdisciplinary focus of the series.

Richard Young
University of Wisconsin-Madison

Acknowledgments

I want to thank colleagues and friends—Lou Cozolino, Zoltán Dörnyei, Bob Jacobs, Hans Miller, Regina Pally, Arnold Scheibel, Richard Schmidt, Allan Schore, Dan Siegel, and the many graduate students in Applied Linguistics at UCLA—who provided helpful discussion and commentary on various versions of this book.

I am extremely grateful to Chizu Kanada, Barbara Hilding, Donna Mah, Garold Murray, Mayumi Noguchi, and Susan Rowlands Shrimpton for allowing me to include their language learning autobiographies in this volume. However, I must take responsibility for the interpretations that are presented in the commentaries on their language learning experiences.

I also want to thank Catherine Masaquel and Susanna Chow who typed the manuscript, my assistant, Shannon Cish, who supervised the project, Mila August, who always made sure help was available, and Lyn Repath-Martos, who provided assistance in numerous ways.

Also, many thanks to Richard Young, editor of the *Language Learning Monograph Series,* for inviting me to write the book and providing helpful guidance at every stage, and also to Rebecca Carr, the production editor at Blackwell Publishers, for her patience, guidance and advice, and to Alexander Z. Guiora, who, as general editor and executive director of *Language Learning,* initiated the monograph series with this book as its first publication.

Finally, I want to thank the Conservatory in Culver City for the wonderful coffee and the pleasant place to work.

The research for this book has been supported by a series of grants from the Committee on Research of the Academic Senate of the Los Angeles Division of the University of California.

Introduction

All normal children in monolingual settings acquire the core grammar of their native language by the age of five to seven. Thus, it would appear that the acquisition of grammar is inevitable for all normal first language learners. However, success is never inevitable in second language acquisition. It is generally recognized that if children are exposed to a second language during childhood, they have the ability to acquire both their native language and the second language fully. However, this potential is frequently not realized. In some cases, the second language is rejected or only partially acquired. In other cases, the primary language may be rejected, and only the language of the new environment is learned. In addition, it is known that adolescent and adult learners of a second language vary greatly in the degree of proficiency they achieve. It is important to note that the issue here is not the critical period for second language acquisition, which is supposed to come to a close at puberty. The problem addressed is variability in success both before and after puberty. A critical period may limit one's ultimate achievement in a second language, but the range of achievement in postcritical period learners is enormous, and it is this variability that this book seeks to explain.

It will become clear that I believe that emotion underlies most, if not all cognition, and I will argue that variable success in second language acquisition (SLA) is emotionally driven. Because I also believe that researchers often have a personal stake in the questions they ask and that it is helpful to know the source of the researcher's interest, it is perhaps worthwhile to explain why I am concerned with variable success and why I take the position I do.

In my life, I have pursued the study of three languages—French, Russian, and Persian—and have not come close to mastering any of them. In fact, I might fairly be considered low-intermediate to intermediate in all three. I studied French for two years in high school and did very well. My mother had been a French major and was very enthusiastic about French language and culture. This attitude influenced me, and I planned to major in French in college. However, during freshman orientation, the director of the university's Russian Institute gave a talk on the value of knowing Russian, and I decided to study that language instead, thinking that perhaps I could minor in French. But the university was Jesuit and we were required to take 36 units of philosophy and 16 units of theology so these subjects became virtual minors, and I found it impossible to continue French. I received a BA in Russian studies and stayed another year and completed an MA in Russian language and linguistics. But after those five years of study, I realized that even though I had done extremely well in my Russian classes, I did not know the language. I had applied to both the Peace Corps and to several doctoral programs in Russian. I was admitted to Berkeley and also received an invitation from the Peace Corps to go to Iran. I chose the latter. In Iran I acquired a working knowledge of spoken Persian, but never learned to read or write the language. Essentially I learned enough to get by, but because it wasn't clear how the language would be useful after the Peace Corps service, I never learned more than what came effortlessly. I returned to Iran for two months in the mid-1970s to work on a project for UCLA. During that time, and in the Persian course I took before I went, I made substantial efforts to improve my vocabulary, grammar, and reading, but the period was short and I didn't make substantial progress.

After receiving an MA in Russian and having spent two years in Iran, I often wondered why I had not achieved greater proficiency in either language. I knew something about language aptitude because all Peace Corps volunteers were required to take the Modern Language Aptitude Test, and during Peace Corps training we were grouped in language classes according to our scores. I was in one of the middle groups, but at the end of the two years in Iran I spoke Persian better than many of the volunteers who were in the top group. So it was clear that aptitude wasn't everything, but I wasn't sure how important it was or to what extent I might lack it. After two years as a volunteer, I returned to Washington, D.C. and worked for a year at Peace Corps headquarters. Then I returned to Iran for a year and worked as director of the Teaching English as a Foreign Language program. During that time, I read an article by Bernard Spolsky (1989) in *Language Learning,* which showed that motivation played a powerful role in second language acquisition. From that time I was hooked. It seemed to me that it was integrative motivation that controlled second language learning. Successful learners would be those who wanted to get to know, speak with, and perhaps become like speakers of the target language.

Later, I learned about pidgin languages,which are spoken by people who have only very limited and utilitarian contact with target language speakers. These forms of speech are agrammatical and often unsystematic versions of the target language. They facilitate denotative referential communication with target language speakers. Pidgin speakers usually lack either the opportunity or the desire to integrate with the target language community, and therefore seem to provide evidence for the role of integrative motivation in second language proficiency.

After I had begun doctoral work, I undertook a longitudinal study of an adult second language learner who, after more than a year of living in the United States, ended up speaking a reduced and simplified version of English that had many characteristics of pidgin languages. I explained his limited language acquisition as the result of lack of integration with (i.e., exposure to, input from) target language speakers. Essentially, he did not integrate because he was not motivated to do so.

The theoretical position that evolved from this study was called the pidginization hypothesis. A few years later, I expanded that perspective by viewing second language acquisition as the product of acculturation. In this model, the crucial variable was integration (contact) with target language speakers. Such contact could result either from necessity, as through immigration, the desire to integrate with target language speakers, or both. The pidginization and acculturation perspective came to be called the pidginization/acculturation model (McLaughlin, 1987; Schumann, 1978a, 1978b, 1978c, 1978d, 1986).

In this model, the learner is seen as acquiring the second language to the degree he or she acculturates to the target language group. Pidginization refers to the grammatical forms in the speech of the second language learners during the early stages of learning. There are two sets of forces influencing acculturation, one social and one psychological or affective. The social forces are such things as dominance patterns and integration strategies. It is generally the case that in a language contact situation, the group that is politically, culturally, technically, or economically superior (dominant) to the target language group will not acculturate and therefore will not acquire the target language. Groups that are subordinate along the same dimensions may also resist acculturation, but those that are nondominant or roughly equal to the target language group are likely to acculturate well. In terms of integration patterns, the language learning group may choose either a preservation, an adaptation, or an assimilation strategy. In preservation, the group strives to maintain its own lifestyle and values and rejects those of the target language group. With adaptation, the learner group maintains its own lifestyle and values for intragroup use, but adopts the lifestyle and values of the target language group. Finally, in assimilation, the learner group gives up its lifestyle and values and adopts those of the target language group. Assimilation fosters maximum acculturation and thus a high degree of language learning. Preservation is an anti-acculturation strategy and results in a minimal level of language acquisition. Adaptation produces varying degrees of contact with the target language group and therefore varying degrees of acquisition of the target language (Schumann, 1976).

The psychological or affective factors that influence second language learning center around the issues of attitude and motivation (Gardner, 1985). The language learner may value the characteristics of the target language speakers and thus have a positive attitude toward them, leading to contact with members of the target language group and fostering language acquisition. A negative attitude would have just the opposite effect. Motivation is generally viewed as either integrative or instrumental.

Integratively oriented learners are motivated by an interest in the speakers of the target language; instrumentally oriented learners have more utilitarian goals (e.g., getting a job).

In the late 1970s, along with several graduate students, I attempted to measure acculturation and to relate it to proficiency in SLA. This proved to be very difficult. Many of the constructs that comprised acculturation were extremely difficult both to operationalize and to measure. It was also clear that the degree of an individual's acculturation changed over time, but a methodology to measure acculturation longitudinally was not available. In addition, there was no principled means to weigh the various social and psychological components of acculturation. In the mid-1980s, I became interested in the cognitive and neurobiological processes that underlie the social and psychological factors of the pidginization/acculturation model. At this time, I began studying neuroanatomy with the goal of discovering whether there was some mechanism in the brain that allowed emotion to influence (or perhaps even control) cognition. In 1989, I attended the McDonnell Summer Institute in Cognitive Neuroscience at Dartmouth. There I learned that in the temporal lobe there is a structure called the amygdala, which assesses the motivational significance and emotional relevance of stimuli. On the basis of such appraisals, the brain allocates attention and memory resources to various problems, and the variability in such allocations affects learning.

In this book I present a theory of how the psychology and neurobiology of stimulus appraisal influence variability in second language acquisition, and then I extend the notion of affect developed for second language acquisition to primary language acquisition and to cognition in general. Toward that end, I lay out a psychological framework in Chapter 1 that develops the notions of value, emotional memory, and stimulus appraisal. In Chapter 2, I suggest a neurobiological mechanism that would subserve the psychological constructs described in Chapter 1. The neural system consists of the amygdala, the orbitofrontal cortex, the body proper, and the connections among them. In Chapters 3, 4, and 5, I offer evidence for the idea that stimulus appraisal constitutes the affective basis for motivation in second language acquisition (and, indeed, for all sustained deep learning). I do this first in Chapter 3 by showing how questionnaires that are designed to determine a learner's motivation for SLA do so by assessing the learner's appraisal of the language learning situation. I also show how the stimulus appraisal perspective is compatible with recent efforts to understand motivation in SLA in terms of alternative motivational frameworks such as need theories, instrumentality theories, equity theories, self-efficacy theories, and theories of intrinsic motivation. In Chapter 4, I examine introspective diary studies and autobiographies of second language learners and show that they are, in fact, chronicles of the learners' appraisals of the target language, its speakers, their culture, and of the teacher, the method, and the materials. In this chapter, I also show how language learning aptitude influences proficiency and how appraisals of proficiency influence motivation.

In Chapter 5 on the implications of this approach, I suggest that the neurobiological stimulus-appraisal perspective provides a common denominator for all motivation studies—the brain makes stimulus appraisals, and patterns of appraisal constitute motivations. Because SLA takes place over a long period of time (five to eight or more years) and because each individual's stimulus-appraisal system is based on her experience, each individual's affective trajectory in SLA is unique. Finally, I outline some methodological and educational implications of this perspective and examine the question of whether appraisals are cognitive or affective processes.

In Chapter 6, I explore affect in first language acquisition and use. I argue that the affective relationship between caretaker and child forms the basis for first language acquisition. In addition, I argue that the same neural system involved in stimulus appraisal (amygdala, orbitofrontal cortex, body proper) also subserves attachment, affect regulation, and social cognition, and through these functions, it controls decision making in language pragmatics.

The final chapter discusses the role of affect in cognition in general. It shows how emotions frame problems by helping constrain the information that is seen as relevant to them. It also describes the kinds of processing strategies that are fostered by positive and negative affective states. In this chapter, I also examine the idea that logical, scientific thought may have evolved by abstracting categories and concepts from an affectively based social cognition.

1

The Theory

Overview

This chapter presents a theoretical framework for understanding the biological foundations of motivation in SLA. Through evolution all humans inherit two systems of motivation: homeostatic and sociostatic regulation. The brain and the body proper contain mechanisms that control respiration, heart rate, and body temperature as well as hunger, thirst, and sexual desires. These systems, called homeostats, place hedonic value on certain stimuli (Edelman, 1989). In other words, those stimulus situations in the world that allow the organism to maintain homeostatic balance will be valued. Thus, the organism will seek out survival-enhancing conditions that allow it to breathe, feed, stay warm or cool, and maintain an appropriate heart rate.

In addition to regulation by homeostats, organisms are motivated by other inherited systems called sociostats. Sociostats are the innate tendencies of the human organism to seek out interaction with conspecifics (members of the same species). They are the inherited drives for attachment and social affiliation, which are initially directed toward the infant's mother or caregiver and are gradually extended to others in the individual's network of social relations.

These two sets of innate motivational tendencies foster the organism's motor activity in the environment. But in addition to innate homeostatic and sociostatic values, organisms develop highly individual value systems over the course of their lifetimes.

Through experience in the world, individuals accrue idiosyncratic preferences and aversions, which lead them to like certain things and dislike others. These preferences are called somatic value. Organisms seem to determine value on the basis of certain criteria. Research indicates that environmental stimulus situations are assessed according to criteria such as whether they are novel, pleasant, enhancing of one's goals or needs, compatible with one's coping mechanisms, and supportive of one's self and social image (Leventhal & Scherer, 1987).

These appraisal systems assign value to current stimuli based on past experience. Thus stimulus situations are appraised according to the accrued history of an individual's preferences and aversions. The value mechanisms influence the cognition (perception, attention, memory, and action) that is devoted to learning. Since each individual's experience during development differs, each person's appraisal system is different. Because of these motivational differences, the same stimulus situation may be evaluated differently by different people.

The appraisal mechanism guides SLA. It appraises the teacher, method, and syllabus, as well as the target language, its speakers, and the culture in which it is used. Because each appraisal system is different, each second language learner is on a separate motivational trajectory. Consequently, inconsistency across individuals in the measurement of affective factors and SLA proficiency is to be expected. When consistency is found, it is only because groups of people, for cultural reasons, occasionally make similar appraisals about language learning.

Homeostats

Basic biological regulation, that is, homeostatic regulation, provides the value system that guides early motor and somatosensory behavior in the environment. The organism moves in order to maintain homeostasis—to feed, to breathe, to fight, to flee, to procreate, to care for kin, to seek light or darkness, to get warmth or coolness. Movement in the environment under the motivation of basic homeostatic drives brings the organism into contact with an unlabeled world (Edelman 1989, 1992). The organism must provide labels, and it does so by categorizing the components of the environment. But each category is formed on the basis of value.

Categories emerge according to how environmental agents, objects, and events influence the homeostatic value system.

Sociostats

In addition to its regulation by survival-enhancing homeostats, I would like to suggest that behavior is also directed by other inherited systems, which we can call sociostats. Sociostats are the innate tendencies of the human organism to seek out interaction with conspecifics. As mentioned in the overview of the chapter, they are the inherited drives for attachment and social affiliation, which are initially directed toward the infant's mother or caretaker and are gradually extended to others in the individual's network of social relations. As Locke (1992, 1993a) reports, children almost from birth crave visual and vocal contact with their mothers. They prefer their mother's voice to that of another woman. The mother's voice is preferred to the father's voice, and the father's speech is preferred to quiet. Two days after birth, infants show a preference for their mothers' faces. Within the first 36 hours after birth, children can discriminate and imitate happy, sad, and surprised facial expressions. If infants do not find their mothers' faces within their normal visual range, they will expand their gaze to engage other adults in the area.

Infants appear to vocalize to get the attention of others, and they coordinate their vocalization with those of adults. Mothers respond to infant vocalization with referential speech containing adjustments for pitch and duration. These suprasegmental features are important to the infant because they communicate indexical information about the mother's affective state. Mothers, in turn, are also able to infer information about the infant's emotions from their facial expressions and sounds during vocalization. Infants become involved in turn taking because they naturally vocalize in bursts. Their mothers treat the infant's sounds as meaningful and respond between bursts. Turn taking is reinforced by the infant's recognition that, by ceasing vocalization, she will become the recipient of adult speech.

Thus, homeostats and sociostats initiate children's activity in the world. Of course, the two are not independent because the adults who meet the child's sociostatic needs are the same individuals who assure the maintenance of the child's homeostats.

Schore (1994) points out that the mother or caregiver is not just the child's source of food, but she also acts as the primary provider and moderator of the light, sound, pressure, and temperature that impact the infant.

Somatic Value

The notion of value goes beyond that generated by innate homeostats and sociostats. An additional value system, which can be called somatic value, is not inherited, but rather it develops in the lifetime of the organism (Edelman, 1992). At about the age of 10 months, when the child begins to walk, an extension of the sociostatic process called social referencing begins. The toddler wanders away from the mother to explore the nearby environment. After a period of independent movement, the child will glance at the mother who with her eyes, facial expression, and sometimes voice will communicate her feelings about the child's movement and the agents and objects the child may be encountering in the environment. If the mother's expression indicates pleasure, the child will feel safe and the elements in the event will be positively valued. On the other hand, if the mother communicates alarm or concern, the child will read that expression as a negative appraisal, which will be incorporated into his value system. According to Schore (1994), through such interactions the mother teaches the child what to feel about his physical and social environment and what is of interest in that environment. This dyadic social referencing between child and mother promotes the development of the child's value system. As Schore (1994, p. 110) argues, "the emotional communication of social referencing transactions provides access to the mother's appraisal of objects in the animate and inanimate world, and this influences the development of an internalized system in the infant that can appraise the personal and emotional meaning of any particular environmental event." Schore (1994) also points out that the mother's hedonic response to people, objects, and events in the child's environmental situation can, by association, imbue neutral elements in that environment with the same value.

Value continues to develop as the child moves from dyadically entrained appraisals of the environment to nondyadic exploratory-investigatory behavior in her surroundings. As the child experiences the world, stimulus situations that enhance homeostatic and sociostatic regulation will be preferred, and those that frustrate them will receive negative appraisals. Since each individual's experience is different, each biological value system will be impacted differently, and the individual will acquire a set of preferences and aversions, likes and dislikes, that are uniquely his or her own. It is this somatic value that results in our liking some foods and not others; it produces our preferences in music, sports, academic subjects, movies, flowers, colors, clothes, behaviors, and so forth. But all these likes and dislikes are derived from our innate homeostatic and sociostatic value systems. The somatic value system is expanded by associations. In a particular experience, a person may find some element positively rewarding or pleasant. In such situations, other elements of the experience, which had previously been neutral, can acquire the affective valence of the valued element. Damasio (1994) explains, "if a given entity out in the world is a component of a scene in which one *other* component was a 'good' or 'bad' thing . . . the brain may classify the entity for which no value had been innately preset as if it too is valuable, whether or not it is" (p. 117). Then the neutral entity that has acquired somatic value, when it is experienced in the future in association with another neutral item, may result in the novel item receiving a similar value. Thus "the repertoire of things categorized as good or bad grows rapidly, and the ability to detect new good and bad things grows exponentially" (Damasio, 1994, p. 117).

Damasio (1994) also points out that the rules of culture and society also provide humans with regulation that goes beyond biological drives. But when an individual learns these rules, the system they are built on is the system for basic homeostatic and sociostatic regulation. In the same way, an individual's preferences and aversions developed during her lifetime (i.e., somatic value) have their origins in the inherited homeostats and sociostats: "Neural representations [for the rules of society] . . . are inextricably linked to the neural representation of innate regulatory biological processes" (Damasio, 1994, p.125). Damasio argues that the source of social regulation is biological regulation because they are both designed to enhance survival.

Memory for Value

In order for an individual to operate in the world, she needs a memory for the associations that are made between homeostatic, sociostatic, and somatic value and experience. Edelman's extended theory of neuronal group selection offers the concept of value-category memory to address this issue. He argues that in the brain there are two sets of circuits involved in memory for value. The first responds to internal signals based on homeostatic, sociostatic, and acquired somatic value. The second responds to stimuli from the world. In Edelman's terms, the internal signals represent the self and the world signals represent the non-self. The two sets of signals are correlated in the brain as the internal system appraises hedonic value of external stimuli. The association is then stored in what Edelman (1989, 1992) calls value-category memory, which is reentrantly connected with parts of the brain that make the correlation between self-signals and the world signals. This allows the value-memory system to be updated and modified on the basis of experience with the new stimuli. However, whereas the signals from the world vary widely and change rapidly, the internal signals from the homeostatic, sociostatic, and somatic system are slow to alter, and therefore, value-category memory remains fairly constant over time, producing an individual with a relatively stable set of preferences and aversions. The system is depicted in Figure 1.1.

A similar conceptualization of memory is provided in Leventhal's (1984) perceptual-motor theory of emotion. Leventhal describes what he calls schematic emotional memory on which schemata are formed as analog memories of emotional experiences. For example, the affective aspects of parental interactions with infants, such as smiles, frowns, and vocalizations, are stored in the child's memory along with the memory of the emotional experience accompanying these events (Leventhal, 1984). This continues as the child grows; memory develops for the experiences and the emotions associated with them. The schematic emotional memory provides an automatic appraisal of new stimulus events on the basis of past experience with similar situations. Such appraisals, which are often outside of consciousness, shape the perception of events by coding the situational input into the emotional schemata themselves. Thus, previous

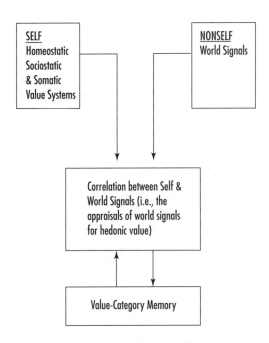

Figure 1.1. The Role of Value-Category Memory in Mediating the Correlation of Self and World Signals (based on Edelman 1992, p. 120).

experiences with noxious or pleasant stimuli are recorded in the schemata, and then act as a filter allowing the organism to focus attention on and generate expectations about subsequent experiences. The salient or modal emotional characteristics of episodes produce prototypes, which allow the schemata to generalize emotional experience. Thus, prototypes can then generate automatic and nonconscious affective attributions about environmental events, agents, and objects. Finally, emotional schemata foster the development of positive and negative attitudes and attachments and aversions which, when imbued with substantial emotional involvement, can be very difficult to alter.

We might propose then that Edelman's notion of special value-category memory corresponds to Leventhal's schematic emotional memory. Value-category memory (and schematic emotional memory) derive from past experience and place value on current correlations of self and non-self signals. This process can be viewed as a mechanism for stimulus appraisal that enables an individual to distinguish between the stimuli that are important and those that are irrelevant. The next question to ask is what criteria does the organism use to place value on current world stimuli.

Models of Stimulus Appraisal

In the 1980s a number of researchers independently began to explore the dimensions of stimulus appraisal in relation to emotional experience. They wanted to determine what sorts of assessments or evaluations of stimulus situations led to various emotions. In other words, they wanted to know the judgments people made about both internal and external stimuli that led to feelings of joy, sadness, happiness, interest, anger, fear, guilt, shame, contempt, disgust, and so forth. In this section, we will examine several models of stimulus appraisal to see possible dimensions along which the biological appraisal may operate. Our ultimate purpose, however, is not to determine which appraisals lead to which emotions, but to explore how stimulus appraisals generate mental activity that enhances or inhibits learning. Thus in this section, we will examine the appraisal dimensions that have been proposed with the assumption that such appraisals reflect the homeostatic, sociostatic, and somatic value represented in schematic emotional/value-category memory. The research will be reviewed to provide a sense of how it was done and what the results were. The two important issues are (a) that emotional reactions influence the attention and effort devoted to learning, and (b) that patterns of appraisal may underlie what has been considered motivation in SLA.

The first psychological model of stimulus appraisal to be considered was developed by Klaus Scherer (1984). He identifies five stimulus evaluation checks: novelty, intrinsic pleasantness, goal/need significance, coping potential, and norm/self compatibility. The novelty check assesses whether internal or external stimulation contains novel or unexpected patterns. An assessment of intrinsic pleasantness determines whether an event is pleasant and thus fosters approach, or whether it is unpleasant and thus promotes avoidance. The goal/need significance check assesses (1) the relevance of the event to the individual's needs and goals (relevance subcheck), (2) the status of the event in relation to what to expect at the current stage in a goal/plan sequence (expectations subcheck), (3) the degree to which the stimulus event is conducive to satisfying the individual's needs or achieving his goals (conduciveness subcheck), and how urgently a response may be required (urgency subcheck). The coping potential check determines (1) the cause of the stimulus event (causation subcheck), (2) the individual's ability to cope with the event (control subcheck), (3) the individual's ability to avoid or change the outcome of the stimulus event (power subcheck), and (4) the ability of the individual to psychologically adjust to the outcome (adjustment subcheck). Finally, the norm/self compatibility check assesses the compatibility of the event with social or cultural norms, or with the expectations of significant others (external standards subcheck).

Scherer's ideas about the antecedents of emotional experience were generated in work he was doing on emotional expression in aggression and conflict. He noted that an appraisal of intrinsic pleasantness was usually an antecedent of a positive or negative emotional dimension, that an activity dimension was preceded by an appraisal of the match between goal expectations and the actual state achieved, and that a potency dimension followed on an assessment of how well an organism could cope with the stimulus situation and its consequences. To these appraisals he added a novelty check to account for startle responses and surprise, and a self/norm compatibility check to account for emotions such as pride, guilt, and shame (Scherer, 1984).

Gehm & Scherer (1988) report research examining the relationship between Scherer's stimulus evaluation checks and the experience of various emotions. This research was part of a larger and multinational project studying several facets of emotional experience. The subjects were 2,235 students between 18 and 35 years of age from 27 countries. The subjects filled out a two-page, closed-answer questionnaire for each of seven different emotions (joy, sadness, fear, anger, disgust, shame, and guilt). The questionnaires were written in the native languages of the subjects. The questions were used to elicit information about antecedent appraisals of the emotional situation and are listed in Table 1.1.

Table 1.1

Questions Eliciting Appraisals of Emotional Situations (from Gehm & Scherer, 1988, p. 65)

Check I: Novelty Check

Now please think back to the situation or event that caused you emotion. Did you *expect* this situation to occur?
1.) not at all   2.) a little   3.) very much   0.) not applicable

Check II: Intrinsic Pleasantness Check

Did you find the event itself *pleasant or unpleasant?*
1.) pleasant   2.) neutral   3.) unpleasant   0.) not applicable

Check III: Goal/Need Significance Check

How important was the event for your *goals, needs or desires at the time it happened?* Did it *help* or *hinder* you to follow your plans or to achieve your aims?
1.) it helped   2.) it didn't matter   3.) it hindered   0.) not applicable

Check IV: Coping Potential Check

How did you evaluate your *ability to act on or to cope with the event and its consequences* when you were first confronted with the situation? Check one, the most appropriate, of the following:
1. I did not think that any action was necessary.
2. I believed that I could positively influence the event and change the consequences.
3. I believed that I could escape from the situation or avoid negative consequences.
4. I pretended that nothing important had happened and tried to think of something else.
5. I saw myself as powerless and dominated by the event and its consequences.

Check V: Norm/Self Compatibility Check

Subcheck a: Compatibility with external standards
If the event was caused by your own or someone else's behavior, would this behavior itself be judged as *improper* or *immoral* by your acquaintances?
1.) not at all   2.) a little   3.) very much   0.) not applicable

Table 1.1 (continued)

Subcheck b: Compatibility with internal standards

How did this event affect your *feelings about yourself*, such as your *self-esteem* or your *self-confidence*?

1.) negatively	2.) not at all	3.) positively	0.) not applicable

The researchers found that appraisals of novelty were particularly relevant to the emotions of fear and anger triggered by the sudden onset of an event. Appraisals of pleasantness were problematic. They were strongly associated with the emotion of joy. However, the researchers are cautious about this result because they question the respondents' ability to distinguish, in such self-reports, the pleasantness of the antecedent event from the pleasantness of the emotional response. Such a distinction is not important for our purposes because we are concerned with how appraisals or appraisals and their emotional responses lead to behaviors (both mental and motor) that produce language learning. Events that were appraised as helping individuals reach their goals were associated with joy, and those hindering goal-achievement were associated with anger. In terms of appraisals of coping potential, the response "I did not think that any action was necessary" was related to disgust; "I believed that I could positively influence the event and change the consequences" was associated with anger and guilt; "I believed that I could escape from the situation or avoid negative consequences" was related to fear, disgust, shame, and guilt; "I pretended that nothing important had happened and tried to think of something else" was associated with disgust and shame; and "I saw myself as powerless and dominated by the event and its consequences" was related to fear, sadness, and disgust. The norm/self compatibility appraisals were especially relevant to shame and guilt, but also to anger and disgust in relation to the external standards criterion.

Another way Scherer (1993) tested his dimensions of stimulus appraisal was through computer simulations. He devised a computer program with a knowledge base containing predictions about which emotions would result from various stimulus evaluation checks (SECs) (i.e., novelty, pleasantness, goal significance, coping potential, and self/norm compatibility). Subjects were asked to recall emotional situations and the computer asked the subjects questions about antecedents of their situations on the basis of the SECs. For example, with regard to intrinsic pleasantness, the computer asked:

> This type of event, independent of your personal evaluation, would it be generally considered as pleasant or unpleasant? (Scherer, 1993, p. 336)

The subjects indicated their answers on a five point scale: (0) not pertinent, (1) very unpleasant, (2) rather unpleasant, (3) indifferent, (4) rather pleasant, (5) very pleasant. With regard to goal relevance, subjects were asked:

> Was the event relevant for your general well-being, for urgent needs you felt, or for specific goals or plans you were pursuing at the time? (Scherer, 1993, p. 336)

The subjects responded: (0) not pertinent, (1) not at all, (2) a little, (3) moderately, (4) strongly, (5) extremely. To evaluate the power aspect of coping potential, the computer asked the subjects:

> Did you feel that you had enough power to cope with the event—i.e., being able to influence what was happening or to modify the consequences? (Scherer, 1993, p. 337)

The reply was given by indicating: (0) not pertinent, (1) not at all, (2) a little, (3) moderately, (4) strongly, (5) extremely. Finally the subjects were asked to indicate the intensity with which the emotion was felt on a 6-point scale ranging from very weak to extremely strong. The computer then presented the subject with a label for the emotion he or she had experienced, and the subject indicated whether or not it was correct. Scherer reported that the computer program generated an accuracy rate ranging between 65% and 80% depending on the analysis used, and observed: "In view of the fact that with 14 emotion alternatives one would expect 7.14% accuracy if the system operated on chance level, this result seems quite respectable" (p. 347).

Smith and Ellsworth (1985) proposed a stimulus evaluation system composed of eight dimensions of appraisal, which they believed were important in distinguishing among emotions. They defined these dimensions as follows:

(a) pleasantness—the extent to which the situation is perceived as being pleasant or unpleasant;

(b) anticipated effort—the extent to which the person feels a need to expend effort (either physical or mental) in the situation;

(c) attentional activity—the extent to which the person wants to attend to or to shut out the situation;

(d) certainty—the extent to which the person understands or is sure of what is happening or is going to happen in the situation;

(e) responsibility—who or what the person perceives as having brought about the situation—either oneself, or someone or something else;

(f) control—who or what the person perceives as currently being in control of the situation—oneself, some other human(s), or uncontrollable circumstances;

(g) legitimacy—the extent to which the situation is perceived as being fair or unfair; and

(h) perceived obstacle—the extent to which the person perceives problems or obstacles in the situation that are hampering the attainment of a desired goal.

(Smith & Ellsworth, 1987, pp. 475–476).

To test this model the researchers asked subjects to describe past emotional experiences related to 15 different emotions (happiness, sadness, fear, anger, boredom, challenge, interest, hope, frustration, contempt, disgust, surprise, pride, shame, and guilt) and then to answer questions about the experience on 11-point scales. For example, with regard to pleasantness associated with the experience of happiness the subjects were asked:

(Pleasant) How pleasant or unpleasant was it to be in this situation?

(Enjoy) How enjoyable or unenjoyable was it to be in this situation?

(Smith et al., 1985, p. 822).

With regard to perceived obstacle, they were asked:

(Problem) Think about what you wanted when you felt happy in this situation. While you were feeling happy, to what extent did you feel there were problems that had to be solved before you could get what you wanted?

(Obstacle) Think about what you wanted when you felt happy in this situation. When you were feeling happy, to what extent did you feel there were obstacles standing in the path between you and getting what you wanted?

(Smith et al., 1985, p. 822).

To evaluate the control dimension, the subjects responded to:

(Situation-Control) When you were feeling happy, to what extent did you feel that circumstances beyond anyone's control were controlling what was happening in this situation?

(Self-Control) When you were feeling happy, to what extent did you feel that you had the ability to influence what was happening in this situation?

(Other-Control) When you were feeling happy, to what extent did you feel that someone other than yourself was controlling the situation?

(Smith et al., 1985, p. 822).

The researchers analyzed these data using a principal components analysis with a varimax rotation and symmetric individual differences multidimensional scaling. These analyses generated a solution consisting of six orthogonal dimensions: pleasantness, anticipated effort, certainty, attentional activity, self-other responsibility/control and situational control (i.e., the extent to which the situation is controlled by circumstances). Of the two remaining dimensions that had been predicted, perceived obstacle was shown to be related to pleasantness, and anticipated effort and legitimacy were associated with pleasantness and human agency.

The experiment reported above relied on self-report of recalled emotional situations. The researchers then wanted to see whether the same dimensions would appear while the subjects were actually experiencing the emotions. Smith and Ellsworth (1987) investigated such on-line appraisals by eliciting reactions from students before a midterm exam and immediately after they had received their grades. At both points the subjects responded to an appraisal questionnaire designed to assess the subjects' appraisals of their current situation and an emotional questionnaire designed to evaluate the subjects' current emotional states.

The appraisal questionnaire was very similar to the one used in Smith and Ellsworth (1985), but it elicited information relevant to the examination. The preexam questionnaire also contained two additional items inquiring about the importance and the anticipated difficulty of the exam. Four additional questions were constructed for the preexam questionnaire. They inquired about how many hours per week the subjects had studied for the test, how well prepared they felt, what their expectations were about how well they would perform, and what grade they expected to receive. On the post feedback questionnaire, the subjects reported their actual grade and their satisfaction with this result. The emotion questionnaire was identical both in the preexam and post feedback situations. The subjects rated on 9-point scales how well 25 emotional adjectives characterized how they felt at that time. The results indicated that the subjects usually experienced blends of two emotions both before the exam and after feedback, but that the patterns of appraisal were very similar to those that were found in Smith and Ellsworth (1985).

Based on earlier research such as Lazarus and Folkman (1984), and Smith and Ellsworth (1985, 1987), Lazarus and Smith (1988) proposed a two-component model for stimulus appraisal. A primary appraisal assesses the relevance of an encounter to the person's well-being. It has two dimensions that determine (1) the degree to which the encounter is relevant to the individual's concerns and goals (motivational relevance), and (2) the degree to which the encounter will promote or hinder the individual's personal goals (motivational congruence). A secondary appraisal assesses the individual's coping resources with regard to the encounter. It has four dimensions. The first involves judgments about who should be blamed for harm or credited for benefit (accountability). The second evaluates the individual's ability to manage the demands and realize the personal commitments of the encounter (problem-focused coping potential). The third assesses the individual's ability to cope with the emotional state that the encounter may generate (emotion-focused coping potential). The fourth determines the possibilities for psychological adjustments to make the encounter motivationally congruent (future expectancy).

Lazarus and Smith (1988) and Smith and Lazarus (1993) make a distinction between knowledge and appraisal. Knowledge is an individual's construal, understanding, or beliefs about the factual nature of the stimulus event—what is happening. Appraisal is the assessment of the personal relevance of this knowledge. It involves judgments about how the stimulus agent, action, or object might be personally harmful or beneficial. Positive emotions are seen as products of appraised benefit and negative emotions as products of appraised harm. In terms of the earlier discussion of value, the appraisal process involves tapping into homeostatic, sociostatic, and somatic values systems. They characterize appraisals in the following way:

> Appraisal is an evaluation of what one's relationship to the environment implies for personal well-being. Each positive emotion is said to be produced by a particular kind of appraised benefit, and each negative emotion by a particular kind of appraised harm. The emotional response is hypothesized to prepare and mobilize the person to cope with the particular appraised harm or benefit in an adaptive manner, that is, to avoid, minimize, or alleviate an appraised harm, or to seek, maximize, or maintain an appraised benefit. Whether a particular set of circumstances is appraised as harmful or beneficial depends, in part, on the person's specific configuration of goals and beliefs. Appraisal thus serves the important mediational role of linking emotional responses to environmental circumstances on the one hand, and personal goals and beliefs on the other. (Smith & Lazarus, 1993, p.234)

Roseman (1984) also presents a framework for understanding the appraisal antecedents of emotion. The perspective developed out of research designed to see what sort of perceptions led to various emotions. About 300 subjects were asked to recall in detail an emotional situation (e.g., anger, fear, love) they had experienced. They were asked to describe the events leading up to the emotional feeling, the manner in which they expressed the emotion, and what followed from the emotional experience. An examination of these reports suggested a framework consisting of five dimensions of appraisal. Roseman tested that formulation (1991), by having 120 college students read stories in which the various appraisals were manipulated. The students then rated how intensively the protagonist may have felt the emotions that were being investigated (joy, relief, hope, warmth-friendliness [liking], pride, distress, sorrow, fear, frustration, coolness-unfriendliness [disliking], anger, regret, and guilt). On the basis of the results of this research, modifications were made in the original appraisal formulation, and the following four-dimension framework was proposed: motivational state, probability, power, and agency. Motivational state appraisals determine whether the stimulus situation is consistent with the individual's motives and thus construed as a rewarding state to be attained (motive-consistent) or whether the stimulus situation is inconsistent with an individual's motives, and therefore construed as an adversive state to be avoided. Probability appraisals assess whether a given outcome is definite (certain) or possible (uncertain). Power appraisals determine whether the individual feels powerful or in control of a negative event (strong) or whether he feels powerless or out of control in relation to a negative event (weak). Appraisals of agency assess whether the stimulus situation is caused by oneself, another person, or by circumstances.

In later research (Roseman, Antoniou, & Jose, 1996) the power dimension was reconceived as an appraisal of control or influence potential that assesses the individual's perceived ability to control or manage motive-inconsistent aspects of an event and thus to contend with the situation rather than to accommodate to it. Based on this research, the investigators also suggested a characterological appraisal, which assesses the problem as intrinsic to the self, another person, or to an object.

Another model of stimulus appraisal developed by Ortony, Clore, and Collins (1988) examines appraisal of the consequences of events, the actions of agents, and aspects of objects. Consequences of events are evaluated according to how they facilitate or interfere with the individual's goals. This evaluation is made in terms of whether the event appears to have desirable (i.e., beneficial) or undesirable (i.e., harmful) outcomes. Actions of agents are evaluated according to moral, behavioral, or performance standards. This evaluation is made in terms of whether the action is viewed as praiseworthy (i.e., upholds valued standards) or blameworthy (i.e., violates valued standards). Aspects of objects are evaluated according to attitudes (including tastes), which are dispositions to like or dislike things. This evaluation is made in terms of the appealingness of an object.

Global variables (sense of reality, proximity, unexpectedness, or arousal) can affect the intensity of emotions resulting from all three appraisal dimensions. An event, agent, or object will generate a more intense emotional experience:

1. if it is perceived as real, rather than just as an imagined possibility or fantasy;
2. if it is perceived as psychologically proximate in terms of space or time;
3. if it is unexpected, i.e., if there was no expectation that the particular event would occur;
4. if it generates or is experienced along with a high level of physiological arousal.

Ortony et al. (1988), also argue that emotions that result from the appraisal of events are influenced by local variables such as likelihood, effort, realization, desirability for other, deservingness, and liking; emotions generated by the appraisal of agents are influenced by local variables such as strength of cognitive unit and expectation-deviation; and emotions produced by appraisals of objects are influenced by a local variable called familiarity. Likelihood refers to the degree of an individual's conviction that a particular event will occur. Effort involves the physical, mental, or material investment an individual makes to achieve or avoid a particular outcome. Realization refers to the degree to which a goal or an anticipated event is accomplished, achieved, or confirmed. Desirability-for-other involves the degree to which an event is seen as desirable in terms of another person's goals. Liking refers to the degree to which one is attracted to or likes the other person whose goals are at issue. Deservingness involves the degree to which one believes another deserves the good or bad things that happen. Strength of unit refers to how much an individual identifies with another agent or an institution which is the source of the event. Expectation-deviation involves judgments about how much an agent's actions uphold or deviate from what is expected of him or her, as someone having a particular role. Finally, familiarity involves the intensity of an affective response one has to an object based on the frequency with which one has been exposed to it.

Ortony et al.'s (1988) account of the appraisals that generate emotion is based on a logical or conceptual analysis. Their book does not report empirical investigation of the implicit predictions in the model, but they outline the kind of research that has informed or would be relevant to their theoretical framework. They consider a valuable source of data to be the intuitions subjects have about what emotions others might experience in various stimulus situations. The authors also suggest an automated diary method in which they have subjects complete a questionnaire administered by a computer that elicits information about emotions, which the subject experienced during the preceding 24-hour period. Such assessment is conducted on a daily basis for periods as long as two months. The researchers also use a technique in which they elicit information about the types and intensity of emotions subjects feel while watching sports events. Such assessments are made periodically during the event. Finally, the authors suggest the development of an artificial intelligence system that would be able to predict what kinds of emotion people would feel in various stimulus situations.

Another appraisal theory is also relevant because it focuses on appraisals of the outcomes of events. Second language learning, which is examined in the first part of this book, involves performance or use of the language at various stages of the learning process. This performance or use can be seen as an outcome that is assessed by the learner's stimulus appraisal system.

Attribution theory (Weiner 1982, 1985, 1986) offers an understanding of how outcomes are appraised in terms of causal attributions. A learner's causal ascription can have several dimensions: locus, stability, and controllability. In terms of the locus dimension, success may be ascribed to an internal cause (e.g., ability or effort) or to an external cause (e.g., task difficulty or problems with other people). With regard to stability, effort would likely be considered unstable because degree of effort can change over time. However, ability would generally be considered a stable cause unlikely to change substantially in the future. In the controllability dimension, effort would generally be regarded as within the learner's control, whereas ability would be seen as uncontrollable. These dimensions are summarized in Table 1.2. The stability of a cause affects the learner's expectations about whether the outcome is likely to be the same in the future or whether it will change. If the learner ascribes his success or lack thereof to ability, a stable cause, a similar outcome will be expected in the future. On the other hand, if the learner makes a causal attribution that is unstable (e.g., effort, mood, or situational variables), future outcomes can be expected to be either the same or different.

Weiner (1985) provides evidence that first, a primary appraisal of success or failure is made and a "primitive" emotion is generated—either happy for success or sad and frustrated for failure. Then on the basis of the causal attributions and their dimensions (locus, stability, controllability), more distinct emotions are generated. These emotional reactions thus "play a role in motivated behavior" (Weiner, 1985, p. 559). Weiner (1982, 1985) reports that pride and self-esteem are generated when a positive outcome is seen as resulting from an internal locus and controllability (self). Thus a learner experiences pride and self-esteem

Table 1.2

Dimensions of Causal Attribution in Relation to Ability and Effort

	LOCUS	STABILITY	CONTROLLABILITY
ABILITY	internal	stable	uncontrollable
EFFORT	internal	unstable	controllable

when successful performance is ascribed to his ability and/or effort. Anger is the emotional reaction when a negative outcome is seen as arbitrarily caused by others (i.e., external locus and controllability). Such an attribution might lead to withdrawal if the source of the anger were seen as stable (e.g., a teacher, a curriculum) or it might be seen as unstable and avoidable in the future and thus be regarded as a temporary impediment. Intuitively, anger might also be self-directed if, in spite of ability or effort, the outcome were negative. Weiner (1985) reports that failure seen as resulting from lack of ability (internal locus and uncontrollable) has been shown to generate shame and may result in withdrawal and motivational inhibition. Finally, hopelessness can result from attributions for negative outcomes in which the cause is seen as stable.

Scherer (1988) presents a comparison of appraisal criteria (see Table 1.3) that have been proposed by several theorists as the antecedents of emotion. Five of them have been discussed above (Ortony, Clore, and Collins, 1988; Roseman, 1984; Scherer, 1984; Smith and Ellsworth, 1985; and Weiner, 1985) and Scherer also includes Frijda (1986) and Solomon (1976). In this comparison, Scherer adds familiarity/strangeness and predictability to his characterization of the novelty dimension. Novelty had initially been seen as essentially an orienting response to unexpected stimuli. In addition, in this formulation, he broadens the dimension of intrinsic pleasantness to include outcome probability, an assessment of the likelihood of a particular positive or negative result in relation to one's goals.

As can be seen from Table 1.3 goal significance and coping potential are elements in six of the seven systems, and aspects of novelty, pleasantness and self/norm compatibility are elements of four out of the seven. Of course, all these researchers were looking for appraisal dimensions that are antecedent to emotional experience. They wanted to see which appraisals resulted in which emotions. Our task here, however, is different. We want to see how appraisals, as products of the language learner's value systems, assess the personal relevance of stimuli associated with language learning and thus lead to action patterns that enhance or inhibit language acquisition. Therefore, there is no way we can decide which system is correct for our purposes. In fact, the researchers studying emotion are not prepared to settle on any

Table 1.3

Comparison of Emotion-Antecedent Appraisal Criteria Suggested by Different Theorists (from Scherer, 1988, p. 92)

Scherer	Frijda	Ortony/Clore	Roseman	Smith/Ellsworth	Solomon	Weiner
Novelty	Change			Attention		
Suddenness						
Familiarity	Familiarity					
Predictability		Unexpectedness				
Intrinsic Pleasantness	Valence	Appealingness		Pleasantness		
Goal Significance						
Concern relevance	Focality		App/Ave Motives		Scope/Focus	
Outcome probability	Certainty	Likelihood	Probability	Certainty		
Expectation	Presence	Prospect realization				
Conduciveness	Open/Closed	Desirability	Motive Consistency	Goal/Path Obstacle	Evaluation	
Urgency	Urgency	Proximity		Anticipated effort		
Coping Potential						
Cause: Agent	Intent/Self-Other	Agency	Agency	Agency	Responsibility	Locus of Causality
Cause: Motive				Agency		Stability
Control	Modifiability					Controllability
Power	Controllability		Power		Power	Controllability
Adjustment						
Compatibility Standards	Value Relevance	Blameworthiness				
External				Legitimacy		
Internal						

one formulation. Frijda (1993a), in assessing the state of the field, noted that "the theory of appraisal-emotion relationships is still in flux" (p. 227). Of the comparison presented in Table 1.3 Scherer (1988) himself says, "Obviously, this table may need to be revised in due course to correct possible misinterpretations and to accommodate revisions in the theoretical proposals reviewed here" (p. 93).

Some of the debates about the dimensions identified by various researchers concern whether the particular appraisal is antecedent to the emotion or part of the emotional response itself. For example, Frijda (1993b) asks whether the emotion of joy follows from an antecedent event being appraised as beneficial and controllable or whether the meaning of joy is simply "the experience of something appraised as beneficial and controllable" (p. 359). In addition, Lazarus and Smith (1988) raise the question of whether the attentional dimension identified by Smith and Ellsworth (1985) is antecedent to certain emotions or whether it is an aspect of the emotional response. Attention might also be viewed as a cognitive consequence of the emotion. In addition, Frijda (1993b) notes that experiencing an agent, action, or object as pleasant or unpleasant can be viewed as part of the emotional response, not as its cause. Frijda (1993b) also observes that appraisals may elicit an emotion, but they then may, in fact, be elaborated during the emotion and thus become part of the emotional experience. For example, "guilt emotion may be precipitated by the appraisal of having caused harm with the risk of loss of love; the experience includes one's sense of responsibility and blameworthiness" (p. 371). Here the appraisals of responsibility and blameworthiness are elaborations of the original appraisal and are part of the emotion experience. However, whether a particular appraisal dimension is antecedent to or part of an emotion is not of concern to the position being presented in this book. As will be shown in Chapter 3, studies of motivation in second language acquisition determine a learner's motivation by eliciting his or her appraisals of the language learning situation. In addition, diary studies and autobiographies of language learners demonstrate that learners constantly appraise the target language, the target culture, its speakers, the language teacher, the method, the text, and their own performance in the target language. In this chapter we have suggested that appraisals are a product of homeostatic, sociostatic, and somatic value and in

Chapter 2 a neurobiological system will be described that may be responsible for these appraisals. The purpose of this book is to explore the possible role of stimulus appraisal in producing variable success in second language acquisition. Therefore it is too soon to decide what dimensions of appraisal are the right ones for SLA. But as a heuristic, I will rely on the five categories of appraisal suggested by Scherer because they seem to be broad enough to orient the investigation and can be supplemented by elements of other appraisal systems or new dimensional formulations where they are warranted and appropriate.

As indicated above, our purpose is to see how appraisals influence efforts to learn a second language. Recent work by Frijda (1987) and Frijda, Knipers, and ter Schure (1989) on action tendency or action readiness that is consequent on appraisal and emotional experience is thus relevant for the discussion. Frijda (1986, 1987) argues that events that are appraised as emotionally relevant because they are beneficial or harmful to an individual's concerns (i.e., important vis-à-vis the individual's goals, motives, or sensitivities) elicit states that he defines as the "readiness to engage in action for establishing, maintaining or breaking the relation with particular aspects of the environment ('action tendency'), or as readiness to engage in relational action generally" (Frijda, 1987, p. 132). Frijda (1986) also notes that "action tendency is not necessarily readiness for overt action. Action tendency can actualize in mental actions having similar intent to overt ones: turning toward an object in thought, or away from it; disengaging emotionally from it; turning toward or away from the thoughts themselves" (p. 76). From this theoretical perspective, Frijda et al. (1989) argue that there is a causal relation between appraisals and the elicited action readiness such that the latter can be predicted from the former. Frijda et al. (1989) report two studies in which they examine how appraisals and patterns of action readiness are related to various emotions (i.e., emotion names) and how action readiness patterns are related to stimulus appraisals. In this research, subjects recalled instances in which they experienced each of eight emotions. They then completed an appraisal questionnaire and an action readiness questionnaire for each emotion. Table 1.4 presents hypothesized appraisal variables and the question items that elicited them. Subjects responded to these items on 7-point bipolar scales (e.g.,

Table 1.4

Appraisal Variables (from Frijda et al. 1989, p. 215)

Variable[a]	Item
Pleasantness (Valence)	Was it a pleasant or unpleasant situation?
Bearable (Valence)	Did you feel you could bear the situation?
Goal-conducive (Valence)	Was the situation conducive or obstructive to your goals?
Self-esteem	Did the situation decrease or enhance your self-esteem?
Fairness	Was what happened something that is generally regarded as fair or as unfair?
Interestingness	Was the event or situation interesting?
Clearness (Certainty)	Was the situation clear; did you understand what was going on and what the consequences would be?
Outcome (Certainty)	Did you know how the situation would end?
Stand (Certainty)	Did you know where you stood in the situation, what the situation meant?
Suddenness (Expectedness)	Was it a situation that had already lasted for some time, or one that had developed all of a sudden?
Expectedness (Expectedness)	Was it an expected or an unexpected situation?
True (Expectedness)	Were expectations involved that came true?
Anticipated effort	Did you feel the situation would or would not require effort?

Table 1.4 (continued)

Personal (Importance)	Did the situation affect you personally?
Importance (Importance)	Was the situation important or not important to you?
Modifiablity	Was the situation's outcome immutable, or could someone or something still change it in some way?
Controllability	Could you still affect the situation in any way?
Self-responsible (Agency)	Were you responsible for what happened or had happened?
Other responsible (Agency)	Was someone else responsible for what happened or had happened?
Familiarity (Familiarity)	Had you experienced the situation before; were you familiar with it?
Knowledge (Familiarity)	Was the situation a known or a novel one?
Time of event (Familiarity)	Was your emotion elicited by something that had occurred in the past, occurred now, or was to occur in the future?
Someone else	To what extent did the event affect someone else's well-being?

[a]*Dimension names are given in parentheses to distinguish alternative questions intended for the same dimension.*

"very good conducive" to "very good obstructive"). Table 1.5 presents the action readiness variables and their elicitation items to which the subjects responded on unipolar 7-point scales, which ranged from "not at all" to "very strongly so." (In this summary, I will only discuss the second of the two studies.)

The authors report the appraisal items predicted emotion categories/names with 40% accuracy, and action readiness predicted the emotions with 46% accuracy. Together the predictions' accuracy was 60%. The authors also ran multiple correlations to see how appraisals predicted action readiness. They found an

Table 1.5

Action Readiness Variables (from Frijda et al., 1989, p. 214)

Variable[a]	Item
Approach (Moving Toward)	I wanted to approach, to make contact.
Be with (Moving Toward)	I wanted to be or stay close, to be receptive to someone.
Protection (Moving Away)	I wanted to protect myself from someone or something.
Avoidance (Moving Away)	I wanted to have nothing to do with something or someone, to be bothered by it as little as possible, to stay away.
Attending	I wanted to observe well, to understand, or I paid attention.
Distance (Rejection)	I wanted to keep something out of my way, to keep it at a distance.
Rejection (Rejection)	I did not want to have anything to do with someone or something.
Disinterest	Things going on did not involve me; I did not pay attention.
Don't want	I wanted something not to be so, not to exist.
Boiling inwardly (Moving Against)	I boiled inside.
Antagonistic (Moving Against)	I wanted to oppose, to assault; hurt or insult.
Reactant (Moving Against)	I wanted to go against an obstacle or difficulty, or to conquer it.
Interrupted (Interruption)	I interrupted what I was doing, or I was interrupted.
Preoccupied (Interruption)	I could not concentrate or order my thoughts.
In command	I stood above the situation; I felt I was in command; I held the ropes.
Helping	I wanted to help someone, to take care of someone.

Table 1.5 (continued)

Disappear from view	I wanted to sink into the ground, to disappear from the Earth, not to be noticed by anyone.
Inhibition (Inhibition)	I felt inhibited, paralyzed, or frozen.
Blushing (Inhibition)	I blushed or was afraid to blush.
Submitting	I did not want to oppose, or I wanted to yield to someone else's wishes.
Apathy (Hypoactivation)	I did not feel like doing anything; nothing interested me, I was apathetic.
Giving up (Hypoactivation)	I quit; I gave up.
Shutting off (Hypoactivation)	I shut myself off from the surroundings.
Helplessness (Helplessness)	I wanted to do something, but I did not know what; I was helpless.
Crying (Helplessness)	I cried, had to cry, or wanted to cry.
Excited	I was excited, restless, could not sit still.
Exuberant (Exuberance)	I wanted to move, be exuberant, sing, jump, undertake things.
Laughter (Exuberance)	I laughed, had to laugh, or wanted to laugh.
Rest	I felt at rest, thought everything was O.K., felt no need to do anything.

[a]*Dimension names are given in parentheses to distinguish alternative items intended for the same dimension.*

average multiple correlation of .55, which accounts for 24% of the variance in action readiness. They note that this correlation supports, but of course cannot prove, their causal hypothesis. The authors also report that a canonical analysis indicated that appraisal variables accounted for 30% of the variance of the action readiness variables.

States of readiness, which one might intuitively see as conducive to language learning, are listed on the left side of Table 1.6.

Table 1.6

Action Readiness Variables That Might Promote or Inhibit Language Learning

+Language Learning	−Language Learning
Approach (Moving toward)	Protection (Moving away)
Be with (Moving toward)	Avoidance (Moving away)
Attending	Distance (Rejection)
In command	Rejection (Rejection)
	Disinterest
	Don't want
	Preoccupied
	Disappear from
	Inhibition (Inhibition)
	Apathy (Hypoactive)
	Giving up (Hypoactive)
	Shutting off (Hypoactive)
	Helplessness (Hypoactive)

Frijda et al.'s research indicates that these states of readiness are generally associated with stimulus situations appraised as personally important, bearable, fair, pleasant (value), interesting, sudden, requiring effort, other responsible, and situations where the meaning of the situation could be viewed as either understandable or ununderstandable. From this perspective, "approach," as a state of readiness is associated with stimulus situations that may develop suddenly and that are seen as fair. In terms of learning, "approach" would involve mental engagement. "Attention" is associated with a stimulus event that is appraised as interesting but for which another person is responsible and the meaning of which is not certain. "Be with" in the sense of mentally or physically "moving toward" is related to situations that are appraised as pleasant, goal conducive, certain, bearable, personally important, and for which effort is expected. Being "in command" is associated with learning situations that are appraised as "bearable."

States of readiness that intuitively would not be conducive to language learning are listed on the right side of Table 1.6. They are associated with appraisals of stimulus situations that are generally viewed as unfair, uninteresting, obstructive of goals, unbearable, unpleasant, having negative valence and generating negative self-esteem.

Following on Frijda's (1993b) suggestion that appraisals are frequently elaborated as part of the emotional response, Lewis (1996) offers a dynamic nonlinear perspective on appraisal-emotion interaction. He suggests that coupling and feedback between appraisals and emotions result in a process whereby stimulus appraisals cause emotions and emotions cause appraisals. Reciprocal causation in nonlinear interactions among successive appraisals and emotions allows the emergence of self-organized stable structures. Lewis (1996) argues:

> There are good reasons why a nonlinear model of appraisal should be informed by dynamic systems ideas. First, reciprocal causation or feedback among system components is essential for self-organisation, and is the means by which novel structures emerge and stabilise over time (Prigogine & Stengers, 1984). Feedback between cognition and emotion is therefore sufficient to generate cognitive appraisals (or appraisal-emotion gestalts) that are elaborate and coherent, that emerge out of simple precursors, and that coalesce into holistic structures. Secondly, self-organising systems have the potential for enormous sensitivity and diversity, as do cognitive appraisals. However, self-organising processes also tend toward stable forms, represented by *attractors*, and these forms denote the emergence of co-operativity among system elements. Attractors help to model the recurrent associations between situations, appraisals, and emotions that account for stable personality differences as well as normative emotional forms. Moreover, the concept of attractors links feedback with stability, and reconciles the fixed and fluid characteristics of everyday emotional experience. (Lewis, 1996, p. 10)

As appraisals of particular environmental or internal events repeatedly select and are selected by particular emotions, classes of responses become typical. These "attractor" states "describe increasingly probable interpretations of emotion-eliciting situations, reflecting an increasingly specific repertoire of appraisals in individual development" (p. 15). They may represent the emergence of motivations from lower order appraisal-emotion interactions and may be characteristic of an individual or even of a culture or group. (Studies of motivation in SLA may be tapping just such emotion-appraisal attractor states.) Lewis suggests:

> When an appraisal builds on itself through feedback with emotion, it may incorporate cognitive elements that include an evaluation of the emotional state itself. When this happens, the valence of the emotion becomes an important determinant of the self-organising trajectory of the unfolding appraisal. The evaluation and expectancy of a negative emotion produces the secondary emotion of anxiety. Although all emotions can participate in positive feedback, highlighting interpretations that amplify and sustain them, fear and anxiety are peculiar in that they also give rise to negative feedback. An interpretation that engenders anxiety sets the occasion for its own cessation. First, anxiety couples with painful expectancies in a self-orgaising appraisal, augmenting attention to helplessness and vulnerability. As it does so, however, it begins to highlight plans, goals, and scripts that facilitate escape—an attempt to get away from the painful attractor. Escape is the aim or action tendency attributed to fear or anxiety by many emotion theorists (e.g., Frijda, 1986; Oatley & Johnson-Laird, 1987). (Lewis, 1996, p.18)

Such negative escape goals, of course, result in withdrawal, which would negatively affect learning.

Finally, such a nonlinear model has important implications for the frequently proffered dichotomy between cognition and emotion. Lewis argues that "reciprocal causation between cognition and emotion makes each entirely dependent on the other as both gain in coherence and articulation. Emotions cannot be identified without some cohesive attentional focus, and appraisals cannot be identified without some coherent emotion to guide them. Thus, whenever the system is sufficiently organized for u to identify an appraisal, an emotion should already be eviden (p.21). From this perspective, cognition and emotions are, in fac separate but, nevertheless, highly interconnected (LeDoux, 1996), with each bootstrapping the other in the production of states of action readiness that generate another level of cognition—that necessary for learning. Here the cognition-emotion interaction in stimulus appraisal is seen as modulating the perception, attention, and memory that allow facts and skills to be encoded in the brain and that result in variable success in what I will call sustained deep learning.

Sustained Deep Learning

In this book, Scherer's five stimulus evaluation checks are used as general categories for stimulus evaluation criteria. This theory then argues that people's actions in the world are guided by their stimulus appraisals. They generally approach that which they appraise positively and avoid agents, objects, and events that they evaluate negatively. A major claim of the theory is that sustained deep learning (SDL) is controlled by stimulus appraisal. This learning is characterized as sustained because an extended period of time (often several years) is required to achieve it; it is characterized as deep because, when it is complete, the learner is seen as proficient or expert. I want to distinguish this kind of learning from that which is inevitable or even uniform across individuals. In other words, I am not referring to learning to see, learning to walk, or learning the grammar of one's native language. The theory pertains to the acquisition of knowledge and skills in which a great deal of variation is evidenced among individuals. Mathematics, history, celestial navigation, cooking, calligraphy, martial arts, bridge, gymnastics, auto mechanics, scuba diving, life insurance, and second language acquisition are all areas where individuals differ in knowledge and/or skill. The question to be answered is why people differ in these areas even when they have had identical opportunities to learn and have identical talent for the particular endeavor. In schools individuals develop varying proficiencies in different areas. Even the most talented individuals do not become expert or even proficient in everything. Individuals exposed to the same education devote their time and energy differently to various subjects and therefore develop different proficiencies and expertise. This variation seems to stem from learners' different goals, preferences, and talents. Aptitude, of course, enforces the inclination to prefer certain areas; therefore, talent and preference are not independent.

The learning I am talking about contrasts radically with that which is required in most psychological experiments in which the subject is asked to learn a small amount of material that is generally not relevant to her life. In other words, if the subject were left on her own, she probably would not learn the material.

Some SDL occurs because the learner is forced to acquire the material (as in some school subjects) but, as we will see, this learning will not exceed the level necessary to fulfill a requirement to an institution's satisfaction, unless the learner desires to pursue it to a higher degree. Of course, the learner may opt not to satisfy even the institution's minimal criterion for success.

In understanding SDL, a distinction must be made between canalized and noncanalized learning (Waddington, 1975). The former is learning that is guided by innate mechanisms and that is acquired by all appropriate members of a species with the provision of rather limited environmental input. Gallistel studies such specialized learning mechanisms in animals. One of the examples (Gallistel, 1995) he uses to illustrate these specialized learning systems is the path integration mechanism of a Tunisian desert ant (*Cataglyphis bicolor*). To search for food, the ant emerges from his nest and moves in a twisting and turning path until it finds the carcass of an insect. It bites off a piece and then runs in a nearly straight line back to its nest. Experimenters have shown that if, after finding the food, the ant is removed to some unfamiliar territory, it will orient and run toward its nest as though it were in the place it had been before it was moved. From this evidence, Gallistel argues that ants must have a specialized mechanism for path integration that allows them to integrate "the velocity vector with respect to time to obtain the position vector" (p. 1258).

He shows that examples of such specialized mechanisms abound. Migratory birds that fly at night do so by reference to circumpolar constellations that define the celestial pole. The birds learn the location of the pole as nestlings by observing the rotation of the relevant star clusters in the night sky. They then use this information to guide their migrating flights.

Ducks have a specialized mechanism that allows them to apportion their time between sources of food according to the abundance of food at each source. Research has shown that if,

> two experimenters stand 30 yards apart on the bank of a pond and throw chunks of bread into the water, the ducks in an overwintering flock divide themselves 50-50 between the experimenters when they throw equally sized chunks equally often. . . . But when one experimenter throws twice as often as the other, they divide 2:1 in favor of the "food patch" that is twice as rich. . . . And when the experimenters throw equally often but one throws chunks twice as big, the ducks initially divide themselves in accord simply with the more readily perceptible relative rates of throwing. However, they soon correct for the more difficult to detect difference in chunk size. Within 10 minutes, they are divided between the experimenters in accord with the relative abundance of bread. (Gallistel, 1995, pp. 1260-1261)

Another example, which most people are familiar with is the specialized learning mechanism that allows forager bees both to learn and to indicate the direction and distance of a food source from the performance of the waggle dance (Frisch, 1967).

The development of grammar in human children is another example of canalized learning. As indicated earlier, all normal children acquire the core grammar of their native language by the age of five. On the other hand, language pragmatics, the ability to use grammar, prosodics, and lexicon in appropriate and effective ways varies across individuals and is acquired throughout life as individuals encounter different domains of language use. For example, there are different language pragmatics appropriate to law, medicine, selling cars, telephone marketing, panhandling, tennis instruction, and funerals.

The kind of learning studied by Gallistel was evidently so important to the organism that natural selection fostered the development of innate mechanisms for the development of the particular knowledge, skill, or behavior. In other words, evolution solved the framing problem (De Sousa, 1987) for these organisms by making the development of this knowledge part of evolutionary inherited homeostatic and/or sociostatic value.

It is, therefore, important to distinguish between different kinds of learning in order to understand the SDL. Affect (i.e., somatic value) guides cognition in learning and problem solving in areas for which we do not have innate mechanisms. It is also required in domains for which we have neural specializations such as the one we have for social cognition. Such specializations facilitate learning, whereas innate mechanisms make relevant learning inevitable. Sustained deep learning is never inevitable and therefore is highly dependent on affect, emotion, and motivation.

The type of learning I am describing cannot be accounted for by cognition alone; it clearly has a strong emotional and motivational component. SDL in a particular field occurs because one is attracted to the field, likes it, or perhaps less frequently pursues it because of a sense of duty or obligation. The affect that supports or even drives such learning is generated and modulated by phylogenetically older neural structures such as the brain stem, the limbic system, and paralimbic areas. These structures interact with the neocortex, which is sometimes seen as the seat of cognition, particularly that of higher cognitive processes involved in certain kinds of memory, conceptual activity, and symbolic computation. Therefore, this model attempts to identify mechanisms for affective/cognitive interaction in the brain that are responsible for the perception of stimuli, the appraisal of stimuli, attention to stimuli, the movement of information in stimuli into memory, subsequent expression or use of that information in some kind of performance, the evaluation of one's performance, and the formulation of casual attributions for the success of the performance or lack of it. These processes are depicted in Figure 1.2. The model seeks to characterize key neural structures in the stimulus appraisal system and, therefore, has selected the most important candidate mechanisms; however, the model is certainly not exhaustive. Variable success in SLA is used in the theory as a paradigm case of SDL.

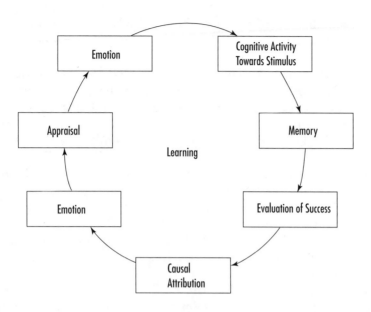

Figure 1.2. Components of Sustained Deep Learning.

Summary

In this chapter, I have argued that innate homeostatic and sociostatic value establish the basis for somatic value—preferences and aversions acquired in the lifetime of the individual. These three value systems form an emotional memory, which acts as a filter that appraises current stimuli according to novelty, pleasantness, goal/need significance, coping mechanisms, and self and social image. These appraisals guide our learning and foster the long-term cognitive effort (action tendencies) necessary to achieve high levels of mastery or expertise. The appraisals also curtail learning, producing variable success. This stimulus–appraisal system, then, is a major factor in the wide range of proficiencies seen in SLA, and SLA, in this formulation, serves as a model for all SDL.

2

The Neural Mechanism

In this chapter, the neural mechanisms responsible for stimulus appraisals will be described. The mechanisms form a three part system: the amygdala, the orbitofrontal cortex, and the body proper (see Figure 2.1). The amygdala is a phylogenetically older part of the brain, which is located in the temporal lobes. It is probably most involved in assessing value based on inherited homeostats and sociostats. The orbitofrontal cortex, located in the brain's prefrontal area, is phylogenetically more recent but is highly connected to the amygdala. This part of the brain presumably subserves somatic value, that is, preferences and aversions acquired in the lifetime of the organism. It is also the area that probably encodes the value associated with culture, religion, and education. The body proper becomes involved in stimulus appraisal when the amygdala and orbitofrontal cortex foster bodily states that produce positive or negative feelings about agents, objects, and events in the environment. Thus, the amygdala and orbitofrontal cortex generate stimulus appraisals that contribute to cognition (decision making) by correlating bodily states with stimulus situations (Allman & Brothers, 1994).

The Amygdala

Some of the earliest evidence for the emotional function of the amygdala comes from what is called the Klüver-Bucy syndrome (Klüver & Bucy, 1939). Monkeys whose temporal lobes are removed typically display a decrease in aggressiveness, a loss of

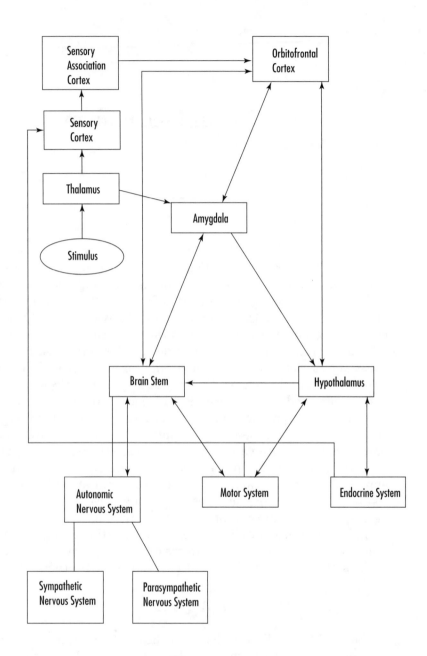

Figure 2.1. The Neural System for Stimulus Appraisal.

fear of humans, a tendency to examine objects repeatedly with the mouth, including inedible objects and aversive objects such as feces. In addition, these monkeys have an abnormally heightened sex drive that leads them to attempt copulation with conspecifics of the same sex and with animals of different species. Mishkin and Appenzeller (1987) report that in later studies the same behavior resulted when only the amygdalas were removed. They suggest that the monkeys are unable to integrate various kinds of memory. The sight of an object does not lead to a memory of its smell, and the smell of an object does not produce a memory of its taste. Amygdalectomies essentially leave these animals emotionally unresponsive to visual, tactile, auditory, and gustatory stimuli. In addition, the animals' loss of fear of humans and a lack of aversion to repugnant stimuli seem to indicate that "a link between familiar stimuli and their emotional associations had been severed" (Mishkin and Appenzeller, 1987, p. 88). This led to the speculation that the amygdala is responsible for assigning an emotional significance to an experience. Clinical evidence indicates that human subjects with amygdala damage have emotional behavior similar to that of the nonhuman primates described above (Aggleton & Mishkin, 1986). These patients are characterized by flattened affect and a rapid dissipation of emotion if aroused. This hypoemotionality can be either global or specific to a single sensory system.

It does not, however, appear that mechanisms of emotional expression are contained in the amygdala itself. Instead, the hypothalamus and related areas are generally assumed to be responsible for this function. Aggleton and Mishkin (1986) report that in cats whose amygdalas have been removed, direct electrical stimulation of the hypothalamus will produce fear and aggressive behavior. Thus, the sources of emotional behavior are still intact in amygdalectomized animals. This observation is consistent with the view that the amygdala directs highly integrated sensory information from the cortical sensory systems to the hypothalamus and to related structures involved in the expression of emotion.

Aggleton and Mishkin (1986) provide a description of the cortical projections to the amygdala, internal connections within the amygdala, and projections from the amygdala to other areas of the subcortex. When sensory information for

vision, audition, taste, and touch enter the brain, the information is first projected to the thalamus and from there it is
relayed to the primary processing areas for each modality. This
information is further processed at various stations along the
particular sensory pathways. From the final stations on these
pathways, where the sensory information is most fully processed, it projects to the amygdala. The amygdala itself consists
of about 12 subnuclei. Each of the final sensory processing
areas projects to one particular subregion with little overlap
among them. The cortex also contains several polysensory areas
that integrate more than one kind of sensory information. Most
of these cortical regions also project to the amygdala. They terminate in specific amygdaloid subnuclei, but they differ from
the sensory-specific projections in that they terminate in two or
more subregions. Within the amygdala. itself, there are extensive projections among the various subnuclei. Finally, the
amygdala. sends fibers to several subcortical sites: the basal
forebrain, the hypothalamus, the thalamus, the midbrain, pons,
and medulla. Amaral, Price, Pitkänen, and Carmichael (1992)
report that, in addition to these subcortical projections, the
amygdala has extensive projections back to the neocortex itself.
For example, it projects to all the temporal and occipital areas
involved in vision. Amaral et al. (1992) note that on the basis of
this connectivity "it is reasonable to predict that the amygdaloid complex might influence both early stages of sensory processing as well as higher level cognitive processing" (p. 41).

The neural circuit described above is a corticofugal pathway
in which projections begin at the final sensory processing stations in the cortex and flow to the amygdala. LeDoux (1986)
points out that there is also a precortical pathway, in which sensory input is received by the thalamus and then projected
directly to the amygdala without passing through the sensory
processing areas in the cortex. This pathway is illustrated in
Figure 2.2.

LeDoux (1986) argues that the pathway from the thalamus
to the neocortex and down to the amygdala assigns emotional
significance to complex, highly discriminated perceptual information. The subcortical pathway from the thalamus to the
amygdala, however, evaluates the emotional significance of

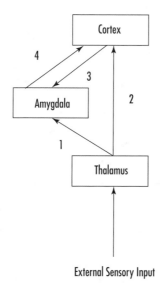

Figure 2.2. The Precortical and the Corticofugal Pathways of the Amygdala (based on LeDoux, 1986, p. 332).

simple or crude stimulus features. Both pathways operate in parallel. LeDoux argues (1986, pp. 345–46):

> Two implications of these parallel emotional processing channels should be considered. First, the subcortical areas that receive thalamic inputs also receive neocortical inputs. The two pathways thus converge. The thalamic pathway, though, is several synapses shorter. Input reaching target areas such as the amygdala may therefore prime the area to receive the better analyzed neocortical inputs, providing a crude picture of what is to come, narrowing the affective possibilities, and perhaps even organizing possible and actual responses.

Another important source of information about the role of the amygdala in emotional processing comes from the research of LeDoux (1994) on classical fear conditioning in rats. In this research, a rat hears a tone, which is paired with a mild shock tc its feet. The shock is referred to as the unconditioned stimulus (US), and the tone is called the conditioned stimulus (CS). After several trials the rat will respond to the sound alone (the CS). This research has revealed the neural pathway that allows fear conditioning to take place (see Figure 2.3). The sound enters the rat's ear and is then projected to the auditory areas of the midbrain and from there to the auditory thalamus. The thalamus is a relay station for all sensory information reaching the brain except olfaction (i.e., for sound, sight, taste, touch). From here, in one synapse, the circuit projects to the lateral nucleus of the amygdala (the thalamo-amygdala pathway referred to above) and then to the central nucleus via the basolateral nucleus and the acccessary basal nucleus. In the amygdala, the crude features of the stimulus are processed. From the central nucleus, the output region of the amygdala, the circuit projects to the brainstem, which leads to the autonomic responses and to the hypothalamus, where endocrine responses are stimulated. These will be described in more detail later.

At the same time the stimulus goes from the thalamus to the amygdala, it goes to the auditory cortex (the thalamo-cortical pathway), where it is analyzed in more detail and then projects back to the lateral nucleus of the amygdala (the corticofugal pathway). From the auditory cortex, the stimulus is transferred to the hippocampus, where the context in which it was heard is recorded and a declarative memory of the event is formed. The processing in the hippocampus allows the cortex to form a record of the event that may be available to consciousness at a later time. Once again, from the hippocampus the circuit projects to the amygdala, where the stimulus can be further processed for its motivational relevance and emotional significance.

If the auditory cortex is lesioned, fear conditioning will still occur because of the projection from the thalamus to the amygdala. However, lesions to the auditory areas of the midbrain and thalamus prevent conditioning because the auditory signal never reaches the amygdala.

As mentioned earlier, the importance of the hippocampus in the circuit is that it records the context in which the stimulus is perceived. Lesions to the amygdala disturb the response to the tone and to the environment in which it occurs (i.e., the experimental chamber for the rat). A lesion to the hippocampus only

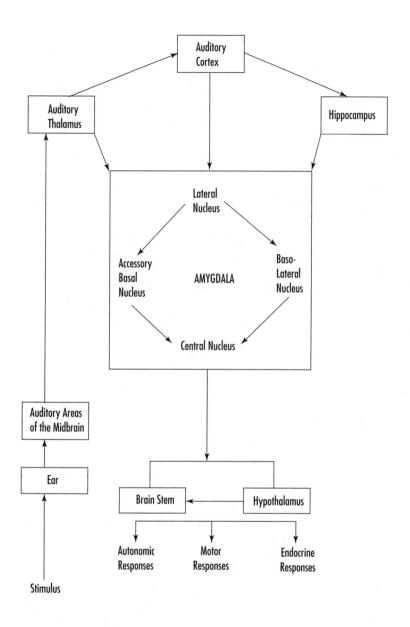

Figure 2.3. The Neural Pathway for Fear Conditioning (based on LeDoux, 1994, p. 54).

interferes with the animal's response to the context. This is because the hippocampus modulates memory for events, which, of course, include context.

It is interesting to note that people often have no declarative memory for events that occur very early in life. Such infantile amnesia is thought to result from the fact that the hippocampus does not become fully operational until between the ages of one and a half to three years (Jacobs & Nadel, 1985). The amygdala, however, functions from early infancy. Therefore, the event may be recorded as an unconscious emotional memory in the amygdala and related areas, and may, nevertheless, affect the individual's behavior.

Research on the function of the amygdala in humans has been more difficult because damage exclusively to that area is rare. Halgren (1981) reports the effects of electrical stimulation on the amygdala, which has been done prior to surgery. He reports that such stimulation can provoke fear, hallucination, aggression, and pleasure. These reactions correlate with the subjects' responses on the Minnesota Multiphasic Personality Inventory (MMPI). Subjects reporting fear had higher scores on psychaesthenia, and those reporting hallucinations had higher scores on the schizophrenia scale. (None of the subjects, however, was psychotic.) The responses to electrical stimulation also correspond to the subject's psychodynamic orientation as indicated in psychiatric interviews and post hoc clinical assessments. Aggressive patients show aggression with amygdala stimulation; patients who have intense pain report pleasure, and patients who appear apprehensive about the stimulation report fear. Finally, the content of psychiatric interviews seems to correspond to the content of complex hallucinations. According to Halgren (1981), the "hallucinations are interpreted as symbolizing ongoing psychodynamic concerns, both implicit in the interpersonal exchange immediately preceding the stimulation, and more long-standing unresolved conflicts" (p.399). Recent research on human subjects with very localized amygdala damage corroborates the picture developed in primate research, which has demonstrated that neurons in the amygdala are sensitive to socially significant signals such as direction of gaze, bodily movements, and interactions occurring between other primates (Allman & Brothers, 1994; Brothers & Ring, 1993; Brothers, Ring, & Kling, 1990).

A subject known as SM, studied by Adolphs, Tranel, Damasio, and Damasio (1994), incurred bilateral damage to the amygdalas as the result of Urbach-Wiethe disease, which created calcium deposits in those nuclei. SM is unable to recognize the expression of fear in other people's faces. She is also unable to recognize blended emotions in a single facial expression, although she can identify simple or prototypical emotions (happiness, surprise, anger, disgust, sadness) in facial expressions (except, of course, fear). Her ability to identify a face (i.e., recognize whose face it is) is undisturbed.

Another subject, DR (Allman & Brothers, 1994; Young et al., 1995) has partial lesions in both amygdalas resulting from treatment for epilepsy. DR has difficulty matching the names for emotions with photographs of faces expressing those emotions. This patient also has difficulty matching a photograph of a face depicting an emotion with another photograph expressing the same emotion. DR also cannot tell when another individual is looking at her or looking away. In other words, she cannot tell whether someone's gaze is directed at her. This research demonstrates that the human amygdala is sensitive to direction of gaze and the expression of emotion in others' faces. Of this ability, Allman and Brothers (1994) say:

> The direction of one's gaze signals the object of one's attention (that is, what one "has in mind") while facial expression indicates how one is disposed to behave. When mutual eye contact is established, both participants know that the communication loop between them has been closed, and for primates of all species this is the most potent of all social situations. The discovery that the human amygdala is involved in detecting both gaze direction and facial expression shows that it is indeed part of a brain mechanism for representing the intentions and dispositions of others. (pp. 613–14)

The ability to place appropriate emotional valence on the perceived intentions and dispositions of agents in the environment allows one to appraise these agents in terms of one's goals and needs, coping strategies, and self and social image.

The Orbitofrontal Cortex

Another area of the brain, which is highly connected to the amygdala, is also important in stimulus appraisal. The orbitofrontal cortex has been shown by Antonio Damasio (1994) to be involved in reasoning about social and personal issues. Individuals with damage to this area of the brain have difficulty making decisions about their personal lives and social relations. They also often behave inappropriately, showing a general disregard and disrespect for social conventions. Damasio explains that "some part of . . . [their old] value system remains and can be utilized in abstract terms, but it is unconnected to real-life situations" (p. 11). Nevertheless, these patients have intact perception, memory, attention, language, and intelligence.

The function of the orbitofrontal cortex is well illustrated in two case studies presented in Damasio (1994) and Damasio, Grabowski, Frank, Galaburda, and Damasio (1994). The first case is the classic neurological case of Phineas Gage. Gage was a railroad construction foreman. In 1848, an explosion sent a tamping iron, 3 cm thick and 109 cm long through his face, skull, and the orbitofrontal cortex of his brain. Gage survived and in many ways was normal. His intelligence was undisturbed, his speech was normal, his past memory was intact, he was able to form new memories, and he was physically healed and able-bodied. However, his personality changed. On the basis of the reports by Dr. John Harlow, the physician who treated and then studied Gage, Damasio indicates that prior to the injury Gage had been a responsible, temperate, and respected citizen and a highly skilled and efficient employee of the Rutland & Burlington Railroad. He was also regarded as an astute businessman who pursued his goals with energy and persistence. Damasio (1994), citing Harlow (1868), characterizes Gage's behavior after the accident:

> He was now "fitful, irreverent, indulging at times in the grossest profanity which was not previously his custom, manifesting but little deference for his fellows, impatient of restraint or advice when it conflicts with his desires, at times pertinaciously obstinate, yet capricious and vacillating, devising many plans of future operation, which are no sooner arranged than they are abandoned. . . . A child in his intellectual capacity and manifestations, he

has the animal passions of a strong man." The foul language was so debased that women were advised not to
stay long in his presence, lest their sensibilities be
offended. The strongest admonitions from Harlow himself failed to return our survivor to good behavior. (p. 8)

Gage had to be dismissed from his job, not because his skill
had diminished but because of character flaws. He then worked
on various horse farms but would, after a short period, quit or be
fired. He took a job at the Barnum Museum in New York City
where he displayed his wounds and the tamping iron that had
caused them. Throughout the remainder of his life, he kept his
tamping iron with him and ultimately he was buried with it.
Four years after the accident, Gage moved to South America
where he worked on horse farms and as a stagecoach driver. In
1860, he returned to the United States and lived off and on with
his family in San Francisco while he took jobs as a laborer on
farms in the area. He died in 1861.

Five years after Gage's death, Dr. Harlow asked to have his
body exhumed so that the skull could be preserved for future
study. Gage's family honored the request and the skull and the
tamping iron were stored at the Warren Anatomical Medical
Museum at Harvard. Recently, Damasio et al. (1994), using measurements of the skull and neuroimaging technology, determined
the trajectory of the tamping iron and the location of the lesion.
The reconstruction indicated the damage was largely in Gage's
orbitofrontal cortex.

The second case, reported in detail in Damasio (1994), presents a neurobiological study of Elliot, who had a brain tumor
that destroyed the orbital areas of his frontal lobes. The tumor
and damaged tissue were removed in surgery, but Elliot was profoundly altered. Damasio (1994) provides the following characterization of Elliot's day:

He needed prompting to get started in the morning and
prepare to go to work. Once at work he was unable to
manage his time properly; he could not be trusted with a
schedule. When the job called for interrupting an activity
and turning to another, he might persist nonetheless,
seemingly losing sight of his main goal. Or he might
interrupt the activity he had engaged, to turn to something he found more captivating at that particular

moment. Imagine a task involving reading and classifying the documents of a given client. Elliot would read and
fully understand the significance of the material, and he
certainly knew how to sort out the documents according
to the similarity or disparity of their content. The problem was that he was likely, all of a sudden, to turn from
the sorting task he had initiated to reading one of those
papers, carefully and intelligently, and to spend an entire
day doing so. Or he might spend a whole afternoon delib-
erating on which principle of categorization should be
applied: Should it be date, size of document, pertinence to
the case, or another? The flow of work was stopped. One
might say that the particular step of the task at which
Elliot balked was actually being carried out *too well*, and
at the expense of the overall purpose. One might say that
Elliot had become irrational concerning the larger frame of
behavior, which pertained to his main priority, while within
the smaller frames of behavior, which pertained to subsid-
iary tasks, his actions were unnecessarily detailed. (p. 36)

Elliot lost his job and then began jumping around from one
business enterprise to another. He ultimately joined a disreputa-
ble character in a business scheme and lost all his savings. He
seemed no longer able to make business decisions. He and his
wife divorced, he remarried and that marriage also ended in
divorce. He began drifting. He was unable to plan for the immediate future or for the long-term. His decision making with regard
to his personal and social life was profoundly flawed.

Computerized tomography and magnetic resonance imaging
determined that in the left and right frontal lobes, the orbitofrontal areas were destroyed. On the right, the white matter under
the cerebral cortex was also destroyed. Elliot underwent extensive psychological testing. His IQ was in the superior range. On
all the subtests of the Wechsler Adult Intelligence Scale, he demonstrated no abnormalities. His scores for immediate memory for
digits, short-term verbal memory, visual memory for geometric
designs, visual perception and construction, and language were
all in the range of normal to superior. Damasio (1994) makes the
following summary of Elliot's intellectual abilities: "perceptual
ability, past memory, short-term memory, new learning, language, and the ability to do arithmetic were intact. Attention, the

ability to focus on a particular mental context to the exclusion of others, was also intact; and so was working memory" (p. 41).

On a neurological test that is known to assess frontal lobe function, Elliot performed normally. In this test, called the Wisconsin Card Sorting Task, a patient has to categorize cards based on feedback from the investigator about whether or not she has done it correctly. When the patient has determined the principle governing the categories, the investigator changes the task. Frontal lobe patients have difficulty altering the basis on which they categorize the cards. Often they can state the categorization rule, but they nevertheless persist with the behavior that is no longer being rewarded by positive feedback from the investigator. Elliot's performance on this test was no different from that of a normal subject. Finally, on the Minnesota Multiphasic Personality Inventory (MMPI) he was also normal. Thus Damasio (1994) reports that nothing in the usual battery of laboratory neurobiological tests could demonstrate that Elliot was deficient in any way.

There was also nothing abnormal about Elliot's emotional life. He was neither particularly sad nor joyful, but was simply emotionally constrained. Damasio, however, noted that Elliot had no sense of suffering about his fate. When he talked about it, it was as though he were merely an observer of the things he reported. He was more mellow after than before his illness. When, as part of his psychological testing, he was shown emotionally disturbing pictures of earthquakes, burning houses, and gory pictures of injured people, he could describe what he saw without any emotional reaction. He was aware that this hypoemotionality was a different response from what he would have had prior to his illness.

Damasio and his colleagues then attempted to determine with additional tests whether Elliot still knew the principles of behavior which he no longer employed, or whether he retained that knowledge but was unable to access it and use it to make a choice. Elliot was asked to solve problems that involved ethical issues and financial decisions; he was given hypothetical social problems and was asked to generate possible solutions; he was asked to consider consequences of the transgression of social conventions. In addition, the researchers assessed his ability to determine effective means to achieve a social goal or to satisfy a social need and his ability to predict the consequences of events. On all of these tests he performed normally or superior to controls. Finally on a measure of moral development (Kollberg's Standard Issue of Moral Development Interview Scale), he scored 4/5 on a five point scale. Damasio (1994) summarizes Elliot's performance in the following way:

> Elliot had a normal ability to generate response options to social situations and to consider spontaneously the consequences of particular response options. He also had a capacity to conceptualize means to achieve social objectives, to predict the likely outcomes of social situations, and to perform moral reasoning at an advanced developmental level. The findings indicated clearly that damage to the ventromedial sector [orbital area] of the frontal lobe did not destroy the records of social knowledge as retrieved under the conditions of the experiment. (pp. 48-49)

Damasio explains these findings by noting that in none of the tasks was Elliot required to make a decision. He only had to generate options for possible courses of action. Thus, he demonstrated social knowledge and access to it, but did not, with these tests, demonstrate the ability to choose. Damasio reports that Elliot himself said he would be unable to choose among the options. Damasio goes on to say:

> Even if we had used tests that required Elliot to make a choice on every item, the conditions still would have differed from real-life circumstances; he would have been dealing only with the original set of constraints, and not with new constraints resulting from an initial response. If it had been "real life," for every option Elliot offered in a given situation there would have been a response from the other side, which would have changed the situation and required an additional set of options from Elliot, which would have led to yet another response, and in turn to another set of options required from him, and so on. In other words, the ongoing open-ended, uncertain evolution of real-life situations was missing from the laboratory tasks. (pp. 49-50)

Elliot's difficulty seems to be an inability to choose and an inability to choose well in real life situations. In Damasio's analysis, Elliot's deficit was the result of a lack of access to emotions or feelings that would help him reject some alternatives and preserve others:

> I was now certain that Elliot had a lot in common with Phineas Gage. Their social behavior and decision-making defect were compatible with a normal social-knowledge base, and with preserved higher-order neuropsychological functions such as a conventional memory, language, basic attention, basic working memory, and basic reasoning. Moreover, I was certain that in Elliot the defect was accompanied by a reduction in emotional reactivity and feeling. (In all likelihood the emotional defect was also present in Gage, but the record does not allow us to be certain. We can infer at least that he lacked the feeling of embarrassment, given his use of foul language and his parading of self-misery.) I also had a strong suspicion that the defect in emotion and feeling was not an innocent bystander next to the defect in social behavior. Troubled emotions probably contributed to the problem. I began to think that the cold-bloodedness of Elliot's reasoning prevented him from assigning different values to different options, and made his decision-making landscape hopelessly flat. It might also be that the same cold-bloodedness made his mental landscape too shifty and unsustained for the time required to make response selections, in other words, a subtle rather than basic defect in working memory which might alter the remainder of the reasoning process required for a decision to emerge. Be that as it may, the attempt to understand both Elliot and Gage promised an entry into neurobiology of rationality. (p. 51)

The Body Proper

Damasio (1994, 1995) argues that not only is the mind embrained, but the brain is embodied, and the body through its autonomic, endocrine, and musculoskeletal systems participates in the organism's emotional and cognitive responses to stimuli. Here the neural mechanism extends beyond the brain to the peripheral nervous system; therefore we are now thinking in terms of the whole nervous system, not just the brain.

The orbitofrontal cortex, both directly and through the amygdala, projects to the brainstem, where autonomic responses are generated in the sympathetic and parasympathetic nervous systems. The sympathetic nervous system places the organism in an aroused state, preparing it for vigorous activity such as fight or flight. This system causes the dilation of the pupils, inhibition of salivation, increase in respiration, acceleration of heart rate, inhibition of digestion, stimulation of glucose release, secretion of adrenaline and noradrenaline, relaxation of the bladder, and inhibition of the genitals (Bernstein, Roy, Srull, & Wickens, 1991). The parasympathetic nervous system has a calming effect on the organism and fosters responses related to protection, nourishment, and growth. This part of the automatic nervous system causes constriction of the pupils, stimulation of saliva-tion, slowing of respiration, slowing of heart rate, stimulation of the gall bladder, stimulation of digestion, contraction of the blad-der, and stimulation of the genitals (Bernstein et al., 1991).

The orbitofrontal cortex also projects to the hypothalamus, both directly and through the amygdala. The hypothalamus con-trols the endocrine system, which consists of glands that influ-ence the body by secreting hormones and peptides, which travel through the blood stream. The hypothalamus controls the pitu-itary gland, which regulates water and salt metabolism and con-trols all of the other glands in the system; the thyroid gland regulates metabolic rate; the adrenal cortex (above the kidneys) controls carbohydrate and salt metabolism; the adrenal medulla (also above the kidneys) prepares the body for action; the pan-creas controls insulin and glucose levels and regulates sugar metabolism; and the ovaries and the testes affect sexual responses (Berstein et al., 1991). Musculoskeletal activity (Dam-asio, 1995) is regulated by the motor systems in the brain and affects body responses such as facial expression, limb position, and muscle tension.

Damasio (1994, 1995) shows how this three part system—orbitofrontal cortex, limbic system (e.g., amygdala), and the body proper (via the brainstem, hypothalamus, and motor systems) cooperates to promote social cognition, that is, reasoning about issues related to one's personal and social life. But Damasio (1994, 1995) also emphasizes that this system contains an essen-tial evaluation component. Because the appraisal of stimulus events, agents, and objects is essential to reasoning about them, the tripartite system also constitutes the organism's stimulus appraisal mechanism. It works in the following way.

Events, agents, and objects that constitute a stimulus situation generate mental images in the early sensory cortices (sight, sound, touch, taste), where they are organized as thoughts under the guidance of dispositional representations (DRs). DRs are potential or dormant patterns of firing activity located in higher order association cortices (convergence zones) in the brain. They are essentially latent memories of all our innate and acquired knowledge. Dispositions that fire in the prefrontal cortex "embody knowledge pertaining to how certain types of situations have usually been paired with emotional responses in . . . [one's] individual experience" (Damasio, 1995, p. 22). Thus, dispositional representations in the orbitofrontal cortex are repositories of somatic value, that is, value acquired in the lifetime of the individual. DRs in the amygdala and related areas of the limbic system may comprise innate homeostatic and sociostatic value, that is, innate dispositions related to survival and interaction with conspecifics.

Thus, DRs in the orbitofrontal cortex contain memories of stimulus appraisals that have been made about similar situations in the past. These DRs both directly and via the amygdala signal the autonomic nervous system via the brainstem, the endocrine system via the hypothalamus, and the musculoskeletal system via the motor system. This signaling creates a bodily state referred to as a somatic marker by Damasio. This somatic state constitutes an emotional reaction to the stimulus situation. The reaction is interpreted by the brain as a feeling, which is juxtaposed to the image of the stimulus situation. Damasio (1995) argues that "by dint of [this] juxtaposition, body images give to other images a quality of goodness or badness, of pleasure or pain" (p. 23). Thus, stimulus appraisals are made when the DRs in the orbitofrontal cortex and the limbic system correlate somatic states with stimulus situations (Allman & Brothers, 1994).

When the stimulus appraisal has been made, neurotransmitter systems in the brainstem and the basal forebrain release chemical messengers such as dopamine, norepinephrine and acetylcholine into various parts of the cortex that regulate perception, attention, memory, and cognitive and motor investigatory-exploratory action toward the stimulus. Positive appraisals generate approach tendencies that involve perception, attention, and cognitive activity toward the stimuli such that the characteristics of the stimuli may be learned. Negatively appraised stimuli are cognized so that they can be dealt with to the extent necessary, recognized in the future, and avoided if possible.

Damasio (1994, 1995) also notes that for some reactions to stimulus situations the generation of an emotional somatic state is unnecessary. For rewards and punishments that are learned through frequently repeated associations of stimulus situations and bodily states during development and for which an appraisal becomes automatic and consistent, an "as-if" loop can be created as a symbol of a somatic state in the brain itself that results in that appraisal. Damasio (1995) states, "there are, thus, neural devices that allow us to feel 'as if' we were having an emotional state, as if the body were being activated and modified. Such devices permit us to bypass the body and avoid a slow and energy-consuming process. We conjure up some semblance of feeling within the brain alone" (p. 23).

Dreaming and Off-Line Appraisals

Ellsworth (1991) indicates that stimulus appraisals are not always immediate. It may take a period of time before such appraisals crystallize and become part of emotional memory. There is evidence that stimulus appraisal and emotional memory formation may continue off-line in the dreaming that occurs during rapid eye movement (REM) sleep (Schumann, 1994). REM sleep generally occurs five times a night. During these periods, brain waves are similar to those of the waking state. REM periods are interspersed with non-REM periods, or slow-wave sleep.

Research by Hobson (1990) and Mamelak and Hobson (1989) indicates that during REM sleep, two sources of aminergic neurotransmitters (norepinephrine and serotonin) in the brain stem are shut down. This disinhibits the forebrain and allows it to assume a state of tonic activation free from the cognitive constraints of attention and memory that are modulated by norepinephrine. It also frees the forebrain from the inhibition of spontaneous neuronal firing, which, in the waking state, is modulated by serotonin. At the same time, another nucleus in the brain stem that is a source of a third neurotransmitter, acetylcholine,

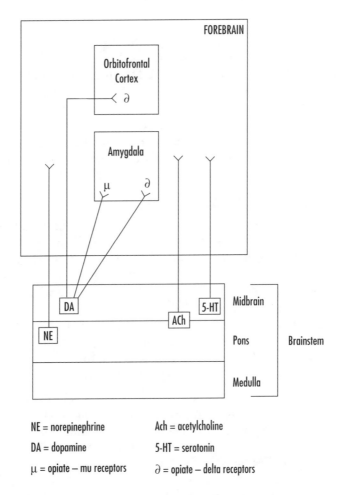

Figure 2.4. Neurotransmitter Systems That May Be Involved in Stimulus Appraisal and Emotional Memory During Dreaming (From Schumann, 1994).

generates bursts of ponto-geniculo-occipital (PGO) waves, which cause phasic activation of the forebrain (see Figure 2.4).

The aminergic demodulation of the forebrain (i.e., the diminished norepinephrine and serotonin) may allow the brain to strengthen information encoded during the day and to integrate it with stored associations and memories. The cholinergic PGO simulation of various parts of the brain may also facilitate the integration, reanalysis, pruning (i.e., forgetting, see Crick & Mitchison, 1983), and strengthening of current information encoded during the waking state. Very recent neuroimaging research (Maquet, Peters, Aerts, Delfiore, Degueldre, Luxen, & Franck, 1996) using positron-emission tomography technology has shown that the left and right amygdala are very active in REM sleep. The authors suggest that during REM periods there may be a reactivation of memories with significant emotional associations and that such activation may result in the long-term consolidation of these memories in various areas of the cortex.

This scenario is consonant with the results of research on dreaming that has been conducted by Cartwright and her associates at Rush-Presbyterian-St. Luke Medical Center in Chicago. Cartwright and Lamberg (1992) argue that in REM dreams the experiences one has had during the day are integrated with past experiences that involved similar emotions. Past and present are blended and, in the process, we review and revise our self-concept. In our dreams, we examine current information in the light of memories of old emotional information relevant to our waking experience. Cartwright and Lamberg (1992) offer the following description of the dreaming process:

> Once we settle into sleep, the second level of the mind, the one that tends to our on-going emotional concerns, seizes the spotlight of our awareness. Emotions that we may not identify in waking life carry over into sleep. When REM sleep arrives, these emotions trigger memories of times when we experienced similar feelings. We weave past and present into the story—like hallucinations of dreams, drawing from a vast storehouse of images filed in our memory networks. Feelings serve as the thread that links one dream image to the next and all dreams of the night to one another. (p. 59)

Dreams are also revealing of our emotional memory schemas and the systems of preferences and aversions by which we evaluate stimuli:

> We start in infancy to make big evaluative discriminations: This feels good; that feels bad. This is warm; that is cold. By the time we reach adulthood, we have added many such distinctions. In dreams, the specific images,

along with their opposites, show how we see people and
events and express our innermost evaluations of them
and feelings about them. Our sense of who we are rests
on where we are on the spectrum of categories revealed
by our most important dream dimensions. (Cartwright
and Lamberg, 1992, p. 42)

Winson (1990) notes that, in certain animals (e.g., cats, rab-
bits, rats), a brain wave called the *theta rhythm* occurs when the
animal is involved in survival behaviors such as exploration,
apprehension, and predation. He also observes that these animals show the same rhythm during REM sleep and also during
the process of long-term potentiation (LTP), which is thought to
be involved in memory formation. On the basis of these observations, he suggests that the theta rhythm may reflect "a neural
process whereby information essential to the survival of a species—gathered during the day—may be reprocessed into memory
during REM sleep" (Winson, 1990, p. 88). Therefore, in REM
sleep, LTP may take place and thus reprocess and strengthen
daytime memories that have survival (or thrival) value by integrating them with past memories and associations. Theta
rhythms have not been observed in primates, and Winson (1990)
suggests that they may have disappeared as vision evolved to
supersede olfaction as the primary sensory modality. He speculates that an equivalent neural mechanism may exist in the hippocampus, where LTP has been observed. In humans, survival
behaviors and self-preservation may be extended to issues of self-
image and self-identity. Cartwright and Lamberg (1992), citing
Snyder (1970), point out that the "I," the individual dreamer,
appears in 95% of our dreams and is almost always the main
character. Thus, a major function of dreams may be to modulate
our self-identity in light of current emotional experience and
stored emotional associations.

Appraisals Made by the Neural Mechanism

I have suggested in this chapter that the amygdala, orbitofrontal cortex and the body proper constitute a stimulus
appraisal system. We might now look a little closer to see how
patients with damage to this system appear to cope with appraisals of novelty, pleasantness, goal significance, coping relevance,

and self and social image. As demonstrated by the characterization previously described, Elliot clearly has problems appraising stimuli in relation to goals. He has difficulty determining whether a particular task, as a stimulus event, is important in relation to a particular goal. He abandons projects before they are finished and perseverates with others beyond what is necessary to accomplish the task. He appears to have problems maintaining goals and determining whether a particular state in their accomplishment is satisfactory or not. Elliot also appears to have problems with the assessment of his coping potential. He evidently is unable to assess the risk involved in the business enterprises he undertakes or to appropriately assess his ability to control events involved in these business ventures. With regard to self and social norms, Elliot's appraisal system also seems to be defective. Damasio points out that Elliot does not seem to suffer. He is indifferent to his plight. A failure in a business or a marriage is a stimulus event that quite reasonably might affect one's self and social image. One might be embarrassed, shamed, or depressed. But evidently Elliot feels no such challenges to his sense of self. It is as though these events had happened to someone else.

From Harlow's account of Gage's postmorbid behavior, we can infer that Phineas had difficulty assessing goal significance. In relation to some need or desire he would generate a plan of operation, arrange for its implementation and then abandon the project. He did so repeatedly. In terms of his ability to assess his coping potential, Damasio (1994) notes Harlow's observation that Phineas seemed always to find work for which he was not suited. He would then be dismissed, but he did not learn from the experience. With regard to appraisals involving of self and social image, Damasio observes, "we can infer at least that . . . [Gage] lacked the feeling of embarrassment, given his use of foul language and his parading of self-misery" (p. 51). Prior to his injury, Gage did not use profanity. We can assume that he didn't do so because such behavior would constitute a stimulus event that he would appraise as diminishing of his ideal self and social image. After the injury, however, that appraisal standard was lost. Phineas, who had been a respected railroad construction foreman, became essentially a circus sideshow freak, and this also left his self and social image appraisals unchallenged.

Another patient studied by Brickner (1936) and briefly described in Damasio (1994), known as patient *A* also sheds light on how orbitofrontal damage affects stimulus appraisal. Patient *A* was a 41-year-old stockbroker who had two operations in 1930 to remove a tumor from his frontal lobe. The tumor and the subsequent surgery damaged the same orbifrontal areas that were affected in Gage and Elliot, but as Damasio (1994) reports *A*'s frontal damage was somewhat more extensive. *A* was studied by Dr. Brickner and his assistant, Dr. Lerner. In fact, Dr. Lerner actually lived for fairly extensive periods with *A* and his family and took detailed notes on *A*'s behavior and verbal interaction with family members. Essentially Brickner and Lerner conducted an ethnographic study of *A*. The conversations between *A* and Dr. Brickner were transcribed verbatim from stenographic records. In *A*'s conversations with Dr. Lerner, Lerner summarized his own statements, but strove to provide verbatim accounts of *A*'s contributions. Damasio (1994) provides an apt characterization of *A*'s overall behavior: "He boasted of his professional, physical, and sexual prowess, although he did not work, did nothing sporty, and had stopped having sex with his wife or anyone else" (p.56). *A*'s verbal intercourse was self-aggrandizing; he boasted of perfection:

December 31, 1931. (A discussion with B.)

> *B.* One thing your illness lost you is the knowledge that you're not perfect.
> *A.* It's a damn good thing to lose.
> *B.* Do you really believe in your heart that you are perfect?
> *A.* Yes. Of course we all have faults. I have faults like everyone else.
> *B.* Name some of your faults.
> *A.* I don't think I have any.
> *B.* You just said you had.
> *A.* Well, they wouldn't *predominate* on the Exchange.
> *B.* I mean personal faults.
> *A.* Yes, I have personal faults. I never give a man an opportunity of doing what he wants to on the Exchange, if I know it.
> *B.* Is that a fault?
> *A.* That's being a good broker.

> *B.* Can you name a personal fault? Do you really
> believe you're perfect?
> *A.* You bet I do—pretty near perfect—they don't come
> much more perfect than I am.
> (B = Dr. Brickner). (Brickner, 1936, pp. 47–48).

The following excerpt illustrates both *A*'s sexual braggadocio and its social inappropriateness:

> *September 2, 1932*
>
> *A.* I'm going over to that meet tomorrow and get me
> a nice girl and I'm going to give her a nice party.
> *Rose.* It's not that kind of meet.
> *A.* I don't care. I don't say I'll do it there—I may
> take her up into the woods. She may have a room
> and invite me up. (*To L.*) I'll leave it to the doctor.
> I just asked my wife if she wants to go upstairs
> and I'll give her a party.
> *Rose.* I don't see what the doctor has to do with it.
> *A.* Neither do I. Say, if you don't come across
> tonight, I'm going to go over there tomorrow and
> get me a nice girl and I'll give her some party—
> maybe two or three.
> *Rose.* Is this blackmail?
> *A.* No. I may do it anyway.
> *Rose.* Well, I'll weaken you up tonight.
> *A.* You can't weaken me. Say, I remember. . . .
> (*Rose interrupted A at this point.*)
> (Rose = *A*'s wife). (Brickner, 1936, pp. 53–54)

A's view of his athletic prowess is illustrated in the following two excerpts:

> (*Discussion of a coming swimming meet.*)
>
> *A.* I think I'll get my bathing suit and enter the meet and
> win a few events, and I can do it too. I'm some swim-
> mer—I'm one of the best swimmers around here.

> August 27, 1932. (*After reading the baseball news.*)
>
> *A.* I think I'm going to take up professional ball play-
> ing. I can sock that ball better than any one else
> and I can sock it too.

(Brickner, 1936, p. 54)

A's friends and colleagues report that things he might have said jokingly in the past, he now wanted to say with conviction, as though he believed them.

A sometimes seemed to know vaguely what is socially appropriate but was not able to exercise that knowledge in his behavior, and once he had acted inappropriately, he then justified his behavior with conviction. At other times, *A* appeared to be relearning (evidently unsuccessfully) how to behave appropriately:

May 11, 1932.

> *B.* What have you done that I've advised you to?
>
> *A.* I've followed out your directions pretty carefully in a general way.
>
> *B.* Can you be specific?
>
> *A.* I've ceased to annoy my father. I've gone up to the medical school and done all the work I was supposed to do. If someone I haven't seen in a long time comes along and makes a remark I don't like, I take exception to it.
>
> *B.* Meaning what?
>
> *A.* Meaning that I make some remark the person may not like. I don't always intend to make those remarks, but I do make them at times.
>
> *B.* You mean that you don't think you should?
>
> *A.* I wouldn't make them if I didn't think I should.
>
> *B.* You say you don't always intend to make them.
>
> *A.* I don't always mean to give them hell. People have different ideas about certain things that I don't always coincide with. But I am following your advice about this to a certain extent. In other words I am making certain *leeways that I ordinarily would take exception to.*
>
> B. What else?
>
> *A.* Well, my attitude toward the women I've come in contact with in the last few weeks has been a more reasonable one. I've done nothing to embarrass them. I don't know if I could have or not *(laughs),* but I didn't.

May 17, 1932. (A had made some hostile remarks to L.)

A. I had no animosity towards you; it was just one of my casual remarks.

L. They aren't the correct ones to make.

A. Well, I don't say I was right in saying it. I sometimes say things that I shouldn't say to people.

L. When did you first come to this conclusion?

A. I began to realize this last summer, and when I feel like making these casual remarks I try to curb myself sometimes.

L. Why?

A. Because I don't think it good form.

(L = Dr. Lerner). (Brickner, 1936, pp. 113–114)

Patient *A*, also had difficulty with the appraisal of goal significance as evidenced by his inability to generate and implement appropriate plans for returning to work at the stock exchange. It would appear that he could formulate goals but could not assign them with sufficient significance to act on them. His boasting about sexual and physical powers, and his lack of performance in these areas indicate that appraisals of his coping potential were also distorted. Finally, his crude and cruel verbal behavior which he occasionally tried to change indicates that he, like Gage and Elliot, had difficulty appropriately appraising his behavior in terms of social norms and his premorbid self-concept.

What we see from the above analysis is that the orbitofrontal damage incurred by Elliot, Gage, and Patient *A* appears to have affected their ability to make appraisals along the dimensions of goal significance, coping potential, and norm/self compatibility. But what about appraisals of novelty and pleasantness? We can assume that all three patients are capable of fear. If they were to start to cross the street and suddenly heard a loud horn they would probably jump back on the curb. In this case, they would be appraising a change in external stimulation. All of the patients also appeared to be able to make appraisals of pleasantness, and they frequently did so to the detriment of achieving their goals. In some sense they appeared to become slaves to current appraisals of pleasantness, abandoning goals to the immediate appealingness of a local stimulus event. It may be the case that appraisals of basic novelty and pleasantness/unpleasantness are made at the levels of the amygdala, and the patients all had intact amygdalas. On the other hand, Elliot was described as perseverating at certain tasks beyond the point at which the effort might have been rewarding in terms of achieving his goals. Here an orbitofrontal override of the activity might have been required but was unavailable.

Gaffan (1992) reports that if a normal monkey is fed until it is sated and is then shown a banana, it will become excited. However, this does not happen after a monkey has been amygdalectomized. Gaffan (1992) argues that experience with bananas in the mouth and in the stomach teaches the monkey about the banana's intrinsic pleasantness. The pleasantness becomes associated with the color and shape of the banana and leads to excitement when the banana is presented. Amygdalectomized monkeys lose such associations and also have difficulty in forming them. An amygdalectomized monkey that is hungry might eagerly eat a banana, but seems not to have a memory for its intrinsic palatability (i.e., pleasantness). Gaffan (1992) also reports that normal monkeys raised in captivity can be exposed to various foods (e.g., olive, lemon, apple, beef) and will acquire a "stable order of preference" (p. 472) for them based on an association between their appearance and their palatability. Amygdalectomized monkeys only establish a weak set of preferences, which do not seem to be based on an association between the perception of the food and its palatability. These observations indicate that the amygdala may be involved in the appraisal of intrinsic pleasantness.

Neuroscientists are still attempting to sort out what kinds of appraisals are made at the level of the amygdala and what kinds are made at the level of the orbitofrontal cortex. Because of the anatomical connections between the two, the levels are clearly not independent. Basic appraisals of intrinsic pleasantness with regard to homeostatic and sociostatic value may be made by the amygdala, but what is pleasant certainly evolves during one's lifetime, and as will be discussed in more detail later, pleasantness can sometimes be linked to goals and at other times may not be relevant to them. However, when the two are associated, the amygdala and the orbitofrontal cortex may be closely involved.

The patients with bilateral amygdala damage reported above (i.e., patients SM and DR) had difficulty with appraisals related to fear, but information is not provided about how they assessed basic hedonic valence. It would be interesting to know whether things they found pleasant before incurring brain damage were still appraised as such afterwards. In general, it would be interesting to have an analysis of these patients' general hedonic tone in relation to familiar agents, events, and objects. Research along these lines, however, is difficult because cases of bilateral amygdala damage are rare. The left and right orbitofrontal cortices are right next to each other along the midline of the brain, and if one is damaged there is a fairly high likelihood that the other will be also. The amygdalas are in the temporal lobes and therefore are on opposite sides of the brain and are less likely to receive bilateral damage. LeDoux (1996) reports research by Bornstein (1992) and by Murphy and Zajonc (1993) which offers some clues that the amygdala may be involved in appraisals of novelty/familiarity and pleasantness. In Bornstein's research subjects were given extremely rapid and therefore subliminal (i.e., nonconscious) exposure to pictures of faces. Later they were asked to indicate which faces they had seen. Because of the brief exposure, the subjects were unable to make such identifications. But when they were asked to say which faces they liked, they chose the ones that they had seen initially. Here an appraisal of pleasantness or appealingness seems to have been made on the basis of familiarity. Murphy and Zajonc (1993) conducted a priming experiment in which subjects were presented with a very brief (subliminal) stimulus such as a Chinese character paired with either a smile or a frown. Later when the subjects were asked whether or not they liked or disliked a particular character, they tended to prefer the stimuli that had been paired with smiles and to dislike those that had been paired with frowns. In this research appraisals of pleasantness are being made. In both experiments the stimuli were so brief that the subjects were not conscious of them. This suggests that the appraisals may have been made via the projection from the thalamus to the amygdala (see Figure 2.1) without being processed by the sensory cortices and the orbitofrontal cortex. If it is the case that stimuli, which are presented so briefly that they are not consciously perceived, can only be appraised by the amygdala via the direct projection from the thalamus, then these experiments may provide some indirect evidence that the amygdala is involved in appraisals of familarity and pleasantness. This issue is being addressed by Robbins and Everitt (1996), who are currently conducting research on monkeys and rats to determine the difference between amygdala focused and orbitofrontal focused appraisals. Much of the amygdala research over the past 25 years has concentrated on the role of this set of nuclei in fear, but Robbins and Everitt are also studying the amygdala in relation to positive reward.

In summary, the research on orbitofrontal patients provides evidence that this area of the hypothesized neural appraisal system is involved in at least three of the five dimensions of appraisal proposed by Scherer (1984), and current research will help resolve how novelty and pleasantness fit into this system.

Summary

The neurobiological basis for stimulus appraisal is hypothesized to consist of the orbitofrontal cortex, the amygdala, and the body proper. The amygdala may be more involved in appraisals based on homeostatic and sociostatic value because it is operating at birth; the orbitofrontal cortex, which develops postnatally and remains quite plastic at least through the second decade of life, may subserve somatic value. Emotional memories of past experiences with events, agents, and objects are encoded via this tripartite system. They serve as a filter which, through signals from somatic markers in the body, determines the personal relevance of subsequent experience. Therefore, it is this neural system that may constitute value category/schematic emotional memory and the mechanism for assessing novelty, pleasantness, and relevance to goals, needs, coping ability, self-image, and social image. Finally, stimulus appraisals that take place in the waking state may be consolidated during REM sleep.

Research on brain damaged patients indicates that appraisals along the dimensions of goal/need significance, coping potential and norm/self compatibility may be mediated via the orbitofrontal cortex and that appraisals on the dimensions of pleasantness and perhaps novelty/familiarity may occur via the amygdala or the amygdala in conjunction with the orbitofrontal cortex (and, of course, the body proper).

The model of stimulus appraisal presented in this chapter is based upon the neurobiologically informed perspectives on emotion offered by Demasio, LeDoux, and others. However, this neurobiological account of stimulus appraisal must be considered speculative because we have no direct experimental evidence, even from the neurobiological perspectives presented, that the system described actually carries out the appraisals that have been hypothesized. The clinical evidence from brain damaged patients and the evidence from animal studies are consonant with the proposed model, but they do not constitute proof.

3

Some Data: Questionnaires

In this chapter, I present some data relevant to the stimulus appraisal perspective hypothesized in Chapters 1 and 2. I begin by showing how questionnaires used to measure motivation in SLA do so by eliciting stimulus appraisals. I then show how the appraisal perspective presented in this book is compatible with other recent approaches to motivation in SLA.

The major work, both theoretical and empirical, on affective variables in SLA has been done by Robert Gardner and his associates in Canada. This research has a forty-year history, which has been devoted to understanding components of motivation in second language learning. Some of the earlier work in their paradigm was concerned with the distinction between integrative and instrumental orientations, which were discussed in the Introduction. However, the central concept in the model has been and is motivation. Gardner (1985) defines motivation as "the combination of effort plus desire to achieve the goal of learning the language plus favorable attitudes toward learning the language" (p. 10). Over the years, Gardner (1985) and his colleagues developed the Attitude/Motivation Test Battery (AMTB), which was designed to measure several attributes of second language learning. The attributes assessed most frequently in this research fall into four categories: motivation, integrativeness, attitudes toward the learning situation, and language anxiety (Gardner & MacIntyre, 1993). I will attempt to show that the scales used to measure the attributes do so by directly eliciting the learner's stimulus appraisals or by assessing the learner's actual, intended, or desired behavior, which is based on stimulus appraisal.

Many of the items in the subscales of the AMTB can be seen as falling within the general appraisal category of pleasantness/valence/appealingness. What Gardner and his associates seem to be assessing is subjects' appraisal of the appeal of various activities, agents, and objects in relation to the goal of language learning. Ortony, Clore, and Collins (1988) view appealingness of objects as a category of appraisal, but clearly activities and agents (people) can also be viewed in terms of their appeal or their pleasantness. Scherer's (1984) original notion of intrinsic pleasantness referred mainly to pleasantness or unpleasantness of the stimulus event in and of itself. A taste, a sound, a color, in its own right may be intrinsically pleasant, but agents, activities, and objects can also be seen as pleasant in relation to their conduciveness to an individual's goals. It is this sense of pleasantness that AMTB taps.

In order to illustrate how the AMTB elicits appraisals, in the section below I analyze the subscales by classifying each item according to what category of stimulus appraisal it elicits. The questionaire item is indicated on the left, and the appraisal category is on the right.

(1) Motivation. Gardner (1985) sees the motivated individual as one who has the desire to achieve a goal, who is prepared to extend effort to achieve that goal, and who gains satisfaction from the task. The AMTB contains three scales designed to measure these components: (a) desire to learn the language, (b) motivational intensity, and (c) attitudes toward learning the language.

The desire to learn the language scale consists of 10 items:

---

1. During French class, I would like:
   a) to have a combination of French and English spoken.
   b) to have as much English as possible spoken.
   c) to have only French spoken.

1. appealingness of an activity

2. If I had the opportunity to speak French outside of school, I would:
   a) never speak it.
   b) speak French most of the time, using English only if really necessary.
   c) speak it occasionally, using English whenever possible.

2. appealingness of an activity

3. Compared to my other courses, I like French:
   a) the most.
   b) the same as all the others.
   c) least of all.

3. appealingness of an activity/object

4. If there were a French club in my school, I would:
   a) attend meetings once in a while.
   b) be most interested in joining.
   c) definitely not join.

4. appealingness of an activity/object

5. If it were up to me whether or not to take French, I:
   a) would definitely not take it.
   b) would drop it.
   c) don't know if I would take it or not.

5. appealingness of an activity

6. I find studying French:
   a) not interesting at all.
   b) no more interesting than most subjects.
   c) very interesting.

6. appealingness of an activity

7. If the opportunity arose and I knew enough French, I would watch French TV programs:
   a) sometimes.
   b) as often as possible.
   c) never.

7. appealingness of an activity

8. If I had the opportunity to see a French play, I would:
   a) go only if I had nothing else to do.
   b) definitely go.
   c) not go.

8. appealingness of an activity

9. If there were French speaking families in my neighborhood, I would:
   a) never speak French with them.
   b) speak French with them sometimes.
   c) speak French with them as much as possible.

9. appealingness of an activity

10. If I had the opportunity and knew enough French, I would read French magazines and newspapers
    a) as often as I could.
    b) never.
    c) not very often.

10. appealingness of an activity/ objects

(Gardner, 1985, pp. 181–2)

The first, third, and sixth items elicit from the learner direct appraisals of the medium of instruction in the French class, appraisal of the French course in comparison to other courses, and assessment of how interesting the learner finds the study of French. The other items assess actual, intended, or desired behaviors that would result from positive or negative appraisal of activities associated with learning French, that is, speaking French outside of school, participation in a French club, studying French, watching French television, speaking French with neighbors, and reading French magazines and newspapers. This scale then elicits appraisals of pleasantness in terms of the appeal of particular activities related to the goal of language learning.

The motivational intensity scale also consists of 10 items:

1. I actively think about what I have learned in my French class:
   a) very frequently.
   b) hardly ever.
   c) once in a while.

1. appealingness of an activity/ object

2. If French were not taught in school, I would:
   a) pick up French in every-day situations (i.e., read French books and news-papers, try to speak it whenever possible, etc.).
   b) not bother learning French at all.
   c) try to obtain lessons in French somewhere else.

2. appealingness of an activity

3. When I have a problem understanding something we are learning in French class, I:
   a) immediately ask the teacher for help.
   b) only seek help just before the exam.
   c) just forget about it.

3. appealingness of an activity

4. When it comes to French homework, I:
   a) put some effort into it, but not as much as I could.
   b) work very carefully, making sure I understand everything.
   c) just skim over it.

4. appealingness of an activity/ object

5. Considering how I study French, I can honestly say that I:
   a) do just enough work to get along.
   b) will pass on the basis of sheer luck or intelligence because I do very little work.
   c) really try to learn French.

5. appealingness of an activity

6. If my teacher wanted some-one to do an extra French assignment, I would:
   a) definitely not volunteer.
   b) definitely volunteer.
   c) only do it if the teacher asked me directly.

6. appealingness of an activity

7. After I get my French assignments back, I:
   a) always rewrite them, cor-
      recting my mistakes.
   b) just throw them in my
      desk and forget them.
   c) look them over, but do not
      bother correcting mis-
      takes.

7. appealingness of an activity/
   object

8. When I am in French class, I:
   a) volunteer answers as
      much as possible.
   b) answer only the easier
      questions.
   c) never say anything.

8. appealingness of an activity

9. If there were a local French
   TV station, I would:
   a) never watch it.
   b) turn it on occasionally.
   c) try to watch it often.

9. appealingness of an activity/
   object

10. When I hear a French song
    on the radio, I:
    a) listen to the music, pay-
       ing attention only to the
       easy words.
    b) listen carefully and try to
       understand all of the
       words.
    c) change the station.

10. appealingness of an activity/
    object

(Gardner, 1985, pp. 180–1)

These items all elicit actual, intended, or desired behaviors that reflect the effort the learner does make or would make to learn French. The level of effort assessed in these behaviors can be seen as a reflection of the learner's appraisal of the acquisition of French in terms of the appealingness of an activity (e.g., studying French) or the appealingness of an activity (e.g., *listening* to French songs) and/or an object (e.g., French vocal music).

The attitudes toward learning French scale consists of five positively and five negatively worded items:

Attitudes toward learning French

Positively worded items.

1. Learning French is really great.	1. appealingness of an activity
2. I really enjoy learning French.	2. appealingness of an activity
3. French is an important part of the school programme.	3. appealingness of an object
4. I plan to learn as much French as possible.	4. goal
5. I love learning French.	5. appealingness of an activity

Negatively worded items.

6. I hate French.	6. appealingness of an activity
7. I would rather spend my time on subjects other than French	7. appealingness of an object
8. Learning French is a waste of time.	8. appealingness of an activity
9. I think that learning French is dull.	9. appealingness of an activity
10. When I leave school, I shall give up the study of French entirely because I am not interested in it.	10. appealingness of an object/ goal

---

(Gardner, 1985, p. 179)

Items 1, 2, 3, 5, 6, 8, and 9 elicit direct appraisals of learning French. Items 4 and 7 assess intended or desired behaviors involved in learning French, and item 10 elicits a combination of direct appraisal of the learner's interest in learning French and a behavior which would result from that appraisal. This scale then assesses attitudes toward learning French along the dimensions of pleasantness in terms of the appeal of activities and objects related to language learning as a goal.

(2) Integrativeness in the AMTB is assessed by three scales: (a) attitudes toward the target language group, (b) interest in foreign languages, and (c) integrative orientation. The attitudes toward French Canadians measure consists of 10 items that are responded to along a 7-degree Likert scale: strongly disagree, moderately disagree, slightly disagree, neutral, slightly agree, moderately agree, strongly agree.

Attitudes toward French Canadians

1. French Canadians are very sociable, warm hearted and creative people.

    1. appealingness of agents

2. I would like to know more French Canadians.

    2. goal/appealingness of agents

3. French Canadians add a distinctive flavor to the Canadian culture.

    3. appealingness of agents

4. English Canadians should make a greater effort to learn the French language.

    4. appealingness of an activity

5. The more I get to know the French Canadians, the more I want to be fluent in their language.

    5. appealingness of agents/ goal

6. Some of our best citizens are of French Canadian descent.

    6. appealingness of agents

7. The French Canadian heritage is an important part of our Canadian identity.

    7. appealingness of an object

8. If Canada should lose the French culture of Quebec, it would indeed be a great loss.

    8. appealingness of an object

9. French Canadians have preserved much of the beauty of the old Canadian folkways.

    9. appealingness of an object/agent

10. Most French Canadians are so friendly and easy to get along with that Canada is fortunate to have them.

    10. appealingness of agents

(Gardner, 1985, p. 178)

On the dimension of pleasantness, items 1, 3, 6, 7, 8, 9, and 10 elicit direct assessment of French Canadians; items 2, 4, and 5 assess intended or desired behaviors that reflect positive appraisals of French Canadians.

The AMTB also contains a 10-item scale assessing Attitude toward European French people.

Attitudes toward European French people

1. The European French people are considerate of the feelings of others.	1. appealingness of agents
2. I have a favorable attitude toward the European French.	2. appealingness of agents
3. The more I learn about the European French, the more I like them.	3. appealingness of agents
4. The European French are trustworthy and dependable.	4. appealingness of agents
5. I have always admired the European French people.	5. appealingness of agents
6. The European French are always friendly and hospitable.	6. appealingness of agents
7. The European French are cheerful, agreeable, and good humored.	7. appealingness of agents
8. I would like to get to know the European French people better.	8. appealingness of agents/ activity
9. The European French are a very kind and generous people.	9. appealingness of agents
10. For the most part, the European French are sincere and honest.	10. appealingness of agents

---

(Gardner, 1985, p. 178)

Again on the pleasantness dimension, on this scale, items 1–7, 9, and 10 elicit direct appraisals of European French people, and item 8 assesses a desired behavior which could result from an appraisal of European French people.

Interest in foreign languages is also assessed by a 10-item scale.

Interest in foreign languages

1. If I were visiting a foreign country, I would like to be able to speak the language of the people.	1. appealingness of an activity
2. Even though Canada is relatively far from countries speaking other languages, it is important for Canadians to learn foreign languages.	2. appealingness of an activity
3. I wish I could learn to speak another language perfectly.	3. appealingness of an activity/goal
4. I want to read the literature of a foreign language in the original language rather than a translation.	4. goal/appealingness of an activity
5. I often wish I could read newspapers or magazines in another language.	5. appealingness of an activity/goal
6. I would really like to learn a lot of foreign languages.	6. appealingness of an activity/goal
7. If I planned to stay in another country, I would make a great effort to learn the language even though I could get along in English.	7. appealingness of an activity/goal
8. I would study a foreign language in school even if it were not required.	8. appealingness of an activity
9. I enjoy meeting and listening to people who speak other languages.	9. appealingness of an activity/agents
10. Studying a foreign language is an enjoyable experience.	10. appealingness of an activity

(Gardner, 1985, p. 178)

Items 1–8 assess desired or intended behaviors that would result from or reflect appraisals of foreign language learning. Item 9 elicits an appraisal of meeting and listening to people who speak foreign languages, and item 10 assesses the learner's appraisal of foreign language study. This scale assesses interest in foreign languages along the dimensions of pleasantness. As in the other scales, a goal dimension is also present, but it is somewhat more explicit here. Because the items are cast mainly in terms of "wishes" and "woulds," it appears that the assessment of pleasantness (appealingness) is the dominant appraisal being made.

Integrative orientation is assessed on a 4-item Likert scale:

Integrative orientation

1. Studying French can be important to me because it will allow me to be more at ease with fellow Canadians who speak French.

    1. goal/appealingness of agent

2. Studying French can be important to me because it will allow me to meet and converse with more varied people.

    2. goal

3. Studying French can be important to me because it will enable me to better understand and appreciate French Canadian art and literature.

    3. goal/appealingness of objects

4. Studying French can be important to me because I will be able to participate more freely in the activities of other cultural groups.

    4. goal/appealingness of activities/agents

(Gardner, 1985, p. 179)

Each of these items elicits the learner's appraisal of his or her goal for learning French in terms of the desire to get to know, meet with, and speak to French Canadians; therefore, on this scale, the goal dimension is the foregrounded appraisal and the appeal of agents, activities, and objects is implied.

Instrumental orientation is also assessed on a 4-item Likert scale:

Instrumental orientation

1. Studying French can be important for me only because I'll need it for my future career.	1. goal
2. Studying French can be important for me because it will make me a more knowledgeable person.	2. goal, norm/self compatiblility
3. Studying French can be important to me because I think it will some-day be useful in getting a good job.	3. goal
4. Studing French can be important for me because other people will respect me more if I have a knowl-edge of a foreign language.	4. goal, norm/self compatibility

---

(Gardner, 1985, p. 179)

The items in this scale elicit the learner's appraisal of learning French in terms of future goals. In addition, items 2 and 4 reflect appraisals on the dimension of norm and self compatiblity.

The next scale contains two items that reflect an instrumental orientation and two that reflect an integrative orientation:

Orientation Index

I am studying French because:

a) I think it will some day be useful in getting a good job.	a) goal
b) I think it will help me to better understand French people and way of life.	b) goal, appealingness of agents/activities
c) It will allow me to meet and converse with more and varied people.	c) goal
d) A knowledge of two lan-guages will make a better-educated person.	d) goal

---

(Gardner, 1985, p. 182)

Appraisals along the goal dimensions are dominant on this scale.

(3) Attitudes toward the learning situation are assessed in AMTB by two measures: (a) the evaluation of the language teacher scale and (b) the evaluation of the language course scale. These two scales directly elicit appraisals of the teacher and the course in terms of sets of 25 bipolar adjectives. Thus, the two scales assess pleasantness in terms of the appealingness of the teacher as an agent and of the course as an activity/object.

My French teacher		
efficient	__ : __ : __ : __ : __ : __ : __	inefficient
insensitive	__ : __ : __ : __ : __ : __ : __	sensitive
cheerful	__ : __ : __ : __ : __ : __ : __	cheerless
competent	__ : __ : __ : __ : __ : __ : __	incompetent
insincere	__ : __ : __ : __ : __ : __ : __	sincere
unapproachable	__ : __ : __ : __ : __ : __ : __	approachable
pleasant	__ : __ : __ : __ : __ : __ : __	unpleasant
trusting	__ : __ : __ : __ : __ : __ : __	suspicious
incapable	__ : __ : __ : __ : __ : __ : __	capable
tedious	__ : __ : __ : __ : __ : __ : __	fascinating
friendly	__ : __ : __ : __ : __ : __ : __	unfriendly
exciting	__ : __ : __ : __ : __ : __ : __	dull
organized	__ : __ : __ : __ : __ : __ : __	disorganized
unreliable	__ : __ : __ : __ : __ : __ : __	reliable
unimaginative	__ : __ : __ : __ : __ : __ : __	imaginative
impatient	__ : __ : __ : __ : __ : __ : __	patient
polite	__ : __ : __ : __ : __ : __ : __	impolite
colourful	__ : __ : __ : __ : __ : __ : __	colourless
unintelligent	__ : __ : __ : __ : __ : __ : __	intelligent
good	__ : __ : __ : __ : __ : __ : __	bad
industrious	__ : __ : __ : __ : __ : __ : __	unindustrious
boring	__ : __ : __ : __ : __ : __ : __	interesting
dependable	__ : __ : __ : __ : __ : __ : __	undependable
disinterested	__ : __ : __ : __ : __ : __ : __	interested
inconsiderate	__ : __ : __ : __ : __ : __ : __	considerate

(Gardner, 1985, pp. 183–4)

My French course

meaningful	___ : ___ : ___ : ___ : ___ : ___ : ___	meaningless
enjoyable	___ : ___ : ___ : ___ : ___ : ___ : ___	unenjoyable
monotonous	___ : ___ : ___ : ___ : ___ : ___ : ___	absorbing
effortless	___ : ___ : ___ : ___ : ___ : ___ : ___	hard
awful	___ : ___ : ___ : ___ : ___ : ___ : ___	nice
interesting	___ : ___ : ___ : ___ : ___ : ___ : ___	boring
good	___ : ___ : ___ : ___ : ___ : ___ : ___	bad
simple	___ : ___ : ___ : ___ : ___ : ___ : ___	complicated
disagreeable	___ : ___ : ___ : ___ : ___ : ___ : ___	agreeable
fascinating	___ : ___ : ___ : ___ : ___ : ___ : ___	tedious
worthless	___ : ___ : ___ : ___ : ___ : ___ : ___	valuable
necessary	___ : ___ : ___ : ___ : ___ : ___ : ___	unnecessary
appealing	___ : ___ : ___ : ___ : ___ : ___ : ___	unappealing
useless	___ : ___ : ___ : ___ : ___ : ___ : ___	useful
elementary	___ : ___ : ___ : ___ : ___ : ___ : ___	complex
pleasurable	___ : ___ : ___ : ___ : ___ : ___ : ___	painful
educational	___ : ___ : ___ : ___ : ___ : ___ : ___	noneducational
unrewarding	___ : ___ : ___ : ___ : ___ : ___ : ___	rewarding
difficult	___ : ___ : ___ : ___ : ___ : ___ : ___	easy
satisfying	___ : ___ : ___ : ___ : ___ : ___ : ___	unsatisfying
unimportant	___ : ___ : ___ : ___ : ___ : ___ : ___	important
pleasant	___ : ___ : ___ : ___ : ___ : ___ : ___	unpleasant
exciting	___ : ___ : ___ : ___ : ___ : ___ : ___	dull
clear	___ : ___ : ___ : ___ : ___ : ___ : ___	confusing
colourful	___ : ___ : ___ : ___ : ___ : ___ : ___	colourless

(Gardner, 1985, p. 184)

(4) Finally, anxiety, is measured on the AMTB by a 5-item French class anxiety scale.

French class anxiety

1. It embarrasses me to volunteer answers in our French class.

    1. coping potential, norm/self compatibility, appealingness

2. I never feel quite sure of myself when I am speaking in our French class.

    2. coping potential, norm/self compatibility, appealingness

3. I always feel that the other students speak French better than I do.	3. coping potential, norm/self compatibility, appealingness
4. I get nervous and confused when I am speaking in my French class.	4. coping potential, norm/self compatibility, appealingness
5. I am afraid the other students will laugh at me when I speak French.	5. coping potential, norm/self compatibility, appealingness

(Gardner, 1985, p. 179)

The five items on this scale assess the learner's anxiety by eliciting appraisals that tap the subjects' coping potential, norm/self compatibility, and the appeal of particular classroom activities.

The point of this analysis of the AMTB is to demonstrate that the perspective on stimulus appraisal is compatible with Gardner's attitude and motivation approach because it is stimulus appraisal that underlies attitude and motivation. What the current perspective provides is an analysis at a level that may help connect variable success with biology. Gardner (1985, and personal communication, April 17, 1995) explicitly recognizes the role of appraisal and defines attitude as "*an evaluative reaction to some referent or attitude object, inferred on the basis of the individual's beliefs or opinions about the referent*" (p.9). He subsequently identified as referents such things as learning French, the other language community, the language learning context, and so forth. Therefore, stimulus appraisal in the current formulation is equivalent to Gardner's notion of "evaluative reaction to referent." The analysis of Gardner's questionnaire shows that attitudes and motivation are the product of stimulus appraisal. We may hypothesize then that attitude and motivation result from particular patterns of stimulus appraisal that derive from the learner's homeostatic, sociostatic, and somatic value systems as encoded in value category/schematic emotional memory. This relationship is depicted in Figure 3.1.

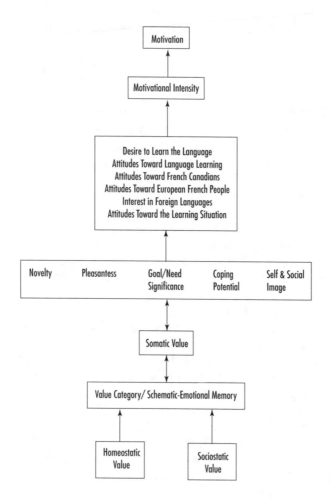

Figure 3.1. The Stimulus-Appraisal Basis for Attitude and Motivation.

Other Views of Motivation in Relation to Stimulus Appraisal

As indicated in the beginning of this chapter, earlier research by Gardner and colleagues on motivation in SLA had stressed the role of the sociocultural context in L2 learning.

Some researchers in the early 1990s began to encourage the exploration of links between motivation and other contexts. From the perspective taken in this book, we would see as valuable the exploration of stimulus-appraisal-context links because, although each individual's stimulus appraisal system is unique, socialization can make whole groups of people appraise certain stimuli similarly. In this section, I review the proposals for other research paradigms on motivation and examine their compatibility with the stimulus appraisal perspective.

In an attempt to examine motivation in a strictly foreign language setting where exposure to native speakers is extremely limited, Clément, Dörnyei, and Noels (1994), examined the motivation to learn English among 301 secondary-school students in Budapest, Hungary. Their study had a social psychological perspective that included the examination of orientations, attitudes, linguistic self-confidence and classroom group dynamics. The authors found a motivational complex consisting of three components: integrative motivation, linguistic self-confidence, and the appraisal of the classroom environment.

The researchers did not provide their questionnaire, but an examination of a sample of the item loadings in the factor analyses offers some indication of the appraisals they elicited to explore motivation in this context. It should be noted that without the actual questionnaire it is difficult to be certain about appraisal designation, but a good approximation can be made using items generated by factor analysis (see Table 3.1).

From Table 3.1, we can see that integrative motivation has four components: a friendship orientation, sociocultural knowledge, instrumental knowledge, and an attitude and effort dimension. The friendship orientation seems to involve patterns of appraisal of goal relevance of the appealingness of agents (foreigners). The sociocultural knowledge component appears to result from appraisals of goal relevance in relation to the appealingness of objects (cultures, nations). The instrumental knowledge element seems to involve mainly appraisal of goal relevance, and the attitudes and effort scale reflects patterns of appraisal of appealingness of agents/activities. Thus integrative motivation seems to emerge from appraisals of appealingness (the pleasantnesss dimension) and goal relevance. On the linguistic self-confidence component, appraisals of coping potential and self-compatibility appear to be particularly relevant, and the

Table 3.1

The Classification According to Appraisal Category of a Sample of the Item Loadings in Clément et al.'s (1994) Factor Analyses

---

1. *Integrative Motivation*

a. Friendship orientation

Make friends with foreigners	appealingness of agents/goal
Meet foreigners	appealingness of agents/goal
Know new foreign people	appealingness of agents/goal
Will help when traveling	goal
Keep in touch with foreign friends	appealingness of agents/goal
Would like to travel	goal
Learn many foreign languages	goal

b. Sociocultural Knowledge

Know various cultures/peoples	appealingness of objects, agents/goal
Learn about English world	appealingness of agents/goal
Understand English nations	appealingness of agents/goal
Know cultures/world events	appealingness of agents/goal
Know life of English nations	appealingness of agents/goal

c. Instrumental Knowledge

Is part of being educated	norm compatibility
To be more knowledgeable	goal
Without it—difficult to succeed	goal
To broaden my outlook	goal
May need later/job, studies	goal
It is expected of me	norm compatibility
To take the State Language Exam	goal

d. Attitudes & Efforts Scale

Attitudes toward the British	appealingness of agents
Motivational intensity	appealingness of activities
Attitudes toward Americans	appealingness of agents
Student's need to achieve	goal?

2. *Linguistic Self-Confidence*

Anxiety in class	coping potential/ self-compatibility
English use anxiety	coping potential/ self-compatibility

Table 3.1 *(continued)*

Self-evaluation of proficiency	coping potential
Frequency of contact	?
Attitudes toward learning English	appealingness of an activity/goal
Quality of contact	appealingness of activity
Satisfaction with competence	self-compatability
Course difficulty	coping potential
Desired English proficiency	goal

3. *Appraisal of Classroom Environment*

Teacher's style	appealingness of an agent
Teacher's competence	appealingness of an agent
Course attractiveness	appealingness of object/ activity
Teacher's motivation	?
Course usefulness	goal
Teacher's rapport	appealingness of agent

appraisal of the appealingness of agents (the teacher) appears to be important in the appraisal of the classroom environment component.

Dörnyei (1994) provides an extensive review of various motivational constructs and synthesizes them into a multilevel framework for L2 motivation (see Table 3.2). The framework consists of a Language Level, a Learner Level, and a Learning Situation Level. The Language Level involves what has already been discussed as integrative and instrumental motivation. These motivations were shown earlier in the chapter to be the product of a particular pattern of stimulus appraisal. The Learner Level consists of two motivational components: need for achievement and self-confidence. In need-achievement, the learner is motivated by the desire to excel either in general or with respect to certain tasks. In terms of stimulus appraisal, the individuals of the first kind find a high level of performance in general to be rewarding and seek that level. By achieving, they avoid negatively appraised average or poor performance. Individuals of the second kind restrict such patterns of appraisal to

Table 3.2

Components Of Foreign Language Learning Motivation (from Dörnyei, 1994, p. 280)

LANGUAGE LEVEL	Integrative Motivational Subsystem
	Instrumental Motivational Subsystem
LEARNER LEVEL	Need for Achievement
	Self-Confidence
	•Language Use Anxiety
	•Perceived L2 Competence
	•Causal Attributions
	•Self-Efficacy
LEARNER SITUATION LEVEL	
Course-Specific Motivational Components	Interest
	Relevance
	Expectancy
	Satisfaction
Teacher-Specific Motivational Components	Affiliative Drive
	Authority Type
	Direct Socialization of Motivation
	•Modelling
	•Task Presentation
	•Feedback
Group-Specific Motivational Components	Goal-orientedness
	Norm & Reward System
	Group Cohesion
	Classroom Goal Structure

certain activities that they assess as novel, pleasant, important for their goals and needs, compatible with their coping abilities, and enhancing of their self and social image.

The second component of the Learner Level involves several aspects of self-confidence including language use anxiety, perceived L2 competence, causal attributions, and self-efficacy. Essentially all these factors are, from the stimulus appraisal perspective, assessments of coping ability. Here the learner assesses his ability to deal with the tasks involved in language learning. The learner's performance becomes an environmental stimulus that is appraised in terms of his goals and needs and self and social image. If the learner feels that his coping capacity is inadequate to enhance these dimensions, anxiety and avoidance result.

At the Learning Situation Level there are several course-specific motivational components, which Dörnyei incorporates from the work of Crookes and Schmidt (1991). Interest relates to how the elements of the learning situation affect the learner's curiosity and desire to know about something. It may involve stimulus appraisals of novelty, familiarity, and pleasantness. Revelance involves the relationship of course-specific components to the learner's goals, needs, and values and would be appraised according to how they affect those dimensions. Expectancy concerns perceptions about the likelihood of success in relation to estimations of task difficulty, effort required, and assistance available. From a stimulus-appraisal perspective, expectancy is an assessment of the learner's ability to cope successfully with the language learning tasks. Finally, satisfaction concerns the rewards (praise, grades, enjoyment, pride) that are generated by the activity. Here, appraisals would be made in terms of pleasantness, goals, and self and social image.

Teacher-specific motivational components involve the learner's desire to please the teacher and the teacher's particular style as an authority on language and on language learning. In addition, this component relates to how the teacher provides feedback, correction, and direction. The learner will assess these components in terms of all five dimensions of stimulus appraisal. The appraisal of the teacher becomes particularly important because of her ability to foster in the student interest, excitement, and validation, or alternatively embarrassment, shame, and humiliation.

The final set of elements at the Learning Situation Level are group-specific motivational components, which concern the dynamics of the learners as a social unit or group. From a stimulus-appraisal perspective, all five dimensions would come into play, but assessments in terms of goals and needs and self and social image would be particularly important.

Oxford and Shearin (1994), also in an effort to encourage additional perspectives on motivation in SLA, review a broad range of motivational paradigms. Their analysis covers need theories, instrumentality theories, equity theories, and self-efficacy theories. Their survey indicates that learners are motivated:

1) by satisfaction of personal needs (safety, security, belonging, etc.), job satisfaction needs, and the need to achieve;
2) by estimates of success in relation to the value they or society place on the results of the effort;
3) by estimates of their contribution to tasks (aptitude, effort, experience, skill) in relation to estimates of the significance of outcomes (proficiency, enjoyment, career enhancement, etc.) according to self and others' standards.

These various motivational perspectives would appear to be compatible with the notion that motivation is the product of appraisals of stimuli and stimulus events. Appraisals according to goal/need significance, coping ability, and self and social image seem to be particularly important in the theories reviewed by Oxford and Shearin.

Crooks and Schmidt (1991) express dissatisfaction with social-psychological approaches to the study of motivation and advocate the examination of motivation in second language acquisition from other perspectives. Schmidt and Savage (1992) explore motivation in SLA from the perspective proposed by Csikszentmihalyi (Csikszentmihalyi & Larsen, 1987; Csikszentmihalyi & Nakamura, 1989; Massimini, Csikszentmihalyi, & Carli, 1987) who suggests that when both skill level and challenge are high, the learner will have high motivation, affect, arousal, and concentration.

Csikszentmihalyi (Csikszentmihalyi & Nakamura, 1989) is essentially concerned with examining intrinsic motivation, which is defined as motivation for undertaking an activity that is neither a response to biological drives nor a response to external punishments or rewards. People are intrinsically motivated when they do something because they want to, that is, because they find the activity itself rewarding.

Csikszentmihalyi and Nakamura (1989) also assume that an activity will be most intrinsically rewarding in situations in which the challenge is higher and the person's skill level is equal to the challenge. This formulation makes sense in terms of stimulus appraisal because people are not likely to pursue something if it presents a challenge that, because of their skill level, they always fail to meet. Of course skill level is, to some extent, controlled by aptitude, and aptitude can place a ceiling on skill that a particular challenge level may exceed.

In terms of stimulus appraisal, a new challenge level might be assessed in terms of its novelty. Perceived skill level is essentially an assessment of one's coping capacity vis-à-vis a stimulus. This assessment evaluates an individual's ability to cope with a task and her ability to psychologically adjust to the outcome. Coping capacity in relation to a challenge will also affect one's self and social image and will affect the assessment of the pleasantness of an event.

In Schmidt and Savage's (1992) study, Thai language learners' motivation was evaluated using the Experience Sampling Method (adapted from Csikszentmihalyi & Larson, 1987, pp. 335-336). This instrument is a 35-item questionnaire that participants fill out at various times during the day in response to a wrist watch alarm programmed to ring at times selected by the researchers. Schmidt and Savage report that they did not find the predicted relationships between challenge and skill, or between challenge and motivation, affect, or activation. They explain their results by the fact that the Thais valued different aspects of their English program than those predicted by the model. Instead of being motivated by a match between challenge and skill, they were motivated by (1) an instrumental desire to improve their ability to communicate in English and thus their performance at work, (2) the classroom atmosphere, which they found relaxed, engaging, and fun, and (3) the methodological procedures and techniques used in the program. Therefore, Schmidt and Savage conclude that for these Thai students the source of intrinsic motivation is not limited to the challenge/skill match, but a task is also intrinsically motivating if it is fun, that is, if it is relaxing and is done with other people. This outcome is also compatible with a stimulus-appraisal perspective, but here the Thai students' appraisal systems are socialized to gain intrinsic motivation from activities that are not only challenging, but that are also social and relaxing. Schmidt and Savage report that Thais have a special word (*sanuk*) for activities that are simultaneously challenging, social, and relaxing.

An examination of the Experience Sampling Method Questionnaire (Schmidt & Savage, 1992, Appendix A, pp. 27–28), which was used in the research, shows the extent to which it elicits stimulus appraisals in order to assess what, in the participant's current experience, is motivation. Part I determines what the participant was doing, what she was thinking, where she was, and why she was engaging in the particular activity.

Code Name: Time beeped: am/pm   Time filled out: am/pm

As you were beeped . . .

What were you thinking about?

Where were you?

What was the MAIN thing you were doing?

What other things were you doing?

WHY were you doing this particular activity?

I had to   I wanted to   I had nothing else to do   1. goal
                do it

(From Csikszentmihalyi & Larsen, 1987, pp. 535-536, as used by Schmidt & Savage, 1992)

Part II contains seven questions that elicit appraisals: questions 1, 2, and 5 assess coping ability, 3, 4, and 6 evaluate self-image (self-compatibility), and 7 elicits an appraisal of one's social image or norm compability.

	not at all			somewhat			quite		very		
1. How well were you concentrat-ing?	0	1	2	3	4	5	6	7	8	9	1. coping potential
2. Was it hard to concentrate?	0	1	2	3	4	5	6	7	8	9	2. coping potential
3. How self-con-scious were you?	0	1	2	3	4	5	6	7	8	9	3. self-com-patibility
4. Did you feel good about your-self?	0	1	2	3	4	5	6	7	8	9	4. self-com-patibility
5. Were you in control of the sit-uation?	0	1	2	3	4	5	6	7	8	9	5. coping potential
6. Were you living up to your own expectations?	0	1	2	3	4	5	6	7	8	9	6. self-com-patibility
7. Were you living up to expecta-tions of others?	0	1	2	3	4	5	6	7	8	9	7. norm com-patibility

(From Csikszentmihalyi & Larsen, 1987, pp. 535-536, as used by Schmidt & Savage, 1992)

Part III uses a semantic differential scale of polar adjectives to assess the participant's mood. In Part IV, items 1, 2, 5, and 7 assess coping ability, and items 3, 4, and 8 assess the activity in terms of the participant's goals and needs, and items 6 and 9 appraise the appealingness of an activity.

Describe your mood as you were beeped:

	very	quite	some		some	quite	very	
alert	0	1	2	3	4	5	6	drowsy
happy	0	1	2	3	4	5	6	sad
irritable	0	1	2	3	4	5	6	cheerful
strong	0	1	2	3	4	5	6	weak
active	0	1	2	3	4	5	6	passive
lonely	0	1	2	3	4	5	6	sociable
ashamed	0	1	2	3	4	5	6	proud
involved	0	1	2	3	4	5	6	detached

	very	quite	some		some	quite	very	
excited	0	1	2	3	4	5	6	bored
closed	0	1	2	3	4	5	6	open
clear	0	1	2	3	4	5	6	confused
tense	0	1	2	3	4	5	6	relaxed
competi-tive	0	1	2	3	4	5	6	coopera-tive

(From Csikszentmihalyi & Larsen, 1987, pp. 535-536, as used by Schmidt & Savage, 1992)

Indicate how you felt about your activity:

	low						high				
1. Challenges of the activity	0	1	2	3	4	5	6	7	8	9	1. coping potential
2. Your skills in the activity	0	1	2	3	4	5	6	7	8	9	2. coping potential
	not at all					very much					
3. Was this activity important to you?	0	1	2	3	4	5	6	7	8	9	3. goal
4. Was this activity important to others?	0	1	2	3	4	5	6	7	8	9	4. goal
5. Were you succeeding at what you were doing?	0	1	2	3	4	5	6	7	8	9	5. coping potential
6. Do you wish you had been doing something else?	0	1	2	3	4	5	6	7	8	9	6. appeal-ingness of an activity
7. Were you satisfied with how you were doing?	0	1	2	3	4	5	6	7	8	9	7. coping potential
8. How important was this activity in relation to your overall goals?	0	1	2	3	4	5	6	7	8	9	8. goal

9. If you had a choice, what would you be doing?	9. appealingness of an activity

10. Since you were last beeped, has anything happened or have you done anything which could have affected the way you feel?

(From Csikszentmihalyi & Larsen, 1987, pp. 535-536, as used by Schmidt & Savage, 1992)

Of the 17 items relevant to stimulus appraisal, 7 relate to coping potential, 4 to goals, 4 to norm or self-compatibility, and 2 to pleasantness (appealingness of an activity in relation to a goal). Since Csikszentmihalyi and colleagues view motivation as a product of skill level and challenge, the focus of the questionnaire on appraisals of coping potential (skill) and goals (challenge) makes sense theoretically.

In response to the suggestions by Crookes and Schmidt (1991), Dörnyei (1994), and Oxford and Shearin (1994) to expand the notion of motivation in second language acquisition, Tremblay and Gardner (1995) examined the roles of expectancy and self-efficiency, valence, causal attributions, and goal setting on the French proficiency of 75 Francophone students with varying degrees of dominance in the language. They assessed the influence of the constructs mentioned above on three variables reflecting motivational behavior: effort, persistence, and attention.

Expectancy relates to an individual's anticipation of events that are rewarding. Within this construct, motivation to do something is assumed to be greater when the individual has a high expectancy that he can achieve a particular goal. Self-efficacy refers to an individual's expectancy that he will be able to achieve a particular goal or standard of performance. The researchers only provide brief illustrative examples of the scales measuring the constructs. Expectancy was assessed on a 7-point Likert scale that elicited the learners' expectations of what they could perform in French by the end of the course (e.g., "'Understand the meaning of most French proverbs,' 'Speak French well enough to be able to teach at the secondary level,' and 'Work as a writer for a French newspaper.'" p.512). These items seem to elicit appraisals related to what Scherer (1984) refers to as a goal/need expectation check (i.e., the expectation of what can be achieved in relation to a desired goal) and the control aspect of the coping potential assessment (i.e., the individual's estimation of his ability to cope with the activities required to achieve the goal). In addition, the expectancy and self-esteem construct seems to involve appraisals along the dimensions of probability and power (control or influence) proposed by Roseman et al. (1996), appraisals of likelihood proposed by Ortony et al. (1988) and internal, stable, and controllable causal attributions proposed by Weiner (1986), which involve the individual's estimation that an outcome is achievable because he has control (i.e., the ability) to achieve it.

The valence construct relates to the attractiveness of a task in terms of the value an individual associates with an outcome that would result from the task. The higher the outcome is valued, the greater will be the motivation. This construct appears to involve appraisals of pleasantness (Scherer, 1984; Smith & Ellsworth, 1985), goal relevance (Scherer, 1984), and the appealingness of an event (task) treated as an object (Ortony et al., 1988).

Causal attributions are judgments about why a particular event (outcome) occurred. Attributions of success to ability or effort (called adaptive attributions) are seen to be motivating whereas attributions to luck or other external events would not be motivating. Attributions to ability are, of course, related to appraisals of self-efficacy and the expectancy of success. This construct would appear to involve appraisals of coping potential (Scherer, 1984), responsibility and control (Smith & Ellsworth, 1985), accountability (Lazarus & Smith, 1988), power (control and influence potential) (Roseman et al., 1996) and agency (Ortony et al., 1988).

In terms of goal-setting, Tremblay and Gardner (1995) hypothesize that success is increased if learners have specific and difficult goals. The idea is that goals mediate the effort that is expended in the tasks leading to the goal. The researchers use two measures of goal-setting. The first elicits information about the specificity of the learner's goal (e.g., "I have a clear idea of the level of French I want to reach"), and the second addresses the extent to which the students organize their study by setting goals for themselves (e.g., "I often make lists of things I have to do in my French course").

Tremblay and Gardner (1995) simply inquire about whether and how frequently learners set goals. In contrast to what is explored by appraisal theorists, they do not examine whether agents or events in the learning environment facilitated or hindered their achievement of those goals. The diary studies and autobiographies of language learners that will be examined later indicate that events in the language environment or language class are appraised as enhancing or detrimental to the learners' goals. These appraisals, of course, influence attention, effort, and thus learning.

Tremblay and Gardner (1995) hypothesized that motivational behavior would have a direct influence on achievement, that adaptive attributions would influence self-efficacy, that self-efficacy, valence, and goal salience would directly influence motivational behavior, that language attitudes would have direct influence on goal salience, valence and self-efficacy, and that French language dominance would have direct influence on adaptive attributions. The authors report that these predictions were largely borne out except that effort attributions did not have significant loadings on adaptive attributions. Based on research by Bandura (1991), the authors point out that while effort may be related to self-efficacy, a learner's report of high expenditure of effort might also indicate low ability.

Schmidt, Boraie, and Kassabgy (1996) undertook research to examine the internal structure of motivation in second language learning. Their perspective was that of value-expectancy theories. They assume that people are motivated to undertake activities that they consider valuable and relevant to their goals and in which they believe they can succeed. Their subjects were 1,464 students between the ages of 15 and 70 (58% were 25–35 years old, 24% were 19–22 years old) studying at a private language institute in Cairo. The research also examined the students' instructional preferences and learning strategies, but only the motivational aspect of the research will concern us here. The students filled out questionnaires consisting of 50 statements related to motivation. Responses indicating agreement or disagreement were made on 6-point Likert scales. The questionnaire was in Arabic. The items were designed to assess intrinsic motivation (e.g., I enjoy learning English very much); extrinsic motivation (e.g., I need to be able to read textbooks in English); personal psychological needs (e.g., I really want to learn more English in this class than I have in the past, One of the most important things in this class is getting along with other students); expectations (e.g., This English class will definitely help me improve my English); locus of control (e.g., If I do well in this course, it will be because I try hard); stereotypical attitudes (e.g., Americans are friendly people); anxiety (e.g., I feel uncomfortable if I have to speak in my English class); and motivational strength (e.g., My attendance in this class will be good).

A factor analysis of the results generated a nine-factor solution consisting of determination and expectation of success, anxiety, extrinsic motivation, sociability, attitudes toward the foreign culture, desire for foreign residence, intrinsic motivation, attribution of failure to extrinsic causes, and enjoyment. This factor analytic solution accounted for 50.3% of the total variance. The authors then submitted the data to a multidimensional scaling analysis that yielded a three-dimensional model, which accounted for 85% of the variance. The three dimensions were affect, goal orientation, and expectancy.

The authors note that the affect dimension could be labeled "enjoyment" or "intrinsic motivation." This dimension indicates subjects experienced learning English as enjoyable when their skill level and challenge were high, and they experienced anxiety when the challenge was high and their skill level was low. The goal orientation dimension seems to involve extrinsic motivation relating to the desire to emigrate, to gain financial benefits, to read textbooks in English, to get a better job, to develop a broader worldview, and to become more educated. The expectancy dimension was associated with issues of determination, confidence, orientation toward success, and positive thinking.

An examination of Schmidt et al.'s questionnaire items (see Table 3.3) indicates that the nine-category factor analytic model and the three-category multidimensional scaling model can be seen to derive from a higher order analysis of appraisals made mainly along three dimensions: goal significance, appealingness (pleasantness) of agents, activities or objects, and coping potential. Some of the items in the questionnaire elicit more than one appraisal. As indicated earlier, value expectancy theories of motivation, which constitute the theoretical perspective of the

Schmidt et al. study, assume that activities that are relevant to people's goals and within their ability are motivating. Therefore, it is reasonable that appraisals along the dimensions of goals, coping potential, and appealingness would scale up into motivations predicted in value expectancy theories, and would suggest that motivations in general may be emergent properties of stimulus appraisals.

Table 3.3

An Analysis of Schmidt et al.'s (1996) Motivation Questionnaire in Terms of Categories of Stimulus Appraisal (pp. 80–83)

Intrinsic motivation

1. I enjoy learning English very much.	1. appealingness of an activity
2. Learning English is a hobby for me.	2. appealingness of an activity
3. Learning English is a challenge that I enjoy.	3. appealingness of an activity
4. I don't enjoy learning English, but I know that learning English is important for me. (reverse coded)	4. appealingness of an activity, goal
5. I wish I could learn English in an easier way, without going to class. (reverse coded)	5. appealingness of an activity

Extrinsic motivation

6. English is important to me because it will broaden my view.	6. goal
7. The main reason I am taking this class is that my parents/ my spouse/my supervisors want me to improve my English.	7. goal, norm compatibility
8. I want to do well in this class because it is important to show my ability to my family/ friends/supervisors/others.	8. goal, norm compatibility

Table 3.3 *(continued)*

9. Everybody in Egypt should be able to speak English.	9. goal
10. Being able to speak English will add to my social status.	10. goal, norm compatibility
11. I am learning English because I want to spend a period of time in an English speaking country.	11. goal
12. I want to learn English because it is useful when traveling in many countries.	12. goal
13. I want to learn English because I would like to emigrate.	13. goal
14. One reason I learn English is that I can meet new people and make friends in my English class.	14. goal
15. I am learning English to become more educated.	15. goal
16. I need to be able to read textbooks in English.	16. goal
17. The main reason I need to learn English is to pass examinations.	17. goal
18. If I learn English better, I will be able to get a better job.	18. goal
19. Increasing my English proficiency will have financial benefits for me.	19. goal
20. If I can speak English I will have a marvelous life.	20. goal

Personal goals

21. I really want to learn more English in this class than I have done in the past.	21. goal

Table 3.3 *(continued)*

22. It is important to me to do better than the other students in my class.	22. goal, self-compatibility
23. My relationship with the teacher in this class is important to me.	23. goal
24. One of the most important things in this class is getting along with the other students.	24. goal
25. This class is important to me because if I learn English well, I will be able to help my children learn English.	25. goal

Expectancy/control components

26. This English class will definitely help me improve my English.	26. goal
27. If I do well in this course, it will be because I try hard.	27. coping potential
28. I expect to do well in this class because I am good at learning English.	28. coping potential
29. If I don't do well in this class, it will be because I don't try hard enough.	29. coping potential
30. If I don't do well in this class, it will be because I don't have much ability for learning English.	30. coping potential
31. If I learn a lot in this class, it will be because of the teacher.	31. coping potential
32. If I do well in this class, it will be because this is an easy class.	32. coping potential

Table 3.3 *(continued)*

33. If I don't learn well in this class, it will be mainly because of the teacher.	33. coping potential
34. If I don't do well in this class, it will be because the class is too difficult.	34. coping potential

Attitudes

35. Americans are very friendly people.	35. appealingness of agents
36. The English are conservative people who cherish customs and traditions.	36. appealingness of agents
37. Most of my favourite actors and musicians are either British or American.	37. appealingness of agents
38. British culture has contributed a lot to the world.	38. appealingness of agents

Anxiety

39. I feel uncomfortable if I have to speak in my English class.	39. coping potential, norm/self compatibility, appealingness of an activity
40. It embarrasses me to volunteer answers in my English class.	40. coping potential, norm/self compatibility, appealingness of an activity
41. I don't like to speak often in English class, because I am afraid that my teacher will think I am not a good student.	41. coping potential, norm/self compatibility, appealingness of an activity
42. I am afraid other students will laugh at me when I speak English.	42. coping potential, norm/self compatibility, appealingness of an activity
43. I think I can learn English well, but I don't perform well on tests and examinations.	43. coping potential
44. I often have difficulty concentrating in English class.	44. coping potential

Table 3.3 *(continued)*

Motivational strength

45. If the fees for this class were increased, I would still enroll because studying English is important to me.	45. goal
46. My attendance in this class will be good.	46. goal
47. I plan to continue studying English for as long as possible.	47. goal
48. After I finish this class, I will probably take another English course.	48. goal
49. I often think about how I can learn English better.	49. goal, coping potential
50. I can honestly say that I really put my best effort into trying to learn English.	50. coping potential

Summary

The analysis of the research on motivation presented in this chapter was designed to demonstrate how motivation is determined by eliciting appraisals of agents, activities, and objects in the language learning environment. The analysis also reveals that different motivational frameworks focus on different appraisal dimensions. For example, in the early research done by Gardner (1985) and associates, approximately 70% of the appraisals elicited were on the appealingness (pleasantness) dimension. In the Clément, Dörnyei, and Noels (1994) research, appraisals of appealingness and goals were dominant. Schmidt and Savage's (1992) work focused strongly on appraisals of coping potential, and to a lesser extent on goal significance, norm and self-compatibility, with appealingness playing a relatively small role. In Schmidt et al. (1996) goal relevance received major focus with a substantial number of items eliciting appraisals of coping potential and appealingness. Tremblay and Gardner (1995) were attempting to expand their motivational perspective and, therefore, elicited a fairly broad range of appraisals.

4

Some More Data: Diary Studies and Autobiographies

Diary Studies

What additional evidence exists for the role of the stimulus appraisal system in producing variable success in SLA? Actually, a rather large body of empirical support can be found in the SLA "diary study" literature. In the mid-1970s, a number of colleagues and I began to try to understand affective aspects of SLA by having learners keep intensive diaries of their reactions to teacher, method, text, target language, its speakers, and the culture in which it is embedded. These studies were conducted in classrooms, in the target language environment, and sometimes in both. Probably 30 or more studies were done in this way. It was felt that the findings of these individual case studies could be aggregated and new generalizations could be made about the role of affective/motivational variables in SLA. Kathleen Bailey was the major researcher in the aggregation efforts, and in a series of publications (Bailey, 1983, 1985, 1991; Bailey & Ochsner, 1983), she reported a variable that strongly influenced second language learning and had not been previously identified. This variable was competitiveness and the anxiety it generated in the language learning situations. However, beyond this successful finding, aggregation across studies has proven very difficult. The diary studies yielded highly individual language learning stories. What emerged were what Schumann and Schumann (1977) called personal variables—influences on SLA that were very often unique to individual learners. But now looking back at those studies, I view them as chronicles of stimulus appraisal. They are accounts of the learner's preferences and aversions, likes and dislikes concerning their language learning. They, in fact, report the learner's perceptions of novelty, pleasantness, goal/need significance, coping potential, and self and social image with respect to the language learning situation. Below I will quote at some length from various diary studies to illustrate their authors' stimulus appraisals.

In the first study, the researcher/learner summarized from the diaries she kept in Tunisia and Iran. She reflects on her coping mechanism vis-à-vis her housing situation and her language learning.

> In both the Tunisia and Iran journals, it is clear that in order for me to be able to devote the time, energy or emotional involvement required in language learning, I must first feel content in the place I am living. My surroundings must be orderly, comfortable and have my imprint on them identifying them as my home away from home. I devote days to putting my nest in order leaving very little energy or even thought for anything else. If I am frustrated in my attempt to build a suitable nest, it will have a negative effect on my pursuing any creative endeavor such as language learning.

> In Tunisia, I was totally unable to fulfill this nesting instinct. We lived in a 300-year-old building in the medina (Arab part of town near the souk). I was never able to adjust to the lack of hot water, comfortable furniture and a suitable place to put away my belongings. I was also frustrated by the constant layers of dirt blowing in and having to put up with a strange type of bug in the house that attacked us all summer causing us to look like smallpox victims throughout our stay. The result was that I felt alienated from and hostile towards my environment, and these emotions usurped my energies such that I rarely could direct any to studying Arabic the entire time we lived there.

> Again this nesting was an issue with me upon our arrival in Iran. Fortunately, the accommodations there lent themselves to fulfilling this instinct and doing so

within a reasonable period of time. Because we lived in a hotel, I was free of cleaning responsibilities and the room was put in order for me daily. The furniture both accommodated our belongings and was comfortable and even provided a very suitable work area. Thus, it was only a matter of unpacking and deciding on convenient places to put things away. Within a week of our arrival I was content that things were to my satisfaction. I was then able to begin to direct my energy to the task of studying Persian. (Schumann & Schumann, 1977, pp. 243–244)

In the next excerpt, the same learner demonstrates how a negative appraisal of the teaching method led to withdrawal from learning.

A rigid adherence to the audiolingual method was followed in my Arabic class. The TL was used exclusively as the means of instruction. Weekly lessons included full page dialogues followed by approximately 6–8 pages of drills. No translations, grammatical explanations or vocabulary lists were given during lessons nor did the text supply one with these supports. In class students were forbidden to write anything down to aid them in remembering, to copy words or sentences off the chalk-board, to look up things in the text or to consult with fellow learners for clarification. The rule was listen, repeat and respond over and over for four hours. The sole source of language was the teacher. I hated the method. My anger bred frustration, a frustration which I acutely felt as my goal was to be a star performer in class, and I found it impossible to be so under these circumstances.

Instead of resorting to a solution that would allow me to cope with this learning environment and learn in spite of the method, my reaction was to reject it and withdraw from learning. This withdrawal was gradual and displayed itself in a variety of ways. Some days I would assume such a low profile in class, making no attempts to participate, that only my physical presence allowed that I was indeed a member of the group. Other days this withdrawal took the form of cutting-up during the lesson. Eventually the withdrawal led to my leaving class early, walking out on exams and on some days not showing up at all. (p. 244)

In the next segment, the learner/researcher describes how a particular stimulus situation (i.e., transitions from one place to another) challenge his coping mechanisms, and how he uses language learning to reduce his anxiety by diverting his attention from the transition. But he notes that this solution only works when traveling to and within the country. Language study during transitions involved in returning to the United States did not ameliorate anxiety because the goal/need significance was reduced upon returning to the native language environment.

> The Tunisian and Iran experience taught me that I am most vulnerable to culture shock during transitions: i.e., entering the foreign country, leaving it and changing residences while in that country. I find that the details of these transitions (making reservations, buying tickets, getting to the airport, going through customs, finding a hotel, moving to and setting-up an apartment) are emotionally draining and anxiety provoking. Once I am there, I am quite content (even in the absence of many creature comforts), but when I begin to anticipate the next transition, the emotional stress starts again.
>
> I found one reasonably effective way to control this stress during travel to the foreign country. En route to Tunisia and during the first week or so after arrival, I devoted every free minute to working my way through an elementary Arabic reader. On the way to Iran I kept myself occupied by working through a low-intermediate Persian reader. I believe these were productive solutions because they allowed me to learn more of the language while dealing with the anxiety. Learning more of the language gave me a sense of satisfaction and accomplishment that went a long way towards counteracting the anxiety. This approach, however, did not work when leaving the foreign country since during departures, I did not feel motivated to study because I wouldn't be needing the language back in the United States. (Schumann & Schumann, 1977, pp. 245–246)

The next excerpt illustrates the learner's conflict between his goals and his social image. He wanted to learn the language his own way, but in doing so he risked not being able to perform in ways valued by the teacher and also risked performing less well than the other students.

> I discovered that I like to have my own agenda in second language learning. In other words, I like to do it my way. However, I also found that my agenda is often in conflict with the teacher's. Since the teacher's agenda is the standard for the class, then my not following it is failure in the eyes of the other class members. In order not to look like a failure, I have a tendency to compromise my agenda in the direction of the teacher's. For example, in Tunisia the teacher wanted the students to memorize the dialogues perfectly. I felt that to learn them that well was unnecessary and that it required spending time that could be put to better use in other language learning activities. But, if I did it my way and did not memorize the dialogue as perfectly as possible then I would be frustrated and embarrassed because my poor performance would be judged by the class according to what the teacher wanted the students to accomplish and not what I wanted to accomplish.

> My desire to pursue my own agenda was somewhat more successful in the Persian class at UCLA. There the teacher occasionally asked the students to write, but I was only interested in speaking and reading, not writing. In this class I could choose not to do a writing assignment both because I was an auditor and because the teacher was flexible enough to allow it. If on occasion I were forced to write (e.g., during an in-class vocabulary quiz), my failure at this task would not be public, it would simply be between the teacher and myself. Therefore, I would not be embarrassed and could stick to my own language learning agenda.

> As a result of my desire to learn a language my own way, I find I like low key teachers who don't demand too much. What I want in a teacher is someone whom I am confident in, who is an able guide and resource person, but who is flexible enough to allow reasonable latitude for me to achieve my own language learning goals. (Schumann & Schumann, 1977, p. 246)

In this final episode, the same learner describes a preference for a language learning strategy that is compatible with his coping mechanisms, but which is not compatible with most language instruction.

> As a general learning strategy, I prefer eavesdropping to speaking as a way of getting into a language. Some people learn languages by being very socially out-going and by talking with TL speakers. I prefer to get input by listening to the TL without having to become involved in a conversation. This tendency manifested itself in several ways. In Iran I enjoyed listening to the radio, watching television and participating in events where I could hear people speak without having to speak myself. Thus, at faculty meetings, at certain social gatherings and while observing classes that were conducted in Farsi, I listened as attentively as possible and wrote down words which I did not understand. Later I would learn the meanings of these words by looking them up in the dictionary or asking a friend. . . . Unfortunately, most language teaching methods do not allow this approach. I was able to employ it in Iran where I was learning it on my own, but I could not use it in Tunisia where I was taking classes. (Schumann & Schumann, 1977, p. 247)

The excerpts that follow are taken from Bailey's (1983) examination of competitiveness and anxiety reported in several diary studies. In the first segment, from Lynch (1979), the learner appraises his performance and the other students' reaction to that performance. In addition, he contrasts his goal of learning to pronounce correctly to his perception of other students' goal of learning to speak fast.

> Following the exam we went over some oral exercises in which individuals were called upon to deliver a series of substitutions out loud. One of the drills I was called upon for included "trabajo" and "hijas"—the difficult velar fricative which no one in the class seems to be able to produce. At first I did produce the fricative quite well, surprising myself, and I sensed a reaction from the students around me—just recognition, not good or bad—but I was immediately self-conscious and struggled between wanting to produce the correct form and not wanting to sound funny. The next few times I did not produce the

fricative well at all. . . . Here the classroom is not an environment where your peers are producing, or I believe even trying to produce, the correct speech sounds. Most people in the class seem not to care about pronouncing correctly, but do seem to care about speaking fast. (Lynch, 1979, pp. 30-31)

Below we see the learner appraising both himself, the class, and himself in relation to the class.

I have the impression that I speak with a better accent, i.e., produce Spanish phonology better, than almost everyone else in the class. Only two exceptions come to mind—Señorita F., . . . who occasionally makes errors involving the use of French words instead of Spanish, and an Iranian student who seems to have studied Spanish before and has a larger vocabulary than the rest of the class. He is the person who approached me . . . to ask if I thought the teacher was any good. . . . (His) complaint was that the class was moving too slow. My reaction was that if it was moving too slow, no one in the class would be making mistakes on the simple matters that even he was guilty of from time to time. (Lynch, 1979, p. 38, cited in Bailey, 1983, p. 81)

Bailey quotes from another learner who struggles with appraisals of her performance in relation to her self-image and her social image.

When in class I still had the fear of being called on. I was afraid that I would fumble on the material I had worked so hard to learn. Each time I did fumble, I became a little less confident. On the other hand, each time I understood what was being said, I felt better. . . . In almost every class hour, I would fluctuate between feelings of success and failure.

From the beginning I believed that the other students were not struggling as much as me. Very often they would process the question and start to answer before I had a chance. This scared me because I did not know what I was doing wrong not to be able to think as quickly as them. So many of my hang-ups about language learning were my own perceptions of what I do and what others do. Unfortunately, I did not know which were distortions of the truth; maybe others were struggling as much, maybe I was speaking as fluently or at least not any worse than everyone else. So much depended on how I viewed myself and others. Very often I would try to stop concerning myself with how I thought they were doing and try concentrating on me. (Leichman, 1977, p. 3, cited in Bailey, 1983, p. 84)

In the next example, as Bailey reports, the learner withdraws from a Russian course because of a poor performance.

After having failed to perform in a distinguishing manner on the mid-term examination, the learner withdrew and resigned himself to reading Dostoyevsky in English translation. (Bernbrock, 1977, pp. 1-2, cited in Bailey, 1983, p. 85)

Later, the same learner experiences more success when learning Thai. In this endeavor he did not have to appraise himself in relation to the performance of other students because he was working with a teacher on an individualized reading course in Thai.

In this particular course I did not have to worry about my performance compared to other students or what the teacher expected of me. . . . I experienced none of the anxiety or fear of making mistakes that was so detrimental to my attempts to learn languages in the past. (Bernbrock, 1977, p. 9, cited in Bailey, 1983, p. 85)

In the final example, we see how appraisals of the learner's goals, coping mechanisms, self-image, and social image combine to cause her to quit a Persian language class.

As class was dismissed (the teacher) assigned a vocabulary test for the following Wednesday to be derived from the thousand-word glossary that accompanied the first-year Persian text. I said that I felt such a test was unreasonable. . . . I knew that I did not have twenty-five hours to spend studying for such a vocabulary test, yet I was frustrated because I wanted to perform well on the test. I felt torn between wanting to somehow show him that I could do well, yet feeling that such a test at that point would not truly reflect anyone's basic productive capabilities (Walsleben, 1976, pp. 23-24, cited in Bailey, 1983, p. 86)

Later she reports a major conflict with the teacher.

> After the break (the teacher) announced that he would give the vocabulary test, "If that's okay." Shirley stated again her difficulty in studying uncontextualized words for a vocabulary test, and (the teacher) explained that he nonetheless felt that it was a justifiable way of building up our vocabularies. When he repeated that he was going to give the test and looked at me when he said, "If that's okay," I responded tersely, "You're the professor, but in my opinion it's a poor use of time." That was the proverbial last straw. For the next hour and a half the whole class was embroiled in a very emotional exchange of opinions dealing with what the class was and was not, what it could and should be, who would let whom do what.
>
> My seven weeks of pent-up anger and frustration made my voice quaver and my hands tremble so that I could not lift my coffee cup without spilling the coffee. (The teacher's) voice too was unsteady. I was terribly uncomfortable, feeling like the class "heavy" and feeling little or no support from the other members of the class at first. At one point, when I saw David's and Ramona's faces flush with what I interpreted as being discomfort, I tried to stop talking, but by then (the teacher) insisted that we continue.
>
> Gradually our voices became lower and more calm, and one by one, the students expressed their own opinions and suggestions. But when we finished talking, I was feeling an internal conflict between my belief that (the professor) had *heard* our criticisms and suggestions and my doubt that he would actually do anything in response to them. I felt exhausted and empty. (Walslaben, 1976, pp.34-35, cited in Bailey, 1983, p. 87)

Finally two weeks before the end of the course, the learner reports

> By Thursday I knew that I would not go to class again—at least for the remainder of the quarter. . . . All quarter long I had spent hours and hours studying Farsi because I wanted to and was determined to keep progressing. Whenever I had several assignments to do I always did my Farsi

first because to me it really was not work at all, but fun. Reading and translating was like working a puzzle. I had reread all the texts and marked all the relative clauses to see if I could grasp the pattern that was being used; it did not always appear to fit the rules (the teacher) had given us, so I wanted to ask questions about them whenever he reached the point where he intended to explicate grammatical points in the texts. I had also noted other grammatical questions in the text margins. But suddenly—it did not seem to matter. (Walslaben, 1976, p. 36, cited in Bailey, 1983, p. 87)

The diary studies provide rather immediate retrospective appraisals of the learning situation. They also frequently reveal the consequences of these appraisals in terms of whether the learner persists in his study of the language or withdraws from it. The diary studies also show how idiosyncratic personal factors influence learning. Thus, the studies reveal how each learner is on a unique affective trajectory in language learning. And this is exactly what the stimulus appraisal perspective would predict. Each language learner's schematic emotional memory or value-category memory, which may be incorporated in orbitofrontal, amygdala, and body proper circuits, is different because it is based, to a large extent, on somatic value generated by each individual's life experiences. Therefore, the normal case is for there to be individual affective trajectories in SLA. Occasionally, for cultural reasons, groups of people will make similar appraisals and commonalities will appear.

I once abandoned diary studies because they seemed so patternless and because they resisted aggregation. But, in fact, they were data for a theory that did not yet exist. The psychology and neurobiology of stimulus appraisal provides a perspective that allows us to see that the unique affective trajectories of stimulus appraisal are, in fact, the bases of all sustained deep learning.

Autobiographies

Another source of data on stimulus appraisal comes from autobiographies of individuals who focus in those works on their second language learning. These are particularly interesting documents because they are written by individuals who are not applied linguists and who are generally naive about the psychological issues in SLA. In this section, I will analyze three recent works in this genre, and by quoting extensively from the authors' accounts, I hope to show how their stimulus appraisals fueled their language learning.

I

French Lessons is the autobiography of Alice Kaplan (1993), a professor of French at Duke University in North Carolina. This *Bildungsroman* is the account of her life-long study of French. Kaplan was born in Minnesota in 1954. When her father died in 1962, her mother considered moving to Montpellier in the south of France. Kaplan reports her image of France at that time.

> I imagined a house where we would be together near the water. . . . I can see myself there underneath a palm tree. I will be a French girl, like Madeline in the Madeline books who lives in an orphanage with other girls and walks in a straight line and gets a visit from Miss Clavel when she goes into the hospital with appendicitis. (p. 31)

Another early impression of things French that Kaplan reports was her recollection of De Gaulle at the funeral of JFK when she was in the third grade.

> The newscasters commented on the world leaders as they walked down Pennsylvania Avenue. De Gaulle, the president of France, floated over the rest. He wore a hat that reminded me of Abraham Lincoln's stovepipe hat, only shorter. Instead of a band all around it there was a visor in front that stuck out in line with his enormous nose. The newsmen commented on the special relationship of de Gaulle and Jacqueline Kennedy, who was able to speak to him in fluent French. (p. 32)

Her family ultimately never went to Montpellier, but in the fifth grade Kaplan began studying French. She did not have a very positive assessment of her first French teacher, Madame Holmgren.

> She was a tired dowdy woman with very black hair, beige clothes, and an almost sickly pale skin punctuated by a mole. . . . [She] was an object of extreme fascination

because of the hair on her legs—dark whiskery hair, the first hair any of us had ever seen on a grown woman's legs. (p. 126)

Alice describes how she and her classmates were "R Resisters"–either deaf to or embarrassed by the French "r." But Alice did not resist categorically.

I knew what it was supposed to sound like. I heard Holmgren's "r." And I knew that by comparison our resistant "r" was a flat, closed-off smashed version of the truer sound. So let's say I did decide to risk it, make it ok, this foreign "r," I still had a dilemma: the American "r" sounded stupid, Midwestern, but to get the French one right I knew there would be an awkward apprenticeship where it would come out all slobbery and wrong. Like kissing a boy with braces on. (p. 128)

In 1966, at the age of 12, Alice heard the word "existentialism." She reports the following appraisal: "It was the longest word I had ever heard. French was this, too, always—even in beginning French classes you knew there was a French beyond the everyday, a France of hard talk and intellect, where God was dead and you were on your own, totally responsible" (p. 138).

Alice spent the summer of 1968 at a French camp in Bar Harbor, Maine, where the campers were required to speak only French and got demerits if caught speaking English. For each demerit, they had to memorize several lines of French poetry.

In her sophomore year, Alice's mother sent her to Switzerland where she would spend a year in a French medium school. Alice was delighted with the prospect. At the boarding school, the students were awakened by the Swiss news broadcast in French over a loudspeaker system. Kaplan reports her early progress:

Every morning those sounds woke me up. I understood more and more until I could anticipate the morning greeting of the Swiss news, and lip synch, word for word, the standard formulae. I got used to looking at people from a distance, trying to figure out what language they were speaking by the merest shadow of sound floating my way or by their gestures. I always had five or six new words on a personal in-progress list. Each time I heard one of the words on my list, I would notice the context and try to figure out the meaning. When I thought I had the meaning I would wait for the word to come up again, so I could check if my meaning was still right. Finally, I'd try the word out to see if a strange look came over the face of the person I was talking to. If it didn't, I knew I was home free. I had a new word.

I started thinking of my ear as something strong, and precious. I couldn't stand Chris's strutting and whispering, so when the girl in the room next door moved upstairs I moved into her old room, where everyone, a Palestinian and an Italian and a French girl, spoke French all of the time. I had to bottom bunk again, and I lay under the yellow and white striped covers and listened. My ear was getting stronger and stronger. (pp. 47–48)

Alice was very happy at the school and was enthusiastic about studying and learning French. She reports,

I look back at my handwriting from that year, in an assignment notebook that never got thrown out. It is small and round and perfect, no variation from letter to letter. Mostly what I have on record are conjugations. In basement study hall before breakfast I copied verb conjugations like a monk. I had a French Grammar book, *Bled's Spelling,* and I did extra exercises for the exceptions to the rules. I did this work the way someone would run a marathon, waiting to hit the wall at twenty miles, feeling the pain of the wall and running through it. I liked to work before breakfast. I thought I memorized better when my head was light. (p. 52)

At one point early in the year, she and a friend went on a diet together. Alice wrote down everything she ate each day in French in a notebook. She also found other ways to diet. "There was chocolate in every store, on every corner, chocolate bars with colored wrappers showing roses, bottles of milk, nuts in rows of six, three rows deep. For each bar of chocolate I didn't eat I learned a verb. I grew thinner and thinner. I ate French" (pp. 52–53).

Life at French school helped Kaplan forget the sadness in her family after her father's death.

I had come from a house where the patterns had broken down and the death that had broken them was not understood. Now I loved the loudspeaker and the study hall and the marble floor because they made me feel hard and controlled and patterned; the harder I felt the more I felt the sorrowful world behind me grow dim and fake and powerless. (p. 53)

She describes her efforts to find opportunities to speak French.

I went into the village in search of French. I went to the train station. I bought tickets to Geneva, "aller et retour à Genève"—that is what you had to say to get a round trip ticket. I loved to let it roll off of my tongue, "allere-tretour" in one drum roll, "to go and return." I bought tickets just to say it. Most of what I did, in town, I did in order to speak. Complicated conversations at the Tabac, the newsstand, the grocery. (p. 53)

Kaplan compares herself to the American students who grew up in French-speaking countries. To her they seemed sophisticated, but bored.

When called on, they spoke French effortlessly, but begrudgingly—"if you insist, if you insist . . ." I could practically hear it under their breath as they tossed off the sentence. They were bored, the students on the left-hand row, how could they be bored? Frichot, the teacher, calls on me. I feel as if I'm on a stage, the lights go down and the desks disappear. The spot is on me. I'm poised as I speak my lines from the play we're reading. (pp. 53–54)

She describes her efforts to learn the French "r":

So that feeling of coming onto the "r" like a wall was part of feeling the essence of my American speech patterns in French, feeling them as foreign and awkward. I didn't know at the time how important it was to feel that American "r" like a big lump in my throat and to be dissatisfied about it. Feeling the lump was the first step, the prerequisite to getting rid of it. (p. 54)

When she finally got it right, she reports,

I looked up at my teacher, M. Hervé Frichot, former colonial school teacher from Madagascar. He had a goatee and glasses with thick black frames. He was a skeptic but he was looking at me now with deep respect. He hadn't thought I could do it. He said, "You've done it." He added: "Vowels next." But that was minor. I wasn't worried about the vowels because I knew that since I had gotten the "r," I had already started opening up my vowels. I could perfect them with the same method I had used for the "r": First feeling them wrong, like an impediment, feeling them again and again in their wrongness and then, one day, opening up and letting the right sound come. Relaxing. The "r" was the biggest hurdle; my system was now in place. (p. 55)

After this success, she could see the Francophone Americans three dimensionally. "I looked over at the students on the left-hand row; suddenly they seemed less menacing. Chris had a meek nervous look on her face. Eric's hair was greasy and he was scratching a red spot on his neck. I saw them, because I was one of them now" (p. 55).

Kaplan describes the pleasure she got from success and from knowing how to learn:

> That was what woke me up: absorbing a new reality, repeating it, describing it, appreciating it. I felt a pull toward learning I hadn't felt since the fifth grade: quiet mastery of a subject. Knowing I knew the material, that I had it down. Knowing how to find out more. Inventing methods for listening and making them habits. Feeling a kind of tickle in my ear at the pleasure of understanding. Then the pleasure of writing down what I had heard and getting every detail, every accent mark right.

> The French have a verb for the kind of work I did at the Swiss school: *bosser,* which comes from a verb meaning "hunched" and means hunkering down to work, bending down over some precious matter and observing it. (pp. 55–56)

Kaplan appraises the pedagogy employed at the Swiss school. "Memorization, copying, repeating, taking words down in dictation: these practices all come from French schools and they are the practices I excelled in. Don't be original, learn from ready-made reality ready-to-hand" (p.56).

In the winter, the students had ski lessons every day and Kaplan learned well: "At home I was the worst in sports; here, miraculously, I was good. It felt like my life had been given to me to start over" (p. 57). She sums up: "French had saved me" (p. 57), but then she tempers this feeling with the analysis that she "had learned a whole new language at boarding school but it was a language for covering pain [her unhappiness at home in the U.S.], not expressing it" (p. 58).

During her spring break, Kaplan traveled to Paris to meet her mother, who was visiting the city with Kaplan's high school French teacher and her two children. But at the same time, the father of one of Alice's best friends, called Mr. D., was also in Paris. Alice greatly admired this man and, in fact, wished he were her own father. She reports the wonderful day she spent with him visiting museums, restaurants, and art galleries. Mr. D. was a genuine Francophile and his enthusiasm for Paris resonated and amplified Alice's appreciation of French life and culture. He was impressed by her ability to speak French and this gave her a further motivating sense of pride in her language learning.

In June, she returned to the United States, where she exhibited symptoms of reverse culture shock. Her negative appraisals of her native country and language reflect her appraisals of the French life she had been living.

> In June I took the plane home. I could feel the French sticking in my throat, the new muscles in my mouth. I had my ear open, on the plane, for the sounds of anyone speaking French because those were my sounds now. I was full of French, it was holding me up, running through me, a voice in my head, a tickle in my ear, likely to be set off at any moment. A counter language. When I got off the plane the American English sounded loud and thudding—like an insult or lapse of faith. I would have to go hunting for French sounds, if I wanted to keep going. (p. 70)

She continues: "I felt small and neat and the people around me looked messy. In bed at night, I felt exposed, because there was no bunk over me. No loudspeaker to wake me up. No reason to get up" (p. 70).

In her senior year, she was admitted to Vassar College; she attended for one year and then transferred to Berkeley. There she spent a year studying and working in the antiwar movement. Her account of the year shows her increasing appreciation for French poetry and for language in general. In her third year, she took advantage of the University of California's Education Abroad Program and returned to Europe to spend her junior year in France.

The junior year abroad group first went to Paris for a six-week orientation and from there, Alice was to go on to Bordeaux, where she would spend the academic year. While in Paris, she fell in love with a twenty-seven-year-old Frenchman. He was a reckless, impulsive, romantic individual, and Alice was captivated. She immediately began to adopt his style of French:

> I went to classes, part of our six-week orientation to French culture. In class I spent a lot of time with my head on the desk, nothing but André in it. I went to language lab for phonetic testing and they said I was starting to get the regional Gascon accent in my "r"s, I should watch out. I had been studying André too hard. (p. 85)

In a highly romantic mood, she wrote him a love letter. André's response was to correct it. In retrospect, Alice realizes that for her André meant access to French:

> This should have been my first clue that what I really wanted from André was language, but in the short run all it did was make me feel more attached to him, without knowing why I was attached. I can still hear the sound he made when he read my love letter: "T,t,t," with that little ticking sound French people make by putting the tips of their tongues on the roof of their mouths—a fussy, condescending sound, by way of saying, "that's *not* how one says it." What I wanted more than anything, more than André even, was to make those sounds, which were the true sounds of being French, and so even as he was insulting me and discounting my passion with a vocabulary lesson, I was listening and studying and recording his response. (p. 86)

Later, André took her out to dinner and made a speech in which he said, "I want a woman I can express myself with. You understand my words but not my language—you don't even realize how great a problem it is between us" (p. 87). But this only motivated Alice to learn French better:

> That week I kept running over his speech in my mind. What was the difference between his words and my words, his world and my world? When I said a French word, why wasn't it the same as when he said one? What could I do to make it be the same? I had to stick it out with him, he was transmitting new words to me every day and I needed more. In fact, while Barbara and Buffy and Kacy (André dubbed us "l'équipe"—the team) rolled their eyes about what a raw deal I was getting from this creep, I was all the more determined to be with him. He was in all my daydreams now. I wanted to crawl into his skin, live in his body, be him. The words he used to talk to me, I wanted to use back. I wanted them to be my words. (pp. 87–88)

When André took up with Maïté, a Frenchwoman who was part of the orientation staff, Alice's reaction was to be jealous of Maïté's French. "Maïté had something I couldn't have, her blood and her tongue and a name with accents in it. I was burning with race envy" (p. 89). Alice spent a lot of time analyzing what André meant to her. She concluded, "he wanted me to be natural, and I wanted him to make me French" (p. 89). When she thought about him with Maïté, she thought, "'It's because my French isn't good enough' and 'It's because she's French.' When he told me I couldn't understand his language, André had picked the accusation I was most vulnerable to. Afterwards I thought, 'I'll show him. I'll know all there is to know about his language. I'll know his language better than he does someday'" (pp. 93–94).

When Alice moved to Bordeaux, André visited her several times. Alice found these encounters less than satisfactory but observes, "I was still putting up with André, for his beauty and his words" (p. 90). Of her relationship with André, she concludes, "I wanted to breathe in French with André, I wanted to sweat French sweat. It was the rhythm and pulse of his French I wanted, the body of it, and he refused me, he told me I could never get that. I had to get it another way" (p. 94).

In Bordeaux, Alice got to know the family of the pharmacist near her apartment. "They became my French family and I their American friend" (p. 97). Alice frequently had Sunday lunch with them, and on these and other less formal occasions, she learned from her interaction with the father, the grown daughter, and her children, French history, customs, family behavior, and more and better French. Alice continued her relationship with the family after her year abroad, always visiting them on her frequent trips to France. She observes, "There in Bordeaux is where my mouth and my eyes and my ears for France started to work. When I was fifteen and had my first conversation all in French, in Switzerland, it was a religious awakening. In Bordeaux it became regular, boring, real" (p. 103).

During her year in France, Alice was introduced to the work of Céline. She fell in love with his language—his "wandering rhythmic phrases" (p. 105). When she was feeling lonely and anomic on Sunday afternoons in Bordeaux because "the shops were closed, the bourgeois families locked away in their houses . . . [and] the only people on the streets were foreigners—students and workers" (p. 105), she found comfort in Céline.

> What exquisite misery I felt! Disconnected, not belonging, desiring every house, imagining every happy scene behind every stone wall, taking in the lewd empty glances, given and received. Céline could express it all in a sentence through the sound of his words as much as their meaning. When reading him I luxuriated in despair, dark thoughts, and a commitment to eternal exile. (pp. 105–106)

Céline, however, had written antisemitic propaganda in the 1930s and was seen as a Nazi collaborator. Alice's father had been a prosecutor at the Nuremberg trials and Alice, as a young girl, had become familiar with the Holocaust very directly—she had seen photographs of the concentration camp victims among her father's papers. This background was part of what drew her to Céline. She reports:

> That was only part of what drew me to Céline. The rest had to do with what happened while I was reading him, the music I felt in my heart, a sense of lightness and magic, as well as a total confidence in this writer's knowledge of the depths of individual human suffering. Our literature professor wanted us to hear that music. . . . (pp. 107–108)

> Céline made me want to write. (p. 109)

Alice characterizes Céline's role in her acquisition of French: "I want French that's alive. Before Céline, I knew French for buying groceries and doing well in school. I was hollow in French, André told me so. I got hooked on Céline because he was the farthest from official French I could get in a book" (p. 117).

After graduation from Berkeley, Alice went to graduate school at Yale where she wrote a dissertation on the French fascist writers. She said she "loved thinking about France in crisis, France where politics ruled literature, where censors shaped editors, where writers were out of control with hate and prejudice" (p. 160).

When she finished her doctoral work, Alice took a job at a state college teaching

> first year French to students who didn't want to be there but had to be, because it was a requirement. I went home every night and read the want ads—just to know that there were jobs in the world other than the one I had. I saw French mistakes I had never even dreamed of—letters that didn't exist, words that bore no relation to any language. I graded and wept. (p. 165)

Then she spent three years teaching at Columbia in a nonpermanent position. Finally she got a tenure-track job at Duke.

Alice's life as a professor led to some interesting observations about the advanced stages of language acquisition. She talks about the difficulties some American professors may have in French departments dominated by expatriate native-speakers. She notes, "there is invariably trouble when a tyrannical or insensitive native-speaker rules over a department where all of the assistant professors are Americans, forever on guard against the telling mistake that might cost them a promotion" (p. 179). She also speaks of another form of tyranny:

> French colleagues are invariably more generous in assessing the language skills of their American colleagues than we Americans are when we talk about each other ("Really, you know, her French isn't very good"). American French professors, they say, are much too self-conscious about petty details of linguistic performance, which have nothing to do with real intellectual life.
>
> Easy for *them* to say: those details are our second identity. (p. 180)

She wonders whether in French departments attachment to the language might be pathological. She notes how professors and students often adopt the prejudices of the French with whom they identify and then do things like make ethnic jokes about the Belgians or denigrate other varieties of French such as Canadian or Haitian. Alice even suggests that Americans with high levels of French identification and proficiency may make the French disdain for Americans their own. And paradoxically, in their effort to be French they sometimes use that language inappropriately. For example, Alice reports that on one occasion when she was with a French feminist, she used the expression "Que je suis bête" ("How stupid of me," or "I'm so stupid"). The feminist was shocked that Alice had employed such denigrating "woman's speech." Finally, she discusses the tendency of some students and teachers of French to use only that language even when interaction, learning, and sociability would be enhanced if English were spoken.

In her search for the source of her motivation to learn French, Alice suggests several related things.

> Learning French was connected to my father, because French made me absent the way he was absent, and it made me an expert the way he was an expert. French was also a response to my adolescence, a discipline to cover up the changes in my body I wanted to hide. (pp. 203–204)

> Why do people want to adopt another culture? Because there's something in their own they don't like, that doesn't *name them.* (p. 209)

> When I was an adolescent, French was my storehouse language. I collected secrets in French; I spoke to myself in French. I know now that my passion for French helped me put off what I needed to say, in English, to the people around me. (p. 214)

> Why did I hide in French? If life got too messy, I could take off into my second world. Writing about it has made me air my suspicions, my anger, my longing, to people for whom it's come as a total surprise. There was a time when I even spoke in a different register in French—higher and excited, I was sliding up to those high notes in some kind of a hyped-up theatrical world of my own making. (p. 216)

She provides a summary of her motivation to learn French:

> Learning French and learning to think, learning to desire, is all mixed up in my head, until I can't tell the difference. French is what released me from the cool complacency of the R Resisters, made me want, and like wanting, unbuttoned me and sent me packing. French demands my obedience, gives me permission to try too hard, to squinch up my face to make the words sound right. French houses words like "existentialism" that connote abstract thinking, difficulties to which I can get the key. And body parts which I can claim. French got me away from my family and taught me how to talk. Made me an adult. And the whole drama of it is in that "r," how deep in my throat, how different it feels. (pp. 140–141)

Commentary

Alice Kaplan's story is an extraordinary chronicle of positive appraisal. She generally wanted to be as French as the French. She shows no ambivalence in this goal. There seems to be no struggle. Alice likes the *r*; she even pursued it in the fifth grade when she and her fellow students had it presented to them by a teacher they thought was odd and unattractive. She masters it as a teenager in Switzerland and then, when she returns to the states, she appraises the American *r* as flat, unappealing.

Alice appreciates the routine of French pedagogy—the dictations, the exercises, the demand for grammatical accuracy. The French educational practices, which emphasized imitation, repetition, and lack of originality, were sources of security for her. She assesses them positively and thrives in the educational environment they provide. Within this system, she developed a sense of mastery, a knowledge that she could cope successfully with the French linguistic stimuli, which were presented within that pedagogical system.

Alice's French lover, it turns out, is just another French lesson. André's rejection of her does not dampen her desire to learn French; it simply motivates her to master it. Alice has the ability to keep her goal and needs in mind. In fact, she is so good at this that she turns every negative situation into an opportunity to learn more French. In Switzerland when dieting, she substitutes learning French vocabulary for eating Swiss chocolate. Instead of being devastated by André's treatment of her and instead of allowing that negative experience to generate a rejection of French, she uses it to amplify her motivation, to make her French better than his. This ability to turn negative circumstances into opportunities to learn more French is also demonstrated by her reading Céline's discussion of alienation when she herself was feeling anomic. Another person might have escaped into an English novel.

Alice also found herself a French family and through them allowed herself to be further socialized to French life. Such cross-cultural relationships are rewarding but only if one is willing to nurture them and to endure the strains they inevitably generate. Alice did both.

There was one quality of the French that Alice did find noxious. It was their frequent assumption that Americans were naive and prudish. She encountered this view in her research on correspondence between Céline and Milton Hindus, a Jew and a sympathetic scholar of Céline. Alice rejects this notion just as she rejected André's view that she could never speak French with sufficient depth to understand him. Alice is an American who is determined to become French. The French believe they are smart. So if Alice is to become French, she must convince herself that she is as intelligent as they. In her appraisal of the French in relation to her own self-image, Alice concedes nothing. She wants to be one of them; she therefore refused to allow their negative appraisals of Americans to extend to her.

What are some of the unique factors that contributed to Alice's trajectory? She suggests that a French identity allowed her to escape the sadness of her father's death and the awkwardness of her adolescence. Her interest in French Nazis perhaps linked her with her father, a Nuremberg lawyer, but quite remarkably allowed her to find something positive even in the darker side of France.

II

The following second language history is a different story. Eva Hoffman (1989) in *Lost in Translation* describes her immigration from Poland to Canada in 1959 when she was 14 years old. The first part of the book, entitled "Paradise," describes the first decade of her life in Cracow, with all the difficulties of post-war existence in Poland. Hoffman's recollections of that period are extremely positive. The somewhat crowded living conditions, instead of being oppressive, provided a sense of community. The city had a rich intellectual, cultural, and social life which, even as a young adolescent, she was able to appreciate. She had several close friends. Her father, who was adept at manipulating the communist economy, was able to provide the family with reason-able comfort and even a few luxuries. Eva began piano lessons at about the age of nine. She had considerable talent and with the support of a well-known teacher, she devoted herself to her music and received, as a result, the praise and respect of her commu-nity. Even at that early age, Eva delighted at the cafe life of the city. She enjoyed visiting cafes in the afternoon for special treats of ice cream. She and her family joined several other families for what she describes as idyllic summers on a farm in the country-side.

In 1956, after Poland's president, Bierut, died under suspi-cious circumstances in Moscow, political tensions began to develop in the form of nationalistic anti-Russian sentiment, but among the Jewish community there developed concern about war with Russia and even the possibility of pogroms. In 1957 and 1958 several families in Eva's social group decided to leave Poland for Israel, and ultimately, her parents also decided to emi-grate but chose Canada as their destination.

Eva's first impressions of Canada are not positive.

> When I come out on deck, I see a bit of a world that returned all of my sense of loss to me like a sudden punch in the stomach. . . . There is something about the sight that is ineffably and utterly different from the landscape I'm used to. . . . We seem to be in the middle of nowhere. (pp. 92–93)

When her family arrives in Montreal, she reports: "Timidly, I walk a few steps away from my parents to explore this terra incognita. . . . There is this young girl, maybe my age [14], in high-heeled shoes and lipstick! She looks so vulgar" (p. 99).

As they cross the Rockies on the way to Vancouver, her par-ents try to get her to notice the beautiful landscape, but she

resists: "I don't want to. These peaks and ravines, these moun-
tain streams and enormous boulders hurt my eyes—they hurt
the soul. They are too big, too forbidding, and I can't imagine feeling that I'm part of them, that I'm in them" (p. 100). It has been
arranged that in Vancouver, they will stay with a wealthy Polish
family, the Rosenbergs, who had immigrated earlier. Of the
Rosenberg's house, she says,

> To me these interiors seem oddly flat, devoid of imagina-
> tion, ingenuous. The spaces are so plain, low-ceilinged,
> obvious. . . . The only rooms that really impress me are
> the bathroom and kitchen—both of them so shiny, pol-
> ished, and full of unfamiliar, fabulously functional appli-
> ances that they remind me of interiors which we
> occasionally glimpsed in French or American movies,
> and which, in our bedraggled Poland, we couldn't distin-
> guish from fantasy. (p. 102)

She begins to see Mr. Rosenberg not as "[their] benefactor but
as a Dickensian figure of personal tyranny, and [her] feeling
toward him quickly rises to something that can only be called
hate" (p. 103).

Eva reports her response to the first day at school. "Both the
boys and the girls look sharp and aggressive to me—the girls all
have bright lipstick on, their hair sticks up and out like witches'
fury, and their skirts are held up and out by stiff, wiry crinolines.
I can't imagine wanting to talk their harsh sounding language"
(p. 105). At school, her name and her sister's name are changed.
Ewa becomes Eva and Alina becomes Elaine. Eva feels unnamed:

> The twist in our names takes them a tiny distance from
> us—but it's a gap into which the infinite hobgoblin of
> abstraction enters. Our Polish names didn't refer to us;
> they were as surely us as our eyes or hands. These new
> appellations, which we ourselves can't yet pronounce,
> are not us. They are identification tags, disembodied
> signs pointing to objects that happen to be my sister
> and myself. We walk to our seats, into a roomful of
> unknown faces, with names that make us strange to
> ourselves. (p. 105)

Eva reports that each day she acquires new words and expressions. She dislikes phrases like "You're welcome" which "strikes

[her] as a gaucherie" (p. 106). But she becomes fond of other words either because of their sound or because she is pleased to have been able to guess their meaning from written texts. These are words "like 'enigmatic' or 'insolent'—words that are only of literary value, that exist only as signs on a page" (p.106).

She characterizes the problem:

> The process, alas, works in reverse as well. When I see a river now, it is not shaped, assimilated by the word that accommodates it to the psyche—a word that makes a body of water a river rather than an uncontained element. The river before me remains a thing, absolutely other, absolutely unbending to the grasp of my mind.

> When my friend Penny tells me that she's envious, or happy, or disappointed, I try laboriously to translate not from English to Polish but from the word back to its source, to the feeling from which it springs. Already, in that moment of strain, spontaneity of response is lost. And anyway, the translation doesn't work. I don't know how Penny feels when she talks about envy. The word hangs in a Platonic stratosphere, a vague prototype of all envy, so large, so all-encompassing that it might crush me—as might disappointment or happiness. (pp. 106–107)

Eva also feels her Polish has atrophied, and her nighttime conversations with herself in that language are no longer functional. She says she is without an interior language. She summarizes: "I'm not filled with language anymore, and I have only a memory of fullness to anguish me with the knowledge that, in this dark and empty state, I don't really exist" (p. 108).

By the women in the community, Eva is taught to shave her armpits, use shampoos, hair lotions, curlers, and crinolines. She infers from this instruction that they see her as deficient. She goes along with the transformation but it makes her less confident:

> My shoulders stoop, I nod frantically to indicate my agreement with others, I smile sweetly at people to show that I mean well, and my chest recedes inward so that I don't take up too much space—mannerism of a marginal, off-centered person who wants both to be taken in and to fend off the threatening others. (p. 110)

Eva becomes friends with an extremely wealthy Polish woman, Rosa Steiner, and her family. In the Steiner household, Eva is introduced to culture. She is valued for her intelligence and her ability to play the piano. Eva admires and values Mrs. Steiner: "She is . . . a friend who understands where I come from—metaphorically and literally—better than anyone else I know in Vancouver" (p. 111). With the Steiners, Eva is exposed to family dinners and their "jokey banter" (p. 113). She becomes friends with the older daughter, Laurie, and listens to her stories about trips to Austria and other experiences, which are vastly different from her own. But the relationship with the Steiners is a positive one in spite of the vast gulf between their social and economic circumstances and her own.

Eva describes how she resents the implication by members of her immigrant community that everything in Canada is better than in Poland. "Not everything there is old-fashioned, not everything here better! But everyone encourages me to forget what I left behind" (p. 115). When she writes to friends in Poland she praises life in her new home. She reports, "I am lying. But I am also trying to fend off my nostalgia. I couldn't repudiate the past even if I wanted to, but what can I do with it here, where does it exist? After a while, I begin to push the images of memory down, away from consciousness, below emotion" (p. 116). Eva describes her social life. She goes with friends on Saturday night to a drive-in hamburger restaurant. "It fills [her] with a finicky distaste. [She feels her] lips tighten into an unaccustomed thinness— which, in turn, fills [her] with a small dislike for [herself]" (p. 117). She tries to tell a joke and gets lost in the translation; nobody laughs. She observes, "ah, the humiliation, the misery of failing to amuse! The incident is as rankling to my amour propre as being told I'm graceless or ugly" (p. 118). In normal speech, she has to rehearse her utterances before she speaks. She hears herself as monotonous, deliberate, heavy. She sees herself as

> a pretend teenager among the real stuff. There's too much in this car I don't like; I don't like the blue eye shadow on Cindy's eyelids, or the grease on Chuck's hair, or the way the car zooms off with a screech and then slows down as everyone plays we're-afraid-of-the-policeman. I don't like the way they laugh. I don't care for their "ugly" jokes, or their five-hundred-pound canary jokes, or their pickle

jokes, or their elephant jokes either. And the most of all, I
hate having to pretend. (pp. 118–119)

A friend gives her a diary for her birthday. She has to decide
whether to keep it in Polish or English. She chooses English, her
public language, in order to update her self-concept. She reports
that by writing in English she learns English and acquires a
written-self.

She struggles to improve her English pronunciation and says
she'd do anything to be rid of her Polish accent. We get an insight
into the motivation that drives Eva to learn English when we see
how she appraises linguistic performance.

> It's as important to me to speak well as to play a piece
> of music without mistakes. Hearing English distorted
> grates on me like chalk screeching on a blackboard, like all
> things botched and badly done, like all forms of graceless-
> ness. The odd thing is that I know what is correct, fluent,
> good, long before I can execute it. The English spoken by
> our Polish acquaintances strikes me as jagged and thick,
> and I know that I shouldn't imitate it. I'm turned off by
> the intonations I hear on the TV sitcoms—by the expecta-
> tion of laughter, like a dog's tail wagging in supplication,
> built into the actors' pauses, and by the curtailed, cutoff
> rhythms. I like the way Penny speaks, with an easy flow
> and a pleasure in giving words a fleshy fullness; I like
> what I hear in some movies; and once the Old Vic comes to
> Vancouver to perform *Macbeth*, and though I can hardly
> understand the particular words, I am riveted by the tones
> of sureness and command that mold the actors' speech
> into such majestic periods.

> Sociolinguists might say that I receive these language
> messages as class signals, that I associate the sounds of
> correctness with the social status of the speaker. In part,
> this is undoubtedly true. The class-linked notion that I
> transfer wholesale from Poland is that belonging to a "bet-
> ter" class of people is absolutely dependent on speaking a
> "better" language. And in my situation especially, I know
> that language will be a crucial instrument, that I can over-
> come the stigma of my marginality, the weight of pre-
> sumption against me, only if the reassuringly right sounds
> come out of my mouth. (pp. 122–123)

Eva feels that, even though she hasn't mastered the new language herself, she has the ability to distinguish English spoken well from poorly spoken English. She compares this skill to that of a chef who can tell whether some foreign cuisine is well cooked without ever having tasted it before or seen it prepared.

> As I listen to people speaking that foreign tongue, English, I can hear when they stumble or repeat the same phrases too many times, when their sentences trail off aimlessly—or, on the contrary, when their phrases have vigor and roundness, when they have the space and the breath to give a flourish at the end of a sentence, or make just the right pause before coming to a dramatic point. I can tell, in other words, the degree of their ease or disease, the extent of authority that shapes the rhythms of their speech. That authority—in whatever dialect, in whatever variant of the mainstream language—seems to me to be something we all desire. It's not that we all want to speak the King's English, but whether we speak Appalachian or Harlem English, or Cockney, or Jamaican Creole, we want to be at home in our tongue. We want to be able to give voice accurately and fully to ourselves and our sense of the world. (pp. 123–124)

Although Eva does not make much of it, her English is clearly improving. She wins a speech contest, and as a prize she is sent on a bus trip to the United Nations. When she returns, a local newspaper interviews her about her impressions of the cities she has visited. She quite happily gives her opinions, "New York is the real capital of the United States . . . Washington just has the government. It doesn't have the excitement" (p. 133). Then she is invited by a radio talk show host to take fifteen minutes of air time to give her views of Canada.

> At this point in my initiation into the English language, I have an active vocabulary of about six hundred words, but it doesn't occur to me that I should mince any of them. I want to tell Canadians about how boring they are. "Canada is the dullest country in the world," I write in the notes for my speech, "because it is the most conformist." People may pretend to have liberal beliefs, I go on, but really they are an unadventurous lot who never

dare to sidestep bourgeois conventions. With the hau-
teur that can only spring from fourteen-year-old innocence, I take these observations to be self-evident,
because they are mine. (p. 133)

Eva also mentions that shortly afterwards she begins winning poetry prizes in school. Again she doesn't make fuss about it
in the biography, but her English is clearly becoming quite good.
She also reports on her acquisition of pragmatics:

I learn also that certain kinds of truth are impolite. One
shouldn't criticize the person one is with, at least not
directly. You shouldn't say, "You are wrong about that"—
though you may say, "On the other hand, there is that to
consider." You shouldn't say, "This doesn't look good on
you," though you may say, "I like you better in that other
outfit." I learn to tone down my sharpness, to do a more
careful conversational minuet. (p. 146)

In the summer between her sophomore and junior year, she
takes correspondence courses so that she can finish high school
in three years and make up for the year she lost by being placed
a year behind her agemates when she arrived. She says she is
motivated by the "Big Fear" (p. 157).

I know how unprotected my family has become; I
know I'd better do well—or else. The "or else" takes
many forms in my mind—vague images of helplessness
and restriction and always being poor. "The Bowery," I
come to call this congeries of anxieties. The Bowery is
where I'll end up if I don't do everything exactly right. I
have to make myself a steel breastplate of achievement
and good grades, so that I'll be able to get out—and get
in, so that I can gain entry into the social system from
where I stand, on a precarious ledge. I am pervaded by a
new knowledge that I have to fend for myself, and it
pushes me on with something besides my old curiosity,
or even simple competitiveness. . . .

I too am goaded on by the forked whip of ambition
and fear, and I derive a strange strength—a ferocity, a
puissance—from the sense of my responsibility, the
sense that survival is in my own hands. (p. 157)

Eva is overwhelmed by the material wealth she sees in Vancouver and reports "after battering myself again and again on the horns of lust and disgust, I begin to retreat from both. I decided to stop wanting. For me, this is a strange turn: my appetites are strong, and I never had any ambitions to mortify them by asceticism. But this new resolution is built into the logic of my situation. Since I can't have anything, if I were to continue wanting, there would be no end to my deprivation" (p. 136). But she reasons that she can have internal things. "If I know everything, if I understand everything, then even though I can't have a house with a patio opening out onto a swimming pool, or a boyfriend whom I like, in some other way I can have the entire world" (p. 137).

Finally, at the end of the second section of the book, which she has entitled "Exile," she reports that she has been invited to present the valedictory address at her high school graduation and has been offered a scholarship to attend Rice University in Houston.

At Rice, Eva experiences all the strangeness of college life, which, of course, is made stronger by her foreign perspective. But here her account becomes less negative, always critical but milder. She discusses her abilities with English and how they affect her studies. She mentions that in literature classes there are many words and expressions she doesn't know. She has trouble with words such as "bole," "blear-eyed," and "midnight oil." She worries initially that "much of what [she reads] is lost on [her], lost in the wash and surf of inexactly understood words" (p. 180). But then she discovers she is at an advantage for three reasons. First, she has a talent for abstraction, for discovering the structure of a text. Second, the opacity of the words prevent her from getting lost in meanings and therefore allows the form of text to reveal itself all the more easily. Third, during that period, the New Criticism dominated literary studies and form was what was important. Eva says,

> "Form is content," at this time, is taken to mean that there is no such thing as content.

> Luckily for me, there is no world outside the text; luckily, for I know so little of the world to which the literature I read refers. My task, when I read a poem or a

novel, is to find repeated symbols, patterns of words, recurring motifs, and motifs that pull against each other. These last are particularly prized because they have the honorific status of "irony" and "paradox." These are exercises I perform with ease. . . .

I became an expert on this business of symbolic patterns. (p. 182)

Eva also reports that

in a democratic education system, in a democratic ideology of reading, I am never made to feel that I'm an outsider poaching on others' property. In this country of learning, I'm welcomed on equal terms, and it's through the democratizing power of literature that I begin to feel at home in America, even before I understand the literature or America, or the relationship between them, very well. (pp. 183–184)

After she graduates from Rice, she spends a year at the Yale School of Music and then goes on to Harvard to study for a Ph.D. in English literature. At the end of her second year at Harvard, Eva makes the following assessment of her language:

I've become obsessed with words. I gather them, put them away like a squirrel saving nuts for winter, swallow them and hunger for more. If I take in enough, then maybe I can incorporate the language, make it part of my psyche and my body. I will not leave an image unworded, will not let anything cross my mind till I find the right phrase to pin the shadow down. (p. 216)

The thought that there are parts of the language I'm missing can induce a small panic in me, as if such gaps were missing parts of the world or my mind—as if the totality of the world and mind were coeval with the totality of the language. Or rather, as if language were an enormous, fine net in which reality is contained—and if there are holes in it, then a bit of reality can escape, cease to exist. When I write, I want to use every word in the lexicon, to accumulate a thickness and weight of words so that they yield the specific gravity of things. I want to re-create, from the discrete particles of words, that wholeness of a childhood language that had no words.

I pounce on bits of colloquial idiom, those slivers of Americana in which the cultural sensibility is most vivid, as if they could give me America itself. "Hair of the dog that bit me," I repeat to myself with relish; "pork-barreling"; "I'm from Missouri, show me"; "He swallowed it hook, line, and sinker." When I speak, I'm awkward in using such homely familiarities; I still feel the presumption in it. But in writing, I claim territorial prerogative. Perhaps if I cast my net wide enough, it will cover the whole continent. (p. 217)

I sound natural enough, I sound like anybody else. But I can hear the artifice, and for a moment, I clutch. My throat tightens. Paralysis threatens. Speechlessness used to be one of the common symptoms of classic hysteria. I feel as though in me, hysteria is brought on by tongue-tied speechlessness. (p. 219)

Since I lack a voice of my own, the voices of others invade me as if I were a silent ventriloquist. They ricochet within me, carrying on conversations, lending me their modulations, intonations, rhythms. I do not yet possess them; they possess me. But some of them satisfy a need; some of them stick to my ribs. I could take on that stylish, ironic elongation which is X's mark of perpetual amusement; it fits something in my temperament, I could learn to speak a part of myself through it. And that curtailed, deliberate dryness that Y uses as an antidote to sentiment opens a door into a certain New England sensibility whose richness I would never otherwise understand. Eventually, the voices enter me; by assuming them, I gradually make them mine. I am being remade, fragment by fragment, like a patchwork quilt; there are more colors in the world than I ever knew. (p. 220)

Eva marries while in graduate school. She admits that language was part of the attraction. "When I fall in love, I am seduced by language. When I get married, I am seduced by language" (p. 219). "I married him partly for this, for the gift of language, and I listen to him with admiring pleasure. . . . but I know that though I'm captivated by his eloquence, I still can't read the language of his feelings" (p. 227).

Eva reports that she eventually achieves mastery of English: "But it's not until . . . I've finished graduate school successfully, and have begun to teach literature to others, that I crack the last barrier between myself and the language" (p. 186). She makes a trip to Poland in 1977 and when she returns, she reports her dreams are in English. She says,

> this is the most important thing: that it was in English, and that English spoke to me in a language that comes from below consciousness, a language as simple and mysterious as a medieval ballad, a gnostic speech that precedes and supersedes our analytic complexities. . . .
>
> Perhaps I've read, written, eaten enough words so that English now flows in my bloodstream. But once this mutation takes place, once the language starts speaking itself to me from my cells, I stop being so stuck on it. Words are no longer spiky bits of hard matter, which refer only to themselves. They become, more and more, a transparent medium in which I live and which lives in me—a medium through which I can once again get to myself and to the world. (p. 243)

She further elaborates on her sense of mastery.

> I've learned how to size people up; stepping into a room crowded with strangers, I can figure out quickly what species—public species, that is—the people in it belong to; I recognize that self-assured young man who peppers his international technocratic career with a few progressive ideas, that British academic who mutters hilarious remarks without bothering to change the pitch of his voice, that young poet whose posture is stiff with the strain of his sacrifice, that cosmopolitan Indian woman who has made the transition to modernity with evident grace. I've learned to read the signs and symbols governing the typology of the contemporary world.
>
> I take great pleasure in these skills, and the sense of mastery they give me. But how fragile they seem as I step back into that first, most private kind of knowledge. (p. 251)

Finally, Eva reports going into psychotherapy and describes the role it plays in her language odyssey.

> For me, therapy is partly translation therapy, the talk-ing cure a second-language cure. My going to a shrink is, among other things, a rite of initiation: initiation into the language of the subculture within which I happen to live, into a way of explaining myself to myself. But grad-ually, it becomes a project of translating backward. The way to jump over my Great Divide is to crawl backward over it in English. It's only when I retell my whole story, back to the beginning, and from the beginning onward, in one language, that I can reconcile the voices within me with each other; it is only then that the person who judges the voices and tells the stories begins to emerge. (pp. 271–272)

In the end Eva comes full circle. When she first arrived in Canada, her pre-sleep internal dialogue was in Polish. But then as she gained proficiency in English and as Polish became less dominant, she lost a vehicle for nighttime private talk. Now English is the medium for these personal speeches. She says, "So at those moments when I am alone, walking, or letting my thoughts meander before falling asleep, the internal dialogue pro-ceeds in English. I no longer triangulate to Polish as an authentic criterion, no longer refer back to it as to a point of origin" (p. 272).

Commentary

Hoffman's case is extremely important because she seems to violate the assumption that positive appraisals generate action tendencies that facilitate language learning and that negative appraisals lead to withdrawal from language learning. The account of her acquisition of English appears, at least on the sur-face, to be a chronicle of negative appraisals. But these negative appraisals are generally made on the dimension of pleasantness, and we have to ask whether the stimulus appraisal perspective requires positive assessment on the pleasantness dimension in order for learning to occur.

Ortony et al. (1988) point out that appealingness or pleas-antness is closely related to desirability, which is the major characteristic of goal appraisals. They state, "most people consider having a tooth filled to be an intrinsically unpleasant experience. However, beliefs about the long-range benefits and avoidance of harm might make this intrinsically unpleasant experience desirable. This simple example illustrates how something can be both desirable (when treated as an event) and disliked (when treated as an object). Thus, whereas *desirability* of an event entails some sort of understanding of its significance because it involves attention to goal-relevant consequences, *appealingness* does not" (p. 57).

Scherer (1988) also notes that a distinction should be made between intrinsic pleasantness and pleasantness that derives from the appeal of an agent, an activity, or an object in terms of its conduciveness to achieving a goal. Many of Hoffman's language learning experiences involving Canadians and things Canadian may have been appraised as desirable as events beneficial to her acquisition of English but as unappealing or unpleasant when treated as objects. In other words, interactions with Canadians and contact with certain elements of Canadian culture may have been frequently unpleasant for Hoffman, but in terms of her long range goals (i.e., achieving high proficiency in English) many of these unpleasant experiences may have been desirable.

Ortony et al. (1988) discuss the interaction among goals, standards, and attitudes. Goals involve appraisals of desirability; standards involve appraisals of the praiseworthiness of actions of agents; and attitudes involve appraisals of appealingness. Each can influence the other. We saw in the diary studies how appraisals of the actions of teachers and how appraisals of appealingness of aspects of target language culture can cause a person to abandon her goals. This seems most likely to occur when the goal is not particularly strong and when it is not supported by a need. In Hoffman's case, the need to acquire English and her desire (goal) for mastery or even virtuosity may have overridden her negative appraisals of pleasantness. In addition, she may have been able to disassociate these appraisals from her goals.

Eva did make appraisals of pleasantness that were related to her goals. Her positive appraisal of the language used by the Old Vic and by articulate and intellectual English speakers in general was related to her desire to achieve high proficiency. Her negative appraisal of the appealingness of the English spoken by the Polish immigrant community and of the language used in television sitcoms was also related to that same goal. But her negative appraisals of the Canadian landscape, Canadian conformity, drive-in restaurants, crinolines, and blue eyeshadow were either overridden by her proficiency goals or dissociated in her appraisal system from those goals. Her exposure to "ugly" jokes, 500-pound-canary jokes, pickle jokes, and elephant jokes may have been desirable to the extent that they facilitated her learning of English, but they may have been unpleasant as objects, that is, as jokes.

The distinction between the appraisal of pleasantness in terms of goal conduciveness and the appraisal of the intrinsic pleasantness of agents, activities, and objects would have been important for Hoffman to maintain. She was in North America for good; there was no going back to Poland. She had to learn English, and because of her desire to belong to a "'better' class of people" (p. 123), she had to speak "a 'better' language" (p. 123). She fought the image of being poor; she had to achieve in order to avoid "The Bowery" (p. 157). Her high achievement goals and her fear of failure conspired to make appraisals of unpleasantness less influential than they would be for someone with more alternatives. The learners we met through the diary studies (and even Kaplan) were in a position to drop the study of language if appraisals of unpleasantness became too strong. Hoffman did not have this option. Her language learning goals were supported by appraisals of need. To stay out of "The Bowery," she had to be competent; to become a member of the elite intellectual group, she had to be excellent. Thus, Eva's appraisals on the goal dimension are also supported by the appraisals she made on the dimension of self and social image. For her, excellence in English would allow her access to and membership in those groups who had status because of high levels of educational, professional, and artistic achievement.

Ortony et al. (1988) pointed out that goals "tend to live for different lengths of time. . . . Some, because they represent aspirations to possess valued objects or social positions, take a relatively long time to achieve and thus have long lives. . . . Because their realization often takes a long time, . . . [such goals] tend to be far removed from the majority of everyday activities" (p. 42). Hoffman had an appraisal system that allowed her to focus on valued long term-goals without being derailed by local unpleasantness. However, in contrast to Hoffman, learners in situations where there is not an overriding need or learners who do not have a strong goal, may require appraisals of pleasantness (i.e., generally positive appraisals of the appealingness of agents, actions and objects in the second language acquisition environment) to generate and sustain action tendencies that produce language learning.

Hoffman's goals in language learning were also supported by high aptitude; she was capable of achieving her goals. Three years after arriving in Canada she graduated first in her high school class. She makes little fuss about her successes: the winning of speech contests and poetry contests in school, being selected to deliver the valedictory address, admission to college. All these achievements are the consequence of her extraordinary acquisition of English. But for her, they are not big sources of satisfaction because she recognizes the distance between the proficiency she has achieved at that point and the mastery exhibited by highly literate and articulate native speakers. Eva's expectancy appraisals along the goal dimension, by which she assesses her current proficiency in relation to her ultimate goals, are always modest. But at the same time, she is always confident that she can be successful. Negative appraisals of her coping capacity are never an issue.

Eva had probably achieved sufficient proficiency in English by the end of her sophomore year in college to be successful in any profession, but ultimately she chose English itself as her profession. It is interesting to note that her negativity decreases in the third part of the book. It would appear that as she becomes part of the intellectual class, which she sees as her reference group, she can relax somewhat; she can be less critical. But Eva is a professional critic, so the negative edge never fully abates. I think Hoffman's case is remarkable in that it indicates how local negative appraisals can be dissociated from or overcome by positive appraisals of a future goal, especially when that goal would place the individual above and beyond the aspects of life which were appraised as negative.

III

In *The Philosopher's Demise: Learning French,* Richard Watson (1995) describes his attempts to learn French at the age of 55. Watson wasn't starting from scratch. In college he had taken a yearlong, ten-hour-a-week class in reading French. He learned to read French very well and enjoyed the process immensely.

> I loved learning to read this new language. It was all in the mind. The instructor devoted, at most, fifteen minutes of the first class period to French pronunciation, but we were never required to speak or write the language, only to read it. I read it very well, earning an A for the yearlong, ten-hour course. Moreover, some years later when I took the Ph.D. reading exam in reading French, I scored 100 percent. (p. 1)

This success and pleasure motivated him to write his Ph.D. dissertation on aspects of the history of Cartesian philosophy. In doing so he had to visit the Bibliothèque Nationale in Paris several times and through that experience he developed a good receptive competence in spoken French, but only acquired a very minimal ability to speak it.

> I went to France to do library research now and then, and although my ability to speak French improved slightly and I became very good at understanding French spoken to me, I never felt any great need to make a serious effort to learn to speak French, no more than had my former professors and language teachers at SUI [State University of Iowa] felt any need to make me learn to speak (as well as read) the language in the first place. (p. 3)

Nevertheless, as a Cartesian scholar he was able to read French texts fluently and translate them into English. He characterizes his French language ability in the following way:

> I had an enormous reading vocabulary, but I could not connect it to my minuscule speaking vocabulary. When I tried to say something, the words eluded me. They did not come up mispronounced, they did not come up at all, I suppose because I read French rapidly, passing over the printed

words without imagining any sounds at all, going directly from print to meaning. Some years before, I had noticed—not without pride—that I could be reading a book consciously unaware as to whether it was in French or English. But that entire sight-recognition vocabulary was useless to me in my attempt to speak French. (p. 6)

In December 1986, he received an invitation to present a paper the following June at a conference on Descartes sponsored by the Centre National de la Recherche Scientifique in Paris. Watson was expected to deliver his paper in French; he decided to take this opportunity to learn to speak the language. He arranged to be tutored by a native speaker who taught French at Washington University, St. Louis, where he was also a faculty, member. Watson experienced enormous difficulty trying to speak the language. His tutor had not expected him to continue for very long, but Watson was determined to succeed. He had always learned whatever he set out to, and he was shocked at his lack of ability with spoken French. He reports, "It was like diving naked and alone into ice water. I was frozen with panic. I found to my horror that I was not an able student, as I always had been before" (p. 8). He persevered, increased his efforts, but at the end of six months he was not much improved. He offers this analysis of his problem.

It was clear that it embarrassed me to speak French. I knew exactly why that was. I didn't want to sound like Charles Boyer in the movies of my childhood. We hooted and groaned when he breathed down the neck of some woman on the screen. And there was the suggestion that he might do things to them offscreen that no real man would ever be caught dead doing.

A great suspicion came over me: Real Men Don't Speak French. But just as you must survive humiliation and submit to agonizing tension, so also must you overcome embarrassment. Make an ass of yourself. If you want to learn. (p. 12)

But he wrote his conference paper in French, had his tutor and her husband correct it, and set off for Paris.

At the conference, he read his paper in French and was reasonably pleased with his performance, but during the question and answer period he froze. He reports, "when I started to answer . . . [the questions] my mind looked with horror into the bottomless pit of echoing silence where every word of French I had ever known had sunk into oblivion like a lost chord. I had to answer in English" (p. 14). His overall assessment of his performance was:

> My French was far from the worst among the foreigners. On any fair assessment, it was among the best. I noticed that the other American, who spoke far more fluently than I, did not make the elisions between words that are essential for speaking colloquial French. (p. 14)

> The distinguished English historian of science didn't do accents. Instead, he read French words as though they were English, with particular stress on all the endings that are silent in French. (p. 14)

> The Italian read his paper with Italian accents, the Japanese with Japanese gutturals and deletions, and the Spaniard was halfway through his paper before anyone realized that he was reading it in French, not in Spanish. All in all, I was quite pleased with myself, except for having to answer my questions in English. On a scale of 1 to 10, I thought I surely rated no lower than an 8, whereas the Englishman got a 6 for having to have the questions translated for him into English, although he did then, sort of, answer them in French. But I had no illusions. I could not really speak French. (pp. 14–15)

One of Watson's goals at the conference was to speak with a famous Professor Marion. On the first day, Watson met him and spoke to him in French. Marion immediately switched to English and after a few minutes excused himself, suggesting they meet the following day. Marion managed to put off Watson for the whole conference and ultimately avoided meeting with him at all. Watson concludes,

> Perhaps it was just as well. All I had learned in six months of tutoring was how to read French out loud. If I had not already known this, three days at the conference would have convinced me. At the end I could not even speak the few words and sentences that had always been my mainstays in France. Something deep in me dictated that it was

better to say nothing, to be thought bereft of any spoken French, than to expose the limited extent of what I knew. Moreover, to my horror, I discovered that if I did try to use the bits of spoken French that had served me in the past, all the old mispronunciations remained. My new knowledge of how to make the sounds had not transferred. I remained silent and watched the show. (p. 16)

Watson also observes that his problems with inhibition in the oral aspects of foreign language communication may be specific to French and to interaction with certain French speakers. He notes:

My wife, Pat, is an archaeologist and has worked in Iraq, Iran, and Turkey. She is good at languages and has studied Arabic, Farsi, Kurdish, and Turkish as well as French, Spanish, and German. But often in the Near East, she would be tongue-tied while I blithely carried on conversations with a few hundred words and rudimentary grammar that I had gleaned from that wonderful and I am afraid now defunct series of blue-backed books titled *Teach Yourself Persian,* or whatever language you wanted to speak. One could not say that I really spoke Kurdish, for example, but I communicated enthusiastically and well enough. With time to think, Pat could speak these languages correctly, but I just talked, any old way. (p. 17)

Watson also reports that he felt quite comfortable speaking French with a Japanese scholar at the conference and also with a French friend and colleague, Professor Roy. But with the elite clique of French Cartesian scholars, he simply cared too much and became inhibited. Below he characterizes his goal and his failure to achieve it.

What I wanted, was that when I asked a distinguished Cartesian scholar a question, as I did in a discussion period at the conference in Descartes[*], but had not dared to do in Paris, what I wanted was that he understand and answer

---

[*]Here Watson is referring to another conference that immediately followed the Paris conference and was held in the village of Descartes where the philosopher was born in 1596.

my question, that he not look as though the village idiot had spoken to him with all the earnestness of his imbecility and as clearly as a cleft palate permitted. (p. 23)

Watson had decided to remain in France after the conference and to study French at the Alliance Française. He took their placement exam and scored too low to be in any class at all, but managed to convince an administrator to enroll him in a section of Part II of the course. His first teacher, Claire, was a charming and flirtatious woman, and he liked her and the class very much. But when he moved on to Part III of the course, he encountered a teacher who conducted her class in a very traditional French lycée manner. Watson reports, "these sessions were a terrifying experience for most of us" (p. 37). She called the students "imbecile" and "idiot." She went around the class asking students to respond to exercises in order. The students, of course, paid no attention to each others' responses and instead worked ahead preparing for their turn.

In one assignment the students were asked to write an essay in the past tense. Watson, to make his composition coherent, put a few verbs in the future. The teacher gave him a low grade on the paper and changed the verbs in the future tense to the past. This, of course, upset the meaning of the text. When Watson explained to the teacher that he had used the future tense on purpose, the teacher responded, "'But Ree-shar, . . . if you knew they were future tense, why did you use them when I asked for the past tense?'" (p. 42).

Watson provided the following analysis of his reaction to the course.

> I was more tense than I have ever been in my life or ever want to be again. The first time I ever climbed a mountain wall with hundreds of feet of exposure below me, that time we arrived back at the entrance of a cave to find a wall of water roaring in and had to crawl downstream as fast as we could for a long distance to clamber up into passages above water level, my Ph.D. oral exam—none of those times could begin to compete with the state of tension I was enduring now.
>
> And how am I to characterize or express adequately my sensations when with every indication of justified anger and disgust, The Professor called me an idiot and

an imbecile? To be sure, she called others in the class the same as the days went on, but I was the first. I, who had been a professor in charge of my own classes for twenty-five years. In some sense of that maligned word, I suppose the experience was edifying. (p. 39)

It was not the first time in my life that I had been called an imbecile in class. But imbecility is in America, so to speak, a relative thing. In France, it is exactly defined, and certified. (p. 40)

Watson also comments on the structure of French and the notion that one should not innovate, but instead should submit to the rules. In order to communicate, he would frequently circumlocute or translate an English phrase into French. His teachers would respond that what he had said was not French or that one couldn't "say that in French." He hypothesizes that "the great difference between a literary tour de force in English and one in French is that a work of genius in English stretches the language as far as it will go, while genius in French literature is exhibited by superhuman adherence to the rules" (p. 45). He concludes, "It is the French and not the Germans after all who are rule bound (at least in language). This opened to me the dark possibility that although I like to read French, perhaps I don't really like French" (p. 45).

Watson reports that he learned to talk French in interactions with a friend, Claude Chabert, who was a lycée philosophy teacher and cave explorer. Claude was patient and let Watson think out how to say something. Watson found he could actually communicate grammatically if he was given time to think. He found that if he could ignore or be spared corrections, he could keep his arguments in mind and could speak. He noted that an individual Frenchman could understand him, but in groups the French had no patience and refused to understand.

Watson also offers some psychological reasons for his difficulty with French.

I have mentioned a possible psychological reason. Although I loved learning to read French and enjoy reading French philosophers and writers, I have a distinct dislike for the sound of spoken French. Many Americans do. Why? Because it's weak. For American men at least, French sounds syrupy and effeminate. (p. 52)

. . . what made me realize how much I dislike the sound of French was the continual, unctuous, caressing repetition of "l'oiseau" ("the bird"). It is a word the French believe to be one of the most beautiful in their language. It is a word that cannot be pronounced without simpering, a word whose use should be restricted to children under five.

I did not want to speak French because it gave me the bird. (p. 53)

So how does one handle such an irrational response? I wondered if it was just the contrast with the English "bird," which is a strong hard word. How about the German word for bird, "Vogel"? I'm going to get to German in a moment. American men don't like to simper. And as I said, they get their notion of Frenchmen from the movies. Certainly no American boy of my generation ever wanted to grow up to be Charles Boyer. (p. 53)

Watson concedes that he's exaggerating, but maintains his view.

All right. All right. But remember, I'm not trying to be reasonable about it. I'm just giving you my unadulterated, stupid, automatic, response. Real Men Don't Speak French. There has to be something to that. Where did I read that during World War I, French soldiers were known as "WeeWees"? Of course that's French for "Yes, yes" but really . . . (p. 54)

A number of Watson's French interlocutors had remarked that he seemed to speak English sentences with French words. He speculates on his reluctance to accommodate to the French way of saying things.

Why did I resist it so? Because, I think, all my life I have been trying to learn to write. These new French forms threatened to destroy what little progress I had made so far. Not only did I use English forms in speaking French, I was appalled to find myself using French forms when I was writing English. French was undermining my very being! My personality was in danger of disintegrating! A great clanging of alarm bells was set

off in my deep unconscious, irritated by these alien influences seeping down from above. (p. 57)

The other thing I understood is why many writers
resist learning a foreign language. They are defending the
style and form they have perfected in their own language.

The mere reading of another language apparently
does not present the same threat. But speaking is too
close to writing. (p. 58)

Watson also has a reaction to the infamous French teaching
and testing method—the dictée:

I do not spell well in English, again perhaps a function
of reading for meaning, not for the sound of words nor
for how they look on the page. I spell even worse in
French. (Now that I have worked at learning to spell
French words, I spell English words even worse than
before.) On dictations I always made about twice as
many errors as the number the teacher announced as
allowable. I began to worry about passing the dictation
portion of the final exam . . . (p. 59)

Watson describes how the French classes, particularly with
one very severe female teacher, became occasions for shame and
humiliation. (The neurobiology of shaming experiences will be
described in Chapter 6.)

At the Alliance Française, I sank lower and lower to
the bottom of the class. I never missed a session. I sat
there paying intense attention and looking at the
teacher with hopeful eyes.

My transition to this groveling state of supplication
was abrupt. During that first month with Claire, I was
often impatient. I was used to being in charge and had
consciously to hold myself down so as not to behave like
a professor, not to speak up on all subjects like a know-
it-all. I did know many things the younger students did
not on subjects that came up in class discussion. But this
problem evaporated like dew under the desert sun during the first hour with The Professor. By the end of the
first day with her I was so anxious simply to be able to
work out the exercises and answer the questions in class

that I lost consciousness of ever having been a professor—or of knowing anything—at all. In The Professor's
class I saw myself as did the youngest members—as a
funny little old man with a white beard who was earnest
and wanted to learn but who just wasn't very good or
very bright. They liked me and would talk to me at
break, but there was no question who was at the bottom
of the class. (pp. 60–61)

Watson suggests that another reason he has difficulty learning to speak correct French is because to do so, he would have to
sacrifice his individualism. He argues that learning a language
means following rules—that is, the rules of language. This, in
fact, then prepares one to follow other rules—that is, the rules of
society, of authority. He speculates, "I'll bet I was having so much
trouble learning to speak French because I did not want to pledge
allegiance to a foreign language" (p. 79). As we saw earlier, Watson views the French as slaves to the cherished rules of their language. He sees himself as rebelling against becoming such a
slave:

It was a depressing prospect. To learn French I might
have to give up my lifelong adherence to the doctrine of
extreme individualism. I had been attracted by French
radicalism only to discover that in language the French
are hidebound conservatives. (p. 81)

Watson also ponders the question of why the French are (considered) nasty. He suggests that it is not because they don't like
you, but simply because they don't care about you. They have
such a high opinion of themselves that outsiders are irrelevant.
Watson is embarrassed because he is a Cartesian scholar who
cannot speak French. He wants to be accepted by the French
Cartesians.

Once I decided to learn to speak French it became—did I
say?—almost immediately an obsession. All those years
of guilt and embarrassment at being a Cartesian scholar
who could not speak French (even if no one else noticed
or cared), the difference between what I was and what I
appeared to be, combined to drive my ambition to a
frenzy. I would learn to speak French, whatever it took,
however long. One day, by God, I would sit at a table in a

restaurant in Paris with a group of French Cartesian scholars, and we would talk! (p. 65)

But that group is closed and indifferent to outsiders.

Scholars compete for prestige, and each scholar—particularly each and every idiosyncratic French scholar—attempts to make dominant his own views and interpretations. In no place in the world is this competition more intense than in Paris, the intellectual capital of the Western world. Those tight little circles of the sort I was yearning just to look into were closed not through any particularly conscious intent, but because competition is so extreme among the small number who must be admitted that they haven't time to notice outsiders. Even more, in their assurance that the French intellectual circles are indeed the highest in the cosmos—a conviction they hold without ever thinking about it, as other people take for granted the air they breathe—French scholars can ignore the work of foreigners as having no relevance to them. Even French scientists seldom make reference to work in languages other than French. Another reason, of course, is that many of them can read only French. (p. 74)

Watson makes another analysis of why French Cartesians were unwilling to spend time with him at conferences. "The real point of getting together is to make contacts. The fact was, as a contact I was not wired into the Parisian power circuit, so why should any of them plug into me?" (p. 120).

Earlier, we saw Watson had referred to the difficulty he had with English spelling. Here he discusses the problem in more detail:

I have always thought my bad spelling was due to inattention as to whether words end, say, with "an" or "on," and the like. Would not impatient inattention also explain how I can look up the spelling of a word, clamp the dictionary shut, and then turn to my writing and still not know how to spell it? I had gone through the procedure of looking it up; did I have to remember it, too? And doesn't everyone now and then reverse letters and numbers—"57" for "75" and even "Nood Gight"? Just today I asked for the "palt and sepper" at lunch, and as long as I can remember I have made that kind of exchange of initial letters perhaps once a week. Is that a kind of dyslexia? It really is not a serious problem in speaking and spelling. What is serious is my inability to listen to sounds and repeat them back. I was poor at memorizing poems and piano pieces in my youth. Again, this was attributed by both my teachers and me to a combination of laziness and impatience, to that same refusal to spend boring hours practicing that drove me from the chemistry lab when I was a freshman in college.

But now I was trying. I was practicing. I was listening and repeating back. I read Georges Simenon's mystery novels out loud in French, trying to accumulate an auditory vocabulary. But time and again when I wanted to use a French word that I knew I knew, a word I would recognize instantly if I either read it or heard it, it would not come up. I could not hear nor see it in my mind. (pp. 102–103)

Watson notes that although he studied diligently and he *did* know the grammar, he still had problems. He laments, "I *did* know this stuff. Why, then, was I so low in my class? Why did I make stupid, simple errors, one after the other? How much practice did it take, not to be perfect, but to pass" (p. 103).

Watson suggests another psychological contribution to his inability to speak French. He had been told by one of his French friends, Claude, the caver, that it would take about two years of residence in France to learn to speak French comfortably. Watson notes that over the years he had spent more time than that in France already, but explains, "The problem was that I was not very sociable. Pat [his wife] and I had once rented an isolated cottage outside a village where we sat and wrote. We went to the market twice a week for groceries. There wasn't time to natter with the natives. Even if they would have." (p. 110).

Eventually Watson did make contact with one of the major Cartesian scholars in Paris and they even had lunch together. But after that he abandoned the effort. "After scoring with one Cartesian scholar, I did not get around to following up on any more of my calls" (p. 121).

Finally, after preparing diligently for the final examinations for part III of the Alliance course, Watson learned he had failed and would not be allowed to go on to the next level. He was devastated. "I was quite angry. At myself both for flunking the exams and for having thought that I might pass them even though I had earlier anticipated that I would not" (p. 122). As someone who had always been successful in school, now the thought of being a student was noxious.

> I had always liked school. In the past when fall came, and I saw young children setting out with their books and new supplies, I felt kind of a joyful uplift that surely reflects my own childhood experiences. One week after I finished my course at the Alliance Française, school started for French children and the streets of Paris filled with their passage and chatter. I witnessed this advent with a sensation of stomach wrenching horror. Thank God I was not still in school. (p. 127)

But Watson's efforts had not been entirely fruitless. He reports:

> Slowly I recovered. I had been in Paris now for three months and had done almost nothing but study French. We went to the Comédie Française and to another play, and I understood most of the dialogue. We went out to dinner with French friends, and spent entire evenings speaking French.
>
> "Look," Pat said to me, "the transformation is amazing. Before you could hardly say a word. Now you carry on conversations for hours in French."
>
> "Last summer you couldn't say a word," Claude said. "Now you won't shut up."
>
> I started working again in the Bibliothèque Nationale. I had a nice long chat with the woman in charge of the rare books reading room. People asked me for directions in the street and understood me when I told them where to go. I was, after a fashion, speaking French. (p. 129)

Finally, Watson attended a conference on Descartes in Holland where several of the distinguished French Cartesians were presenting papers. The Dutch professor who was directing the conference invited him to a dinner to which the French scholars were also invited. At dinner, Watson was at the table with Marion, the French professor who had avoided him at the Paris conference and several times since. Watson describes his final encounter with the illustrious Marion.

> Anyway, there we were. And there, seated facing me, unable to escape at last, was Professor Marion. Now he would have to talk to me. I spoke to him at length, in French, rather well, I thought.
>
> "Speak English," he said. And he answered me in English.
>
> "Look," I said heatedly, "your English is just as bad as my French."
>
> "But I am French," he said.
>
> "Then speak French," I said.
>
> "Are you sure you can understand?" he asked.
>
> "Of course I can understand," I said. "I'm not an idiot."
>
> "All right," he said, "I'll speak French. But you speak English. Don't try to speak French. Your French is terrible." (p. 133)

Commentary

Richard Watson's story seems to involve three sorts of appraisals. First, he expresses a dislike for the way French sounds. To him the language is effeminate, unmanly. He worries that adopting its sounds and structure will undermine his personality, his writing ability, and his sense of individualism. Second, unlike Alice Kaplan, he dislikes French teaching methods. He rebels at their demand for accuracy, at their insistence on the French way of saying things, and their rejection of one's ability to say things in French, that is, the ability to get one's meaning across in French, but not necessarily in the French way. He finds the French emphasis on form over content an affront. Third, Watson, much to his surprise, finds that he must negatively appraise his ability to cope with spoken French. Because he has always been a good student, his expectation is that he can and will learn to speak French. That expectation is not met and he is shamed, even humiliated. But he can't believe it; this has never happened to him before. So he tries harder, studies diligently for his exams at the Alliance Française and fails again. His French is rejected not only by the Cartesians but also by his instructors. His goal of being validated and respected is totally frustrated. Thus he decides he doesn't really like French. At the end of the book, he appears to have given up. In this sense, he is typical of most learners. Low appraisal of one's aptitude resulting from inadequate performance signals one to stop, to put one's efforts elsewhere. One cannot become an expert in something one does not like, and it is very difficult to like to do something for which one lacks ability. Watson cuts his losses, returns to the States, and writes a fascinating book about his experience—in English. In sum, on the dimension of goal-related pleasantness, Watson makes negative appraisals of French sounds, the French pedagogical demand for accuracy, and the French emphasis on form over content. In terms of coping potential, he is confronted with a major deficit in aptitude for speaking French, and finally, in terms of goal appraisals, the French instruction and the French philosophers themselves prevent him from becoming a respected French-speaking Cartesian.

Watson's case raises the important issue of language learning aptitude in relation to stimulus appraisal. Watson, of course, had extraordinary aptitude. He was able to go from a graphic representation of a second language to meaning with amazing facility. Decoding a printed page and thus deriving meaning from French script was his forte. This skill had allowed him to become an expert in a major area of French philosophy. Watson's aptitude in aural aspects of French were not as high as in reading, but his comprehension ability did not show any deficit and could be considered good. However, he clearly had a problem with language production.

It is well established that there is an aptitude for second language learning, which has been shown by Carroll (1965, 1981; see also Skehan, 1989) to consist of:

1. Phonemic coding ability—the capacity to distinguish sounds and to code them for future use.
2. Associative memory—the ability to learn rapidly the meaning of target language words.

3. Grammatical sensitivity—the ability to recognize the grammatical function of words in sentences.
4. Inductive language learning ability—the capacity to determine patterns of meaning and form in a language sample.

Watson seemed to have difficulty with phonemic encoding and associative memory, that is, he had difficulty either forming oral representations for French sounds and words and/or with converting them to speech. He also appeared to have problems in the ability to determine patterns of grammar and their meaning from an oral language sample, and he definitely had deficits in the ability to generate correct grammatical patterns in his production of spoken French.

But aptitude is not independent of stimulus appraisal and is reflected in the dimension of coping ability. A person is likely to find language learning pleasant and enhancing of his self and social image if he has high aptitude, that is, if he is able to cope well with language learning tasks and learns with facility. Therefore, if acquisition of the language is also important for the learner's goals and needs, he will maintain the long-term effort necessary to learn the language. On the other hand, if an individual finds second language learning difficult, he is likely to experience it as less pleasant and as diminishing of his self and social image. The learner might even find his L2 performance shaming, and there is research that shows that shame experiences generate cortisol in the body, which interferes with cognition. Thus, lack of aptitude is likely to generate withdrawal from language learning. It is probably extremely rare for people to become proficient or expert in an area for which they lack aptitude. This may not be because aptitude always sets a ceiling on what can be learned; it may be that high proficiency could be achieved, but that the process would be so long and so insulting to one's self and social image, that the effort would be abandoned.

Watson's experience in France clearly led to negative appraisals on the dimension of coping potential and to consequent negative appraisals on the norm/self compatibility dimension. He appears to have spent much of his time in France in a shame state that further frustrated his learning. Ultimately, he abandoned the enterprise. But the consequences of doing so were not particularly great. He was a full professor of philosophy with tenure at an American university. If advancement in his career were dependent on his ability to speak French, the situation would have been much worse.

Ehrman (1996) reports just such a case. Her subject is Lewis, a 40-year-old member of the U.S. Foreign Service where language proficiency is important for career advancement. In preparation for his assignment, he took an intensive language class at the Foreign Service Institute. He got sick during the course and fell behind. He went overseas, served his tour of duty, returned to the U.S., was tested, and performed poorly; that is, he scored at about the same level he had at the end of his initial language training. He then took a second course in which he struggled but still did poorly and felt very bad about himself. He indicated that some instructors were friendly, but in general he felt abandoned by the program in the sense that he perceived most instructors as having no confidence in his ability to learn. He began to believe that they were even ignoring him outside of class and wouldn't even speak to him in the hallways. He regarded the efforts that teachers made to help him as babysitting, and by continually comparing himself with other students, he felt inferior, inadequate, anxious and depressed. This psychological state, of course, further interfered with his learning. In anticipation of the end-of-course proficiency exam, he became panicky and even had somatic reactions such as headaches, but with counseling he was able to control his anxiety. He did poorly again on the proficiency test because of grammar errors and insufficient vocabulary knowledge. Lewis was, nevertheless, again sent overseas where he used his language in a variety of professional and social contexts, but upon completion of his tour of duty, he was tested and only showed minimal improvement.

During his periods at the Foreign Service Institute, Ehrman had Lewis take several psychological tests. On the Modern Language Aptitude Test (Carroll & Sapon, 1959) which assesses the four components of language learning ability mentioned earlier (phonemic coding, associative memory, grammatical sensitivity, and inductive language learning), he scored below the average for students in the program. Other tests indicated that he had an intellectual preference for meanings, ideas, and concepts, rather than for facts (and declarative knowledge of language consists of grammatical facts and rules). Testing also indicated that he sought predictability and preferred learning from others in a social setting. He also appeared to be field dependent, that is, he had holistic perceptions and difficulty perceiving patterns embedded in auditory or visual backgrounds. This characteristic may have made it difficult for him to extract phonological and grammatical information from second language input. Ehrman suggests that his linguistic performance may have relied on compensatory strategies such as circumlocution and simplification, which may have been communicative, but not grammatically precise. Such a deficit in grammar would prevent him from ever scoring higher than a 3 on the Foreign Service Institute Oral Proficiency Exam on which scores range from 0 to 5. From Lewis's reports of his study habits, Ehrman also suggests that he may have had a sub-clinical attention deficit disorder. He appeared to be able to overcome this attentional disability only when he had a strong intrinsic motivation. Such motivation had enabled him to become a concert musician in a previous career. But language learning was not intrinsically motivating for him. It was important in terms of extrinsic goals such as furthering his career in Foreign Service, but this was not sufficient to overcome his attentional deficits. (In contrast, Kaplan and Hoffman were motivated by both intrinsic and extrinsic value.)

Ehrman indicates that Lewis's negative appraisal of his ability to cope with language learning led to distortion in other appraisals he made. Because of his perception that he could not do what other people valued, he began to feel discounted and disliked by them. Ehrman suggests that these beliefs led to behavior that may actually elicit the negative reactions he expects. What Lewis's case demonstrates, then, is that negative appraisals of aptitude (coping potential) in situations in which goals are high and important for the achievement of other valued goals (e.g., career advancement) can result in negative spirals of anxiety and shame that further inhibit learning. Aptitude and appraisal are not independent; they interact with each other producing damaging and potentially dangerous psychological states.

Watson and Lewis contrast because Watson could ultimately escape; Lewis, as long as he remains in the Foreign Service, is likely to face the prospects of having to acquire another language or to improve in the one he has been wrestling with. The relationship between stimulus appraisal, aptitude, and proficiency is illustrated in Figure 4.1.

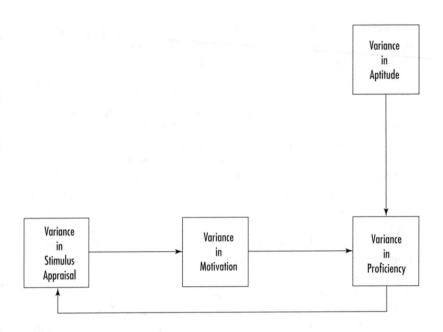

Figure 4.1. The Influence of Aptitude on Proficiency and of Proficiency on Stimulus Appraisal.

These three autobiographies, like the data reported in diary studies, and the student case study that follows, illustrate the wide variation in appraisal systems and the very different trajectories they create for learners.

Elicited Language Learning Biographies

In the summer of 1994, I had the good fortune to be invited by Professor Stephen Carey to teach a course in second language acquisition to graduate students in the Department of Language Education at the University of British Columbia. These students had had extensive experience with second language learning and were extremely insightful about the process. The course lasted for three weeks and was held two hours a day. For an assignment due halfway through the course, I asked the students to write approximately five-page autobiographical accounts of their language learning. As a final project, I asked them to provide the same histories again, but this time analyzing their experience according to the stimulus-appraisal framework I had taught during the second half of the course. I felt these essays demonstrated extremely well how an analysis of one's various language learning experiences from the perspective of stimulus appraisal could provide an explanation for variable success.

With the permission and kind participation of the authors, I present six of these analyses in this book. One is presented here to facilitate direct comparison with Kaplan, Hoffman, and Watson. The other five are in the appendix where they can be examined according to the readers' interest. For five of the contributors, both assignments are reproduced here with as little editing as possible. The two assignments are presented so that the reader can judge the validity of the approach by comparing a naive analysis with one guided by categories of stimulus appraisal. The last contribution in the appendix by Garold Murray is only the first essay. For his final assignment he did a somewhat different project. I included his essay for two reasons. First, it has a wonderful lyrical quality that reminds me of early Françoise Sagan novels, and it allows the reader to make his or her own interpretation of the appraisals that Murray may have made.

Barbara Hilding I

Variable success in learning foreign languages varies within an individual as well as across different learners. I have been exposed to several L2s in both formal and informal settings and have achieved widely varying successes in them.

My first informal exposure to L2 was learning to speak Ukrainian with my grandparents who always spoke it at home. I spent a lot of time with my grandparents before starting school and so I learned to speak and understand Ukrainian quite well in order to communicate with them.

While traveling extensively in Asia after completing my BA, I was exposed to many different languages. I now find it odd that I didn't take advantage of this learning opportunity: I never felt the need or the desire to learn any of the languages, except for the counting system for purposes of bargaining in the market and a few elementary phrases such as "please," "thank you," and "where are the toilets?" The languages changed so dramatically from one area to the next that it never seemed worth the effort to learn them. Perhaps the relative difficulty of learning non-European languages was another factor.

I now know French at a reasonably complete level although I did not really begin to learn it until my late twenties. I had studied French in Grades 6–12 but learned very little. My knowledge of French at that time consisted of a few isolated lexical items and verb conjugations. I would attribute this lack of learning to ineffective instructional methods and the fact that none of my teachers, I now suspect, actually knew French themselves.[1] As it had no connection with my life, I was not motivated to learn the language. Although I enrolled in French in my first year of university, I soon dropped out.

After a hiatus of ten years with no interest in French, I entered into a romantic relationship with a French Canadian. I was also working as a letter carrier, a job which left me plenty of spare time. This fortunate combination of circumstances offered the perfect opportunity for foreign language acquisition so I registered for beginner level French at the university. I remember being very motivated to learn French at this time, even to the point of spending four to six hours daily in the language lab (including weekends). Studying and practicing French was great fun as I was learning so quickly. I also drove my francophone partner crazy at this time by turning every household transaction into an interminable linguistic exercise. When asked to go to the store to pick up some ingredients for dinner, for example, I would insist on being able to list them off perfectly in French, complete with partitive articles, before leaving for the store— much to his exasperation.

My boyfriend's Catholic family disapproved of our non-traditional living arrangement. However, they thought it was rather "cute" that I was trying to learn French, convinced that this was a sign that I would soon accept the other family values. Some-

---

[1] I did this schooling in rural Manitoba where my Grade 11 French teacher pronounced "garçon" as [gar' kon] and where my Grade 12 French teacher had a nervous breakdown near the end of the year.

times I think I learned French just to spite them. I know I did take a certain spiteful pleasure when I began to notice grammatical errors they made or when they mixed English words into their speech. I suppose that this could be considered as a sort of negative integrative motivation—if I couldn't be accepted for myself, I could outdo them in speaking their own language.

I advanced so quickly that I went directly from first semester French into a special intensive section of combined fifth/sixth semester French. On the first day of class, we wrote an autobiographical essay. The next day, when the professor asked to speak to me about it, I was afraid she would say that I wasn't advanced enough for the class. Much to my surprise, however, she wanted to know why my level of French was so much superior to that of the other students in the class. This comment must have appealed to my competitive nature: I was now convinced that I could and would get the best mark in the class. I was also convinced that this was the best French professor in the world. I took up the challenge with boundless enthusiasm, spending many hours every night on my homework, playing the incomprehensible bits on the tapes over and over again, reading dictionaries and verb books in the bathroom, getting up at 6 am before my boyfriend went to work to have his breakfast ready (I never showed interest in cooking before) so that he could have time to go over my homework with me.

I'm sure that the sheer effort expended, plus the enormous amounts of time spent on the task combined with the fact that I had a private francophone tutor contributed to my rapid rate of learning. Also, I felt a sense of personal satisfaction since I could see how quickly I was learning. This spurred me on to even greater efforts.

That summer, I went to Quebec for a six week immersion program. This proved to be a rewarding experience since my confidence in speaking French increased immensely. The following year, I completed enough credits in French to be eligible for graduate studies, then did Byrn Mawr's summer program in Avignon. When I began the graduate program in French literature, I applied for an RA. However, as they needed TAs as a cheap source of labor, I was thrown into the world of teaching French. I was enthralled with teaching from the beginning and was soon spending three hours preparing for every hour of class so as to be ready with the answer to any possible question. By the end of the year, I knew the subject I was teaching very thoroughly. Teaching French while studying it was a particularly valuable experience which allowed me an insightful understanding both of the way the language works and of the problems encountered by language learners.

Although I have since left my French Canadian boyfriend, I still teach French and I continue to visit a francophone area most summers. I enjoy these immersion experiences and consider them necessary for me to maintain a near-native level in the language.

I have achieved a reasonable but much less complete knowledge of Spanish. The impetus for my learning Spanish was a trip to Mexico. Before leaving, I worked with a set of records ("Learn Spanish in Three Weeks") and gained a rudimentary knowledge of the language: I was able to order beer and find the toilets. In the small villages where it was essential to communicate in Spanish, armed with my limited knowledge of Spanish, I could and did communicate. I was most impressed by the friendly and helpful attitude of the Mexican villagers who would gather around when I attempted to ask for something, and in some puzzlement repeat my mispronunciation until someone finally guessed what I was trying to say. We all felt quite pleased with ourselves at the successful conclusions to these conversations. In two months, I learned a significant amount of Spanish because of the combination of the necessity to communicate in Spanish and positive reinforcement from very supportive and patient native speakers.

Encouraged by this success, I enrolled in Spanish 100. Despite an incompetent teacher who did nothing but drill type exercises with us, my knowledge of Spanish increased considerably. By the following year, however, the charm seemed to have worn off. Although I passed Spanish 200 with a mediocre grade, I had lost interest in the language and can remember only a sense of frustration at the amount of work required to memorize those cursed irregular verb patterns. Fond memories of communicating with Mexican villagers had receded, leaving only hours of work for an unimportant goal.

My experience in learning German consists of two years of university courses. In my first year, we started out with 35 students but were down to 12 by week's end due to the professor's techniques of intimidation and humiliation. However, I thought that Fräulein Tampi was wonderful and I learned an incredible amount of German that year. Learning was facilitated in a small class composed of only committed students. Furthermore, the information was presented in a very organized manner. The professor began every class with a review of what we had learned the previous day, did a summary of what we would learn that day, and ended with a preview of the next class. The professor had high expectations of each student with the result that everyone was always prepared and always participated fully. Hardly anyone ever missed class.[2] Every week we had a 15 minute individual oral exam in her office. We soon lost our fear of oral exams, and became quite proficient in conversing under pressure. This regular individual conversational practice contributed to our rapid rate of learning.

The following year, German class was a great disappointment to me. Fourteen of the nineteen students were native speakers. I was silently furious with the professor for allowing the native speakers to answer all the questions. I was unable to learn in this environment since I felt I could not participate and was never allowed to formulate an answer in my own mind before it was provided. I felt intimidated and stupid since I did not compare favorably with native speakers and became extremely frustrated with the class.[3] I soon stopped attending regularly; nevertheless, I received an excellent grade for the course because I had learned so much the previous year.

I also studied Italian for two years and found it very easy because of its similarity to Spanish. As well, by this time I was very interested in languages in general and was also an experienced L2 learner.

---

[2] I once missed class due to illness. Fräulein Tampi then informed me that my grade would certainly deteriorate if I kept up this frivolous behavior.

[3] Once, on leaving the classroom I suddenly remembered that I had said "die" instead of "das." I hit myself on the head, disgusted with myself, saying: "You idiot! How can you be so stupid?" I also remember the professor making fun of a word I'd written on an essay. For "living-room" I had written "lebensraum"—that is what Hitler had been trying to get more of, said the professor. I felt publicly humiliated on this occasion, which is not typical of me, since I would normally find this quite funny.

I find the phenomenon of L2 attrition to be very frustrating. I spent last summer mostly in the francophone area of Switzerland. Although I was soon able to understand the Italian and German TV channels, I seemed unable or unwilling to make the effort required to speak during visits to the Italian and German areas of the country. I felt that I would need a few months of study before I would feel comfortable conversing. I have also lost much of my Spanish, but have noticed that it comes back very quickly when I have the opportunity to use it. I am able to maintain near-native competency in French only because I use it so frequently and spend a considerable amount of time in francophone areas.

I believe I have some natural aptitude for L2 learning. I enjoy both formal and informal study of languages and I enjoy traveling in areas where English is not spoken. The most important factors that have influenced how completely I was able to learn various L2s would seem to be length of time spent on the task, opportunity to live in an immersion setting, and personal interest in learning the language.

Barbara Hilding II

I have been exposed to several foreign languages in both naturalistic and formal settings and have achieved varying levels of completeness in learning them. Aptitude has surely played a role in my ability to learn languages; however, since this factor would remain constant across languages and across time, it cannot account for differential levels of attainment. Additional important variables would seem to be age at time of exposure, attitude toward the target language and its speakers, duration and intensity of time spent on the learning task and, most importantly, motivation.

Acquisition in Natural Settings

Twice in my life I have had the opportunity to acquire second languages in naturalistic settings: for a good part of the first five years of my life I lived with my Ukrainian grandparents and then, during my twenties, I spent two years traveling in Asia. In the first situation, I learned the language to a level typical of a native speaker of that age. In the second situation I learned only a few words or phrases. Age difference at the time of exposure to second languages was surely one important factor which helps to explain this differential success in acquiring L2. The high quality and quantity of comprehensible input must also have positively affected my acquisition of Ukrainian.

In addition, motivation to learn the L2 must have influenced my level of attainment. Since a child's most immediate goals would naturally include communication and interaction with care-givers, I must have been very motivated to learn Ukrainian. I remember living with my grandparents as a very pleasant experience. I am still convinced that I was the center of my grandmother's life: to this day I retain fond memories of baking bread and exploring the forest with her. My grandfather worked on the railway in northern Manitoba and was often away, so my grandmother and I spent a lot of time alone together, isolated except for the occasional passing train. In such an environment with no other children around, I must have considered myself to be a member of a three-person target language community. Speaking Ukrainian would have been a natural part of my psychological and social integration and therefore an integral part of my developing ego and self-image. In fact, my learning Ukrainian could probably be best termed as simultaneous L1 acquisition.

My failure to learn foreign languages while traveling in Asia can most likely be attributed to culture shock and psychological disorientation. Wanting to experience the "real" culture and people, my traveling companion and I deliberately avoided tourist transportation and lodging. This way of traveling led, however, to a state of affairs which meant that dealing with life became a daily test of coping ability. Even the simplest gesture that had always been taken for granted could suddenly take on unexpected meaning (shaking the head, for example, could mean the opposite of "no"). Food was unfamiliar, sanitation was primitive and toilets often filthy, rats and other horrors lurked in dark corners, debilitating diseases such as hepatitis, dysentery, and malaria lay in wait for the unwary traveler.

Moreover, the sight of two women traveling without male companion seemed to be somewhat of a curiosity. We were a constant object of attention and frequently found ourselves in what we perceived to be a rather dangerous position. All our energy had to be channeled into the challenge of just living. Attempting to learn the languages of the area would have meant more strain on coping mechanisms that were already seriously overloaded.

Furthermore, learning these languages never became an important goal. It was not necessary to learn the language in order to communicate; instead, it seemed that anyone who had the slightest smattering of English wanted to practice speaking it. This lack of necessity to learn L2, coupled with the fact that we did not intend to remain in any one area for an extended length of time, made it seem that effort expended learning language would be pointless. Motivation was therefore extremely limited and it is not surprising that I did not learn.

Second Language Learning in Formal Settings

I have also had the opportunity to study several foreign languages in formal academic settings and have learned them to varying degrees of completeness. My knowledge of Spanish, German, and Italian remained at rather incomplete levels. However, I attained advanced proficiency in French and earned a graduate degree in French literature.

I studied French during two separate periods in my life and achieved vastly different results each time. My knowledge of French after having studied it for six years in school was extremely limited. After a second period of studying it, however, I reached a level that Schumann describes as sustained deep learning: "sustained because an extended period of time (often several years) is required to achieve it [. . .] deep because, when it is complete, the learner is seen as proficient or expert."

This differential success achieved at two separate times of studying French cannot be attributed to aptitude for learning L2 since aptitude would not have changed. Clearly, the age advantage ("younger is better for ultimate attainment") cannot have been a determining factor here. I would therefore attribute this differential success in learning French to varying levels of motivation at two different periods of my life. Of course, it can be argued that I devoted greater quantities of time and attention to the task of learning French the second time and thus achieved a superior level of proficiency. However, the very act of spending so much focused time on the task came out of the high level of motivation.

As a teenager, I simply did not have any motivation to learn French. Although it would have been within my intellectual ability to learn the language, it was of no importance to my life and goals. Uninspired by my teachers, I found the experience to be neither novel nor pleasant. Moreover, at that time, learning French was not consonant with my social and self-image: it was not expected by friends and family, and bilingual role models were not readily available.

Living with a francophone boyfriend increased my integrative motivation immensely. All of a sudden, it became my immediate and urgent goal to learn French so that I would be able to understand the French language and culture and interact with native French speakers. I became interested in all aspects of French and French-Canadian cultures: music, cinema, literature, peoples, dialects. An entirely new and intensely interesting world had opened up to me. My all-consuming goal became to master the French language in order to be able to participate fully in the "French experience."

I then discovered the language in and of itself to be intrinsically fascinating in all its manifestations. I began a serious study of French linguistics (phonology, morphology, and syntax as well as history of the French language) and French literature (from the Middle Ages to contemporary authors). The novelty and pleasure just refused to wear off. On the contrary, the more I studied, the more I wanted to learn. I became passionately interested in the variants of the French language spoken in different areas. On a trip to Nova Scotia, I fell in love with the Acadian people and gained an appreciation of the ingenious ways their dialect had evolved. How logical that francophones surrounded by an essentially anglophone environment should have invented the term "donner back" to describe returning a book to the library! I marveled at the linguistic ingenuity demonstrated by a man who couldn't go to the bar because he had to "watcher les kids" or "fixer le clutch." What I formerly would have considered to be errors in the language, I began to see as evidence of delightful and creative linguistic innovation.

My attitude toward non-standard French speakers had become much more tolerant and, in fact, had undergone a complete transformation. I did courses in the structure of Canadian French and discovered that what I had formerly considered to be grammatical and lexical errors in the speech of my boyfriend's family were in many cases forms that had been imported from seventeenth century France to Canada. (Later, when I was teaching French at the University of Alberta, native speakers from isolated francophone areas of the province would enroll in my section as I was the only instructor who didn't make them "feel stupid.")

Academically I was succeeding brilliantly in my study of French. While completing my BA, I had been a competent but uninspired student. All of a sudden, I was the object of constant praise and won several scholarships. I became trapped in a vicious circle of learning French: increased proficiency led to increased rewards which led to increased motivation which led to increased proficiency.

The differential degree of proficiency I achieved in Spanish, German and Italian can also be explained in terms of varying levels of motivation. I am confident that I could now learn them to an advanced level given increased motivation. When I become more motivated to learn these or other languages, I will be willing to devote appropriate amounts of time and energy to the task. In addition, I would be sure to include extended stays in regions where the target language is spoken. I now consider this type of immersion experience to be an essential component of successfully learning foreign languages. Not only are linguistic input and time on task increased, but also integrative motivation is enhanced.

My success in learning French has convinced me that I have the aptitude necessary to learn foreign languages. Furthermore, I have become a rather efficient learner and have developed facilitative learning strategies. My interest in the fields of linguistics and language learning processes remains high. If it were not for competing demands on my time and financial resources, there is nothing I would enjoy more than to continue to learn additional foreign languages.

Commentary

Barbara Hilding is an interesting case because she provides her own control group in a natural experiment comparing the relative roles of aptitude versus appraisal and motivation in second language acquisition. First, I think it is clear that Hilding had high aptitude. She learned French extremely well and is now a professor of French. Second, I think it is reasonable to assume that she had that aptitude throughout her life. Nevertheless, she failed to learn French when she was exposed to it in junior high school, high school and college, but she did learn French when she was exposed to it in her late twenties. She accounts for the difference by the fact that, in secondary school and college, she appraised French as irrelevant to her life goals and irrelevant to her social image in terms of what was expected of her by valued others. She reports that she found French classes neither motivating nor pleasant and, in general, her teachers were uninspiring.

In her late twenties, when she developed a relationship with her French-speaking boyfriend, the situation changed. The relationship created a need. Learning French became important in order to communicate with him, his family, and friends, and to understand French culture. Her autobiography indicates how her need led to enormous effort. She highly appraised her French classes, the language laboratory, and the interactions with her boyfriend as conducive to what had become her goal—to master the French language and to participate in the French experience. Her appraisal of her interactions with her boyfriend and her success in French classes led to the positive appraisal of many things French: French music, cinema, literature, linguistics, peoples, and dialects. Recall Damasio's (1994) notion of how an appraisal of one thing can be extended to related things: "If a given entity out in the world is a component of a scene in which one *other* component was a 'good' or 'bad' thing . . . the brain may classify the entity for which no value had been innately preset as if it too is valuable, whether or not it is" (p. 117). Hilding's initial appraisals of French in terms of pleasantness, goal/need significance, her coping potential and norm/self compatibility led to an expanded network of positive associations to many aspects of French language and French life and she eventually became bilingual.

With the same aptitude for language learning she always had, she also undertook the study of Spanish and German. When it became clear that she would not be having the opportunity to use Spanish, its relevance to her goals and needs was diminished and she lost her motivation to continue. She stopped studying German when she was forced to compete with native speakers in her second year class. This insult to her coping ability and self-image led to a negative appraisal of the course and a decision to abandon the effort to learn German.

Hilding's experience learning French also illustrates the productive interaction of positive assessments of language learning situation in relation to goals, coping abilities, and self and social image. For her, patterns of appraisal generated motivation that led to effort and resulted in success, which generated continued motivation and effort. Finally, from Hilding's case it might be fair to conclude that aptitude without motivation is not much use: the cognition involved in learning seems to require affect/motivation in order for it to operate.

Summary

In this chapter, the role of stimulus appraisal in ongoing second language acquisition was illustrated in the introspective diary studies written by learners acquiring the second language in both classrooms and in the environment where it is spoken. The autobiographies by Kaplan, Hoffman, Watson, and Hilding, which were retrospective analyses of language learning over a lifetime, provide a particularly clear demonstration of how stimulus appraisals enhance or inhibit the cognitive effort necessary to become bilingual. It was also argued that aptitude and stimulus appraisal are not independent factors because our ability to do something influences our appraisal of it. The diary studies and autobiographies reveal the consequences of stimulus appraisals in terms of whether the learner persists in her study of the language or withdraws from it. They also show how idiosyncratic personal factors influence learning. Thus these studies reveal how each learner is on a unique affective trajectory in language learning. And this is exactly what the stimulus appraisal perspective would predict. Each language learner's value-category/schematic emotional memory, hypothesized here to be incorporated in the orbitofrontal, amygdala, and body proper circuits, is different because it is based to a large extent on somatic value generated by each individual's life experiences. Therefore, the normal case is for there to be highly individual affective trajectories in SLA. Finally, it should be noted that although the data presented in this chapter suggest that stimulus appraisal profoundly affects second language learning, at this point, we are only in the position to hypothesize that the neurobiological systems described by LeDoux, Damasio, and others apply to the appraisals made by second language learners. Indeed, the neurobiologically informed perspectives on the amygdala, the orbitofrontal cortex, and related areas presented in Chapter 2 cannot be seen as proof that these systems are responsible for stimulus appraisal because, at this point, we have no direct experimental evidence that an individual's experiences with various agents, events, and objects in life cause alterations in these areas of the human brain.

5

Implications

In Chapter 1, the biological concept of value was presented, and the psychology of stimulus appraisal was described as a manifestation of an individual's homeostatic, sociostatic, and especially, somatic value. In Chapter 2, based on neurobiologically informed research and speculation by Damasio (1994) and others, a neurobiological system for stimulus appraisal was proposed (amygdala, orbitofrontal cortex, body proper). In Chapters 3 and 4, data were presented from motivation questionnaires, diary studies, and autobiographies showing how learners' appraisals enhance or inhibit efforts to learn. However, we cannot claim that these appraisals were made through the neurobiological system described. As mentioned earlier, it has not yet been demonstrated that neural activity in the amygdala and orbitofrontal cortex is responsible for the kinds of stimulus appraisals the subjects made. Experimental demonstrations would be necessary to provide true empirical underpinnings for the role of the hypothesized neural system in appraisals related to sustained deep learning. Nevertheless, it is legitimate to speculate that the stimulus appraisals evidenced in the diary studies and autobiographies are manifestations of the proposed underlying neural systems. Again this is simply a speculation. But such an inference is useful in theory construction, and with the rapid development of neuroimaging technology, the means may soon be available to provide empirical tests of the hypothesis.

Stimulus Appraisals as
the Common Denominator in Motivation

With the above caveat in mind, I would like to explore some implications of the perspective presented in this book with respect to the role of affect in SLA. I have indicated how the neurobiological stimulus-appraisal perspective is compatible with other perspectives on motivation in that motivations are determined on the basis of elicited appraisals of agents, events, and objects. But now I want to ask whether this perspective adds anything other than a view of affect in SLA at a lower level of analysis. I would suggest that the perspective does indeed make a broader contribution. The stimulus-appraisal approach, I believe, provides a common denominator for all motivations and motivational theories.

Neurobiological research on patients with damage to the orbitofrontal area indicates that this part of the neural stimulus-appraisal system appears to be involved in appraisals of goal relevance, coping potential, and norm/self compatibility. This neural region may also be involved in the appraisal of pleasantness when an agent, activity, or object is viewed as appealing in relation to its goal conduciveness. The amygdala has been shown to be involved in appraisals of fearful or threatening situations, and it may also contribute to the appraisal of pleasantness when it fails to register a stimulus as noxious in terms of fear or threat.

Novelty can be viewed in several ways. Scherer (1984) originally viewed the novelty appraisal as antecedent to the startle response or surprise. But novelty can also be contrasted with familiarity. (See Rowlands Shrimpton's language learning autobiography in the appendix.) In the face of boring familiarity, novelty may be appraised positively, but in the face of excessive strangeness or unfamiliarity, novelty may be appraised negatively as a source of anxiety or fear (and would be relevant to the neural appraisal system at the level of the amygdala). Familiarity, on the other hand, may be found and appraised positively when it manifests as routine or predictability. Kaplan refers to this type of familiarity quite often. When talking about her experience at the French school in Switzerland she says, "I wanted life to be the same everyday, and mostly it was" (p. 52). At home, after her father's death, reliable and familiar patterns had broken down. In

Switzerland they were restored by such activities as morning news reports delivered on the loudspeaker and the required study halls. The routine of French pedagogy also offered a familiarity that Alice found comforting. She enjoyed the memorization, repetition, dictation, and the lack of demand for originality. When she returned home, she missed the boarding school routine. Later, when she was living in France, life became pleasant when it became familiar, when she could recognize people in the neighborhood and when her room became a comfortable nest. When that familiarity was achieved she reported: "My room and I were together now; night and morning rituals established themselves with pleasantly passing weeks" (p. 91). More broadly, she says she sought and appreciated "the ritual of France" (p. 102). For Kaplan the dimensions of familiarity and pleasantness are associated, and if pleasantness involves the absence of threat, the amygdala may be relevant to such appraisals.

I would suggest then that Scherer's five dimensions of stimulus appraisal provide a reasonably good characterization of the categories on which the neural system operates. This proposal, of course, is subject to revision as more is learned about the neural system and as more research is done relating appraisals to motivation and behavior. The analysis in Chapters 3 and 4 indicates that motivations may emerge from patterns of appraisals. These patterns involve permutations of a limited set of appraisal dimensions, which Scherer's system seems to capture. For example, Gardner's Attitude and Motivation Test Battery focuses on appraisals of goal related pleasantness, Clément et al.'s (1994) motivation questionnaire focuses on appraisals of general goal relevance and goal related pleasantness of agents and activities, Csikszentmihalyi's assessment of intrinsic motivation used by Schmidt and Savage (1992) relies mainly on appraisals of coping potential and less strongly on goal significance and norm/self compatibility, and Schmidt et al.'s (1996) examination of second language learning from the perspective of value-expectancy theories of motivation focuses on appraisals of goal relevance, pleasantness and coping potential.

The dissatisfaction that some researchers felt with respect to Gardner's early work may have resulted from the ATMB's focus on pleasantness. Pleasantness was certainly appropriate for the North American context in which most of the research was done, but other researchers sensed and later found that different motivations featured more importantly in other settings. Gardner, in his latest research (Tremblay and Gardner, 1995), radically expands the dimensions of appraisal that he elicits to examine the role of expectancy, self-efficiency, valence, causal attributions, and goal-setting in language learning.

The stimulus-appraisal perspective may be relevant in that it suggests that the neural system for appraisal operates along a limited set of dimensions that may pattern differently to generate a variety of motivations, which are identifiable in large populations of learners, and to generate unique affective trajectories when learners are examined individually over an extended period of time. What is being hypothesized here is that motivations may be higher order constructs or emergent phenomena that are reducible to a limited set of stimulus appraisals. The word "reduce" always makes people nervous because it is frequently taken to mean that the analysis at the higher level becomes irrelevant. No such eliminative reductionism is intended here. Without the analyses at the motivational level much of our understanding of the role of affect in SLA would be lost. What the appraisal level provides is a characterization of the components of motivation and thus knowledge of its more basic structure.

Why should there be a limited set of appraisal dimensions, perhaps universal, that permute and pattern to become higher-order motivations? A brief examination of basic brain structure may provide an answer. As shown in Figure 5.1 the brain can be seen as the integration of three systems: a posterior sensory system, an anterior motor system and a ventral appraisal system. The appraisal system is necessary in order that the emotional relevance of sensory information (touch, sight, sound, etc.) can be assessed and appropriate behavorial activity can be taken in relation to that sensory information (e.g., fight, flight, approach, attend, think, learn). An organism that can make more sophisticated and more appropriate appraisals is one that is open-ended, that can adapt to new contexts, and that, although constrained to varying degrees by past experience, has the ability to construe the world in ways that allow it to best achieve its goals. The prefrontal cortex, of which the orbitofrontal area is a part, constitutes one third of the human brain. In our closest rela-

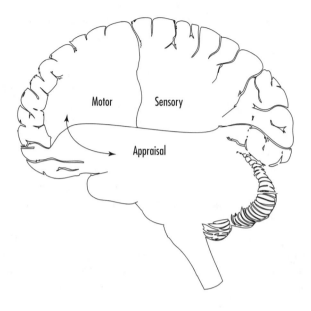

Figure 5.1. Sensory, Motor and Appraisal Areas of the Brain.

tives, chimpanzees, the prefrontal area is only 17% of the brain (Grafman, 1995). In addition, the prefrontal area remains remarkably plastic until late in life and perhaps throughout life (Barbas, 1995). This plasticity allows the appraisal systems to adjust to new reward contingencies encountered in varying contexts as humans mature. These adjustments are seen in the autobiographies of the second language learners. For example, Hilding assessed the value of learning French differently when she had a French Canadian boyfriend than when she was in high school and college. For survival, Hoffman developed an appraisal system that could dissociate the pleasantness of agents, activities, and objects from her appraisals of goal relevance. That the human appraisal system is capable of enormous adaptability may be seen, for example, in great variation in human preferences for food and sexual stimulation. So, although the neural system may operate on a limited set of dimensions, what is novel, pleasant, relevant to one's goals, coping abilities, and self and social image can take on a large or perhaps even an infinite variety of forms.

The stimulus appraisal approach may provide a common denominator for all motivations and motivational theories. As described in Chapter 3, SLA scholars have been searching the literature on motivation to find the best theories and research methodologies to adapt to the study of SLA. On the basis of the perspective described in this book, there can be no best approach. The diary studies and the autobiographies have shown that across learners a wide variety of appraisal patterns guide SLA. In addition, for individual learners, these appraisal patterns can change over time.

Learners' appraisal systems are sometimes constrained by cultural factors such that groups of learners appear to be instrumentally motivated, integratively motivated, intrinsically motivated, or achievement motivated, and so forth. But in the long run, in sustained deep learning, each learner is on a separate affective trajectory guided by her own past, present, and future stimulus appraisals. The thing that may be common to all motivational perspectives, however, is the biological system that does the appraisal. If we understand how the amygdala, orbitofrontal cortex, body proper, and related areas work, then we understand that this system has evolved to allow somatic value to assume a variety of preferences and aversions that can change over time, and that, as a result, cannot be captured by a single motivational perspective. The only approach is biological because the motivational machine is biological. Thus we will never be able to say which kind of motivation is best for SLA because there are as many appraisal trajectories as there are human second language learners. The human biological stimulus-appraisal system has evolved to make it that way.

Methodology

Another contribution of the perspective taken in this book is methodological. Diary studies and language learner autobiographies, like questionnaires, are self-reports, but they allow the learner to reveal what she believes is relevant. Questionnaires

allow the learner to report what the researcher considers important. The two approaches complement each other. It would not
make sense to add to motivation questionnaires subscales on
nesting patterns and transition anxiety (Schumann and Schumann), vocabulary learning through sublimation of the desire for
sweets (Kaplan), romantic relationships (Kaplan, Hilding), reaction to drive-in restaurants, deodorant, and crinoline (Hoffman),
or the reaction to such actors as Charles Boyer or the pronunciation of the word *l'oiseau* (Watson). No motivational research paradigm could tap these highly individual appraisals, except, of
course individual learners' autobiographical accounts.

It might be interesting to speculate about how Kaplan, Hoffman, Watson, and Hilding would respond on Gardner's Attitude
and Motivation Test Battery, which was described in Chapter 3.
Of course, their responses would depend on when in their language learning careers they were tested. Therefore, let's assume
that Kaplan took the AMTB toward the end of her year in Switzerland, Hoffman in her last year of high school, Watson while he
was studying at the Alliance Française, and Barbara Hilding as a
teenager, and then in her late twenties.

Kaplan would certainly show very positive responses on scales
for the desire to learn French, motivational intensity, attitudes
toward learning French, and attitudes toward French speakers. In
addition, she would demonstrate high interest in French and an
integrative orientation. She would probably rate her French
teacher and French course positively. Finally, she would probably
show low French Anxiety. In essence, we would expect Kaplan to
demonstrate all the characteristics of a highly motivated, integratively oriented learner. Hoffman is more complicated. She is learning a second language, not a foreign language, and is an
immigrant, not a sojourner in a foreign country. The AMTB questionnaire might not capture the appraisal system that motivated
her. Her sense of superiority, which coexists with profound feelings
of inferiority in her new country, would probably lead to mixed and
perhaps anomalous responses on many of the scales. Hoffman
would probably not report positive attitudes toward Canadians,
and her response on the integrative orientation scale might be
skewed because she does not want to integrate; she wants to
exceed. She doesn't want to become part of the modal North American culture; she wants to master it and stand above it. She

aspires to elite intellectual circles. She has a drive toward cultural superiority; excellent English is simply a prerequisite.

While at the Alliance Française, Watson would probably show a strong drive to learn French and a strong motivational intensity, and he would report a strong interest in learning a foreign language. His attitude toward French language and French speakers would probably be mixed to negative. All the statements on the integrative orientation scale (e.g., Studying French can be important to me because it will allow me to meet and converse with more and varied people) would reflect his original orientation toward French speakers, particularly French Cartesian scholars, but after the conference, he might not have expressed an integrative orientation because, by then, he would have learned that integration with the French Cartesians was impossible. His response on scales assessing attitudes toward his French teacher and French class would, of course, vary with the class he happened to be in at the Alliance, but in general they would be negative. The questionnaire, however, would not capture Watson's appraisal of French as unmanly and also would not reflect his fear about what conforming to the French way of learning, speaking, and acting would do to his sense of self.

As a teenager, Barbara Hilding had little desire to learn French. She probably had fairly neutral attitudes toward French speakers, little interest in foreign languages, and little or no integrative motivation. In addition, she would probably report little enthusiasm about her French teachers and French classes, which she found uninspiring. As an adult however, when she had a francophone boyfriend, she became interested in all aspects of French culture: French literature, linguistics, dialectology. She devoted enormous energy to learning French; she was successful in classes, returned to graduate school, and amplified her language learning with the academic goal of earning a graduate degree in French. During this period, we would expect her to make very positive responses on scales assessing desire to learn French, motivational intensity, attitudes toward learning French and French speakers, interest in foreign language, and integrative orientation. Also during this period in her life, she had teachers whom she would have appraised very positively.

It is clear that motivation varies over time and that the freeze-frame nature of questionnaire research loses developmental and idiosyncratic information. In other words, we do not know what the learner's motivational profile was a month before the study or what it might be a month later. In addition, there is a danger that the freeze-frame motivational picture might be interpreted as a narrative or language learning history. Here one might incorrectly assume that a group of successful learners who evidenced an integrative orientation or an intrinsic motivation at the time of the study was guided by these same profiles in their past learning and will be guided by them in the future. Language learning histories demonstrate that this is not necessarily the case. On the other hand, questionnaire research allows intensive focus on particular patterns of appraisal in groups of subjects. In addition, questionnaire work is amenable to statistical analyses such as multidimensional scaling and factor analysis, which provide higher-order solutions in terms of categories that can characterize similarities across large numbers of learners. An additional issue then might be whether one type of research is more scientific than another. My own view is that diary studies, autobiographies, and questionnaire studies as self-reports are all subject to the limitations of that kind of research, but they all have the same epistemological status. Each type of self-report has advantages and disadvantages, and the reduction to numbers that we see in questionnaire studies confers no special scientific status on that work.

Are Appraisals Cognitive?

The position taken in this book is that affect and cognition work together to generate mental and motor behavior. A perennial issue in the psychology of emotion is whether or not the appraisals that lead to emotion are cognitive. Lazarus, Averill, and Opton (1970) argue that the cognition in emotion involves the appraisal (and reappraisal) of the stimulus situation. They see appraisal activity as cognitive and maintain that:

> the appraisal process must be viewed as a continual searching for, sifting through, and evaluation of the cues which a person or infrahuman animal confronts. Some appraisals are rejected and others are accepted on the basis of both the steady inflow of information and the

psychological dispositions which influence transactions with the environment. (Lazarus et al., 1970, p. 220)

Smith and Ellsworth (1985) offer the following characterization of the cognitive activity in appraisal:

> We believe that people must answer certain fundamental questions about the changing sensations that impinge upon them not only so as to know what to do, but also as to know what they feel. Their answers may be incorrect, in which case observers might say that their emotions are inappropriate. Their answers may be incomplete, in which case they might be uncertain of how they felt, or might vacillate between different emotions. The emotion, however, is in part the resultant of a series of estimates about the present environment. Finally, we are not proposing that emotion is merely the product of cognitions; instead, we are trying to explore the cognitive aspects of emotion. (p. 819)

Ortony et al. (1988) argue that the appraisals of agents, events, and objects are cognitive processes because "they are determined by the structure, content, and organization of the knowledge representations and the processes that operate on them" (p. 4). They also note that some emotions may make higher cognitive demands than others, but nevertheless such construals and their required cognition may remain unconscious. In addition, some appraisals may involve high levels of socialization and education. Frijda (1993b) characterizes the cognitive work in emotion as the comparison of stimulus information with stored information and expectations about the personal and social relevance of the same stimuli or similar stimuli encountered through past experience. Such cognition may be conscious or unconscious.

Leventhal and Scherer (1987) analyze the controversy over whether emotion is independent of cognition (Zajonc, 1980, 1984) or whether it is necessarily consequent on prior cognitive appraisal of stimuli (Lazarus, 1982, 1984). They conclude the dispute is essentially a semantic one, and offer a solution via an integration of Leventhal's (1979, 1980, 1984) perceptual-motor processing model of emotion with the stimulus evaluation checks in Scherer's (1984) component process model of emotion.

Table 5.1 illustrates this integration. In terms of the model presented in this book, at the sensorimotor level, incoming stimuli are matched against innate information involving basic homeostatic and sociostatic value. In schematic processing, stimuli are evaluated against learned memory schemata containing information about the valence of past experience with the same or similar stimuli. At the conceptual level, appraisals are related to acquired complex scripts, the appreciation of complex stimuli such as music, art, ideas, and procedures, which are acquired via extensive socialization and education, and the appraisal of planned, anticipated, and imagined goals, coping challenges, and personal and social states. At this level, much of the appraisal activity may be under conscious control.

Appraisals at the sensorimotor level are likely to be automatic and, therefore, might not be seen as cognitive, or may only be seen as cognitive to the extent that a computation takes place matching stimuli with innate value. Leventhal and Scherer (1987) point out that computations at the schematic level may also become

Table 5.1

Processing Levels for Stimulus Evaluation Checks (from Leventhal and Scherer, 1987, p. 17)

	Novelty	Pleasantness	Goal/need Conduc- tiveness	Coping Potential	Norm/self Compat- ability
Conceptual Level	Expecta- tions: cause/ effect, probabil- ity estimates	Recalled, anticipated, or derived positive- negative evaluations	Conscious goals, plans	Problem solving ability	Self ideal, moral evalua- tion
Schematic Level	Familiar- ity: schemata matching	Learned preferences/ aversions	Acquired needs, motives	Body sche- mata	Self/social schemata
Sensorimotor Level	Sudden, intense stimula- tion	Innate preferences/ aversions	Basic needs	Avail- able energy	(Empathic adapta- tions?)

automatic in situations where there has been extensive repetition of certain stimulus situations and certain appraisal outcomes. Damasio (1994) calls such automaticity "as-if" loops where somatic states acquire representations directly in the brain and generate emotions without activation of autonomic, endocrine, and musculoskeletal responses. In these situations the determination of emotional or cognitive primacy is difficult. When the matching has become automatic, Zajonc's (1980) famous phrase "preferences need no inferences" may indeed be applicable, and emotion and cognition may become indistinguishable. In the face of such problems, Leventhal and Scherer (1987) and Scherer (1988) conclude that the debate about whether the appraisal process is cognitive or emotional is fruitless.

LeDoux (1993) believes that cognition and emotion are independent. In the generation of emotion he sees cognitive processing involved in "the elaboration of the stimulus input and the generation of 'good' stimulus representations" (p. 62); he argues that emotional processing involves "the evaluation of the significance of the stimulus (determination of the relevance of the stimulus for individual welfare)" (p. 62). If both processes were to be considered cognitive, LeDoux would view emotional processing as involving affective computations, which he would see as fundamentally different from sensory computations.

My own view is along the lines of Leventhal and Scherer (1987) and LeDoux (1993). The problem, as I see it, with calling appraisals cognitive is that the cognition is done in the emotion areas of the brain. In appraisal, stimulus information is matched with stored information about emotional relevance and motivational significance of the same stimuli or similar stimuli encountered in the past (Frijda, 1993b). In other words, new stimuli are appraised in the light of previous information stored via the amygdala and orbitofrontal cortex. The matching provides emotional coloring to the new stimuli. The matching is a computation done by the brain's emotional systems. If all computation is to be seen as cognitive, then appraisal is cognitive. However, if all computations are cognitive then nearly every process in the nervous system would be cognitive and the term would become meaningless.

The computation in which current stimuli are matched with stored valences for such stimuli would consist, biologically, of synaptic strengthening or perhaps the formation of new synapses in the networks where the information about the motivational relevance and emotional significance of the same or similar stimuli are stored. So biologically the computation involves synaptic adjustment of some sort. All computational processing in the brain involves similar synaptic alteration. The issue then is not whether the process invovles a computation but where that computation takes place or where it took place when the information was originally encoded. Synaptic alterations influenced by the amygdala, the orbitofrontal cortex, and related areas that appraise the emotional relevance of stimuli might then be more properly considered affective processes, or affective computations. Following on LeDoux (1993) then, we might see the brain as carrying out cognitive processing in the sensory system, affective/emotional processing in the appraisal system, and each bootstrapping the other to produce attentional behaviors and action readiness patterns necessary to generate the mental and motor behavior involved in learning.

In this regard, there is another distinction to be made. The affective processing of stimulus information by the limbic system must be distinguished not only from sensory processing (LeDoux, 1993) but also from the kind of higher cognitive processing relevant to the development of declarative and procedural memories involved in sustained deep learning. Therefore, we see the sensory systems generating the cognitive elaboration of visual, auditory, tactile, and gustatory representations, the appraisal system determining the personal relevance of such information, and higher-order cognitive systems laying down the factual and procedural information constituting relevant knowledge and skill.

Educational Relevance

An issue that naturally emerges from the position presented in this book is what teachers can do to influence their students' stimulus appraisal systems to improve their language learning. In Los Angeles, I work with a group of psychiatrists and psychotherapists who are interested in the brain and psychopathology. The members of this group all have private practices, and in various ways, their work involves helping to ameliorate the stimulus-appraisal systems of their patients.

One aspect of psychopathology is that patients make unproductive or counterproductive appraisals of agents, actions, objects, and events. They may find intimacy adversive or success threatening. They may appraise male and female associates in the same way they appraise their parents. They may appraise themselves narcissistically or shamefully. They may have fears or phobias that lead to negative appraisals of things that normally would be perceived as benign. The psychotherapist works to make his patients' appraisal systems productive and enhancing of their goals, needs, and self and social image. The psychotherapists receive years of training in order to do this, and even as practicing professionals they seek (and pay for) supervisors to help them improve their art. They consult with colleagues, stay up on the literature, and receive continuing education and training. And in fact, this effort pays off. Many patients' stimulus-appraisal systems are improved and they lead happier, more productive lives.

Language teachers, of course, want to accomplish the same thing; they would like to influence their students' stimulus-appraisal systems to make their learning of the foreign language more productive. But I think the language teacher's task is more difficult than that of the psychotherapist. The language teacher has to deal with 15 to 20 "patients" at a time, each with a different schematic emotional memory and hence a different stimulus-appraisal system. The language teacher has to do this while doing something else—teaching the language. In addition, in a school, the language teacher is in competition with the math teacher, the history teacher, the science teacher and the English teacher—all of whom are striving to have the student appraise their subject, their methods, their materials, and themselves as important to the student's goals and needs, compatible with their coping potential, and enhancing of their self and social image.

Dörnyei (1996), after extensively surveying language teachers, derived the following ten ways to help motivate students.

1. Make the language classes interesting by selecting varied and engaging topics, materials, and activities.
2. Have humor, fun, and games in the class.
3. Create a pleasant and friendly atmosphere.

4. Promote learner autonomy by allowing freedom in the classroom and sharing as much responsibility with the learners as you can.
5. Make the course relevant by doing a needs analysis and adjusting the syllabus accordingly.
6. Set a personal example in being motivated and committed yourself.
7. Develop the learners' confidence by encouraging them, giving them positive feedback, and making sure that they regularly have a feeling of success.
8. Make the foreign language "real" by introducing its culture, using authentic materials, inviting native speakers, and arranging native-speaking penfriends for your students.
9. Develop a good and trustful relationship with the learners.
10. Emphasize the usefulness of the knowledge of the foreign language.

These things are what all teachers would strive to do to motivate their students, but we have to be realistic about what can actually be achieved. Teachers won't be able to please every student all the time.

I think that we also have to recognize that teachers have appraisal systems as well, and they may have appraised certain pedagogical procedures, materials, and methods as relevant and important to their language teaching goals and appropriate to their coping potential and self and social image as language teachers. The teacher has both the right and responsibility to let this appraisal framework guide his teaching. But this framework may conflict with the appraisal systems of some students; accomodations may be possible, but in some cases they won't be.

It may be possible to do research on how some teachers are able to achieve maximum congruence between their appraisals of how language should be taught and their students' appraisals of how the language can be learned. At our department at UCLA we have four lecturers who teach ESL classes and who consistently receive 8+ ratings on a scale of 0–9. Clearly these teachers are conducting their classes in ways that are being appraised positively quarter after quarter, year after year. An understanding of how they accomplish this might be achieved by conducting an ethnography of their teaching. Such research would involve videotaping classes, analyzing the classroom interaction, interviewing students, and asking students to keep day-by-day introspective diary studies of their affective reactions to the instruction and their learning. The teacher might also keep such a diary. This research would reveal the activities and interactions that take place in the class and would also reveal the students' appraisals of them. Such research may reveal how good teachers work productively with their students' varying stimulus-appraisal systems. We know appraisal systems are highly individual and dynamic, changing over time. This characteristic makes the long-term longitudinal study of individual learners virtually impossible. But with the research suggested, we could capture those appraisal systems at work during a limited period of time, and may generate knowledge that could improve teaching. Of course, there is an enormous amount of literature on the study of teachers and classrooms to investigate what constitutes good teaching. So what I am suggesting is nothing new except that here the focus would be on the student appraisal of the teacher, the method, the materials, and how the teacher is able to accommodate the highly diverse preferences and aversions that characterize the students' appraisal systems.

Summary

The theory and research presented in Chapters 1–4 suggest that in learning, which is not controlled by innate mechanisms (e.g., those underlying the acquisition of the grammar of one's native language), cognition is controlled by acquired value. We cognize on value, and value is expressed in stimulus appraisals. Thus in SLA, as in all sustained deep learning, our perception, attention, memory, and behavior are based on value as expressed in our stimulus appraisals.

Variable success in SLA is the product of the history of one's stimulus appraisals, whose influence on second language learning is highly variable, and essentially unique for each individual. The only thing that is universal about affective influence on SLA is the neural mechanism that subserves it. The biological appraisal system starts out with some innate tendencies (homeostats and sociostats) that enhance survival, but very quickly the individual begins to accrue a system of somatic value based on his experience in the world. This value system consists of individual preferences and aversions that cause learners to react uniquely to various language learning situations and to achieve varying degrees of proficiency in the second language.

6

The Role of Affect in
First Language Acquisition

The first five chapters of this book established an affective basis for second language acquisition. The argument was made that differences in learners' neurobiological stimulus-appraisal systems foster variable success in SLA. In primary language acquisition, however, variable success does not seem to be an issue. We do not find children failing to acquire the copula, past tense, or articles because they negatively appraise their mother tongue, its speakers, or the culture in which it is used. Language delay and communication difficulties have been observed in children who have been abused or neglected (Allen & Oliver, 1982; Coster & Cicchetti, 1983), but such children do not fail to acquire the grammar of their native language. The question then is whether there is an affective basis for first language learning.

In this chapter, building on the work of Locke (1992), I will argue that primary language acquisition is, indeed, fostered by the affective attunement of the child with caretakers, and I will hypothesize that failures in that attunement can result in deficits in the communicative competence of first language learners. Locke (1995) suggests that language acquisition is governed by two separate neural systems: a specialization for social cognition (SSC) and a grammatical analysis module (GAM). The SSC has continuity with earlier phylogenetic forms and provides inherited capacities for facial and vocal identification and for the interpretation of facial and vocal affect. This specialization, which is under right-hemisphere control, governs the first two phases of what Locke proposes as a four-phase sequence in the development of a child's linguistic capacity.

The first phase begins in the final trimester of gestation and extends through the last month of the first year. This stage, as described in Chapter 1, is under the guidance of innate sociostatic value. The infant seeks facial and vocal contact with caretakers, most prominently with its mother. The mother and child engage in coordinated eye gaze and coordinated vocalizations. During this interaction, the child is able to assess the emotional state of the mother by listening to her tone of voice and intonation and by examining her facial expression. The mother makes similar appraisals of the child's emotional state by attending to her vocalizations, facial expressions, and body movements.

Under appropriate social conditions, infants may imitate the intonation patterns of caretakers. This vocal accommodation is affect-driven and "appears to be motivated by a desire to incorporate superficial characteristics of individuals to whom infants are emotionally attached" (Locke, 1995, p. 290). At about seven months, the infant's vocalizations become interspersed with consonantal sounds. This results in babbling (e.g., ba, da). During vocal interaction, the infants pay attention to what their interlocutors are looking at while talking. Thus, it would appear that the infant understands that "the object of a mother's attention while vocalizing is probably the subject of her reference" (Locke, 1995, p. 293). This process of shared gaze quite likely facilitates concept formation and later lexical acquisition.

The second phase is also controlled by the right hemisphere and lasts for most of the second year. During this period the child acquires words and whole utterances. However, these speech segments are unanalyzed utterances, which Locke (1993b; 1995) argues are prephonological and under prosodic control. They allow the child to produce speech appropriate to certain contexts and thus to engage in social interactions. But these utterances contain phonemes and morphemes that do not function as single units and cannot be recombined to produce alternate sequences. This formulaic material is learned associatively with respect to context and does not represent generatively produced language.

The third phase is analytical and computational and constitutes a critical period lasting from the age of 20 to 35 months. During this period the right hemisphere's formulaic speech is analyzed by what

Locke (1995) calls the Grammatical Analysis Module (GAM) in the left hemisphere. This "structure analysis system identifies recurring elements within and across utterances, and thereby learns the rules by which utterances are to be synthesized and parsed" (Locke, 1993b, p. 18). It is during this period that the child discovers the phonological, morphological, and syntactic units of language.

In the fourth phase, the functions of the SSC and the GAM become integrated. The rules that developed to analyze and systematize the stored formulaic utterances are used to impose structure on language input the child receives from the environment. At the same time, the SSC directs the acquisition of pragmatic knowledge that guides the social use of language. This specialization continues to operate throughout life as language is used in different social contexts. It should be noted that each phase in this developmental sequence overlaps with the preceding phase.

Locke (1995) argues that the affective basis for this four-phase sequence emerges from the fact that attachment, that is, the affective bond between mother and child, is achieved through the same facial and vocal channels as is language development. Face and voice moderate both language and attachment. Compared to other primates, human infants are born in a very premature state. The infants' resulting helplessness necessitates an extended period of caregiving that is fostered by mother-child attachment, and the attachment itself fosters language development. As Locke (1995) notes:

> In contemporary parlance, this facial-vocal channel "buys" theorists a great deal, for it has the infant paying attention to the things people do when they talk. It has the mother remaining at close range, and providing her infant with facial and vocal behaviors that cement and sustain emotional attachment. Because she happens to use *speech* as the primary vehicle for this affective communication, rather than merely vocalizing nonverbally, we have both parties acting as they should if spoken language is to be the result. (p. 289)

Schore (1994) argues that the visual and vocal interactions between mother and child serve as an "imprinting stimulus for the infant's developing nervous system" (p. 91). He suggests that as a mother views the face of her infant child, a state of pleasure is generated, which causes her pupils to dilate. This dilation causes a reciprocal response in the infant, whose pupils also dilate. The pleasurable affect on the mother's face is registered and imprinted in the infant's right orbitofrontal cortex. This interaction lays the basis for the infant's learning about positive affective states. The mother here is acting as an affect regulator for the child. Her elation, joy, and excitement is communicated to the child and the child feels the state as if it were the child's own.

The mother and child dyadically interact in this way, each increasing the pleasurable affect in the other until the child becomes over-stimulated and looks away, allowing his state of arousal to decrease. Then the interaction begins again. The psychologically attuned mother knows when to allow the infant to withdraw his gaze and reduce his arousal. If the mother persists in stimulation during the infant's gaze aversion the hyperstimulation will result in the child crying. This finely tuned interaction, according to Schore (1994), is actually necessary for appropriate brain development.

As the child's motor coordination improves, the child becomes more mobile and able to explore the environment at some distance from the mother. The exploration immediately provides an enriched environment that fosters dendritic growth in the toddler's brain. But such excursions also leave the child emotionally fatigued and in need of affective refueling. This necessary revitalization occurs in two ways. The child can return to the mother, and through facial, vocal, and tactile interaction, the child's heightened hedonic tone is restored, and the child can once again engage in exploratory-investigatory activity in the environment. Another vehicle for emotional refueling is through social referencing. In this process, the child wanders away and intermittently looks back at her mother for facial and vocal responses to her exploration. When the mother signals positive affect, the child is reassured and energized and continues exploring. The mother's response to both "returns" and "distance reunions" also contributes to the development of the toddler's stimulus-appraisal system. Her facial and vocal reactions to the agents and objects in the child's environment and to the child's interaction with them contribute to the development of the child's emotional memory for these events and allows the child to assign a positive or negative valence to them.

On entering the second year of life, the child becomes more mobile and the mother must behave in ways to get the child to act appropriately and safely. In the early part of the practicing period (8 to 10–12 months, see Malher, Pine, & Bergman, 1975), the mother's affective attunement with the child fosters joy, elation, and interest-excitement. The child's narcissistic urges are supported by the caregiver. But the child must learn that although she is important, she is no more important than anyone else. Thus there are inevitably infant activities and behaviors of which the parent must disapprove. Efforts must be made to discipline aspects of willfulness. The adjustment occurs in what are called shame interactions between mother and child. The elated, narcissistic toddler socially references her mother with the expectation of maternal attunement and approval, but the child instead perceives disapproval on the mother's face (and in her voice) and immediately moves from a state of elation to a state of shame. The child reads the negative affect on the mother's face (constricted pupils, frown, tightened facial muscles) and shifts from a hyperaroused to a hypoaroused state. This affective de-escalation and the behaviors that engender it become imprinted in the orbitofrontal appraisal system and gradually come to be used in the child's autoregulation. The affective dyadic interaction between mother and child socializes the child to appropriate behavior with regard to actions, agents, and objects in her environment.

In socializing the child and constraining his narcissism with affectively engendered shame transactions, the caregiver must signal disapproval of the child's behavior without humiliating him. Shame and its consequent inhibition promote self-regulation. Therefore, disapproval-shame interactions promote healthy emotional development. However, when the caretaker expresses contempt, which consists of disapproval, disgust, and anger, the child responds with hyperactive feelings of humiliation. Humiliation is an overregulated state that is potentially damaging to the child's emotional development.

As mentioned earlier, Schore (1994) argues that the excitatory and inhibitory dyadic interactions between child and caregiver during the practicing period foster the development of the child's stimulus-appraisal system. The facial and vocal reactions of the mother teach the child " 'how to feel,' 'how much to feel,' and 'whether to feel' about particular objects in the environment" (Schore, 1994, p. 108).

> With regard to the development of interest, curiosity, and "excited anticipation," social referencing maternal attention-focusing strategies may also be essential to the practicing caregiver's enduring effect on the infant's learning of "what to feel" about objects in the social environment (including the mother herself and through her the father and other social objects), and "what to be interested in" amongst the objects in the physical environment. These critical period events may induce "topographic familiarity" and begin to generate "personally relevant" aspects of the individual's world (Van Lancker, 1991). Developmental studies of 12-month-olds support the notion that social referencing accounts for the maternal emotional biasing of infant reactions to novel inanimate objects (Hornik et al., 1987). In other words, these early synchronized visuoaffective attunement experiences influence the development of the child's motivational systems. Of special importance at this time is the development of what Lichtenberg (1989) calls the exploratory-assertive motivational system. (Schore, 1994, pp. 108–109)

Thus, we see that the child's innate motivation to interact with the caretaker results in dyadic sociostatic interaction during the second year of life, which allows the child to incorporate her mother's affective reaction to her behavior in the environment into her stimulus-appraisal system.

What is particularly significant about Schore's proposal is his suggestion that some crucial aspects of brain development are dependent on the child's experience in the excitatory and inhibitory interactions with the caregiver in the early and late stages of the practicing period. Specifically, he argues that the affectively positive dyadic interactions at the end of the child's first year actually cause the growth of dopamine pathways from the ventral-tegmental area (VTA) in the midbrain to the orbitofrontal cortex. (See Figure 6.1.) The infant's perception of the positive affect in the face, voice, and touch of the mother is perceived by relevant neural areas, particularly by the face recognition cells in the amygdala, which signal the hypothalamus to

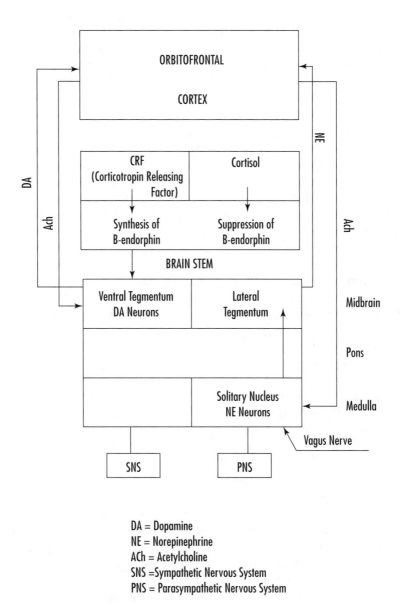

Figure 6.1. A Representation of Schore's (1994) Dual Component Affect Regulation System.

secrete corticotrophin releasing factor (CRF) into the anterior pituitary where ACTH (adrenocorticotropic hormone) and beta-endorphin are then synthesized. The pituitary then releases these two substances into the bloodstream where they travel to the ventral tegmental area of the midbrain. The opiates (endorphins) carried to the ventral tegmental area by the circulatory system promote the growth of axons of dopamine neurons in the ventral tegmental area, which extend to and release dopamine in the orbitofrontal cortex. Schore (personal communication) suggests that this dopamine has two effects on the target area. The first is metabolic and short-term: the dopamine causes an increased arousal in the orbitofrontal area. The second effect is long-term and trophic: the dopamine triggers growth processes of the target area resulting in axonal extension of orbitofrontal cholinergic neurons to other cortical areas and also back to the ventral tegmental area. This growth creates an excitatory circuit between the midbrain and the orbitofrontal cortex that supports interest, excitement, attention, exploratory-motor, and investigatory-cognitive activity toward stimulus situations that generate positive affect and reward. This ventral tegmental limbic forebrain-midbrain circuit between the brain stem and the orbitofrontal area influences the body proper through the sympathetic nervous system, which increases heart rate, respiration, and the release of glucose, adrenaline, and noradrenaline.

During the late practicing period (15–18 months), the misattunement in the mother's shaming interactions with the toddler stimulates the development of a complementary system of affect regulation. In this case the negative affect in the mother's face and voice initiates a chain of events that leads to the release of cortisol into the child's bloodstream. The cortisol suppresses endorphin and ACTH release into the circulatory system. This suppression reduces the activation of ventral tegmental dopamine and facilitates the growth of axons of norepinephrine containing neurons in the nucleus of the solitary tract through the lateral tegmentum to innervate the superficial layers of the orbitofrontal cortex. This process also results in the reciprocal back-projection of cholinergic neurons to the nucleus of the solitary tract, creating an inhibitory loop that influences the body proper through the parasympathetic nervous system, which decreases heart rate and respiration. This system is illustrated in Figure 6.1.

Since development of the sympathetic ventral tegmental and the parasympathetic lateral tegmental limbic forebrain-midbrain circuits is dependent on certain interactional experiences between mother and child during the early and late practicing period, Schore (1994) hypothesizes that absence or inadequacy of these experiences will result in anomalies in the microanatomy of the orbitofrontal area. We know from Damasio's work that the orbitofrontal cortex is a region of the brain that controls decision making about personal and social issues. In addition, we know that normal conversational interaction involves making personal and social decisions on a moment-to-moment basis about such things as: what one should say, how much to say, how to say it, when to take a turn, when to give one up, when to pause, when and how to repair utterances, when and how to give preferred and dispreferred responses, whether to use technical vocabulary, colloquialisms, or jargon and so forth. Therefore, we would predict that failures in affective dyadic interaction between caretaker and child during what Schore (1994) and others argue is a critical period for brain development (10–12 to 16–18 months) would have consequences for language generated by SSC while grammar produced by the GAM might be perfectly intact. In other words, we would predict that people with experience-related deficits in the orbitofrontal area would have difficulties with aspects of discourse, conversation, and pragmatics in general.

Attachment

Based on research by Ainsworth (1985) and Main and Solomon (1986), Schore (1994) proposes the psychobiology of two types of insecurely attached infants: insecure-avoidant and insecure-resistant (ambivalent). Infants of the first type have mothers who find physical contact and interaction with the child to be aversive. Therefore, they rebuff the child by withdrawing or pushing the child away and, in general, resist the infant's attachment behavior. The child reacts by engaging in defensive behaviors in which she avoids eye contact and physical contact with the mother, but nevertheless, feels anger toward her, which is suppressed. The child's physical reaction to the rejection involves "a state of stressful hyperarousal reflected in negative affect and elevated heart rate" (Schore, 1994, p.379). Schore believes that such children develop a parasympathetic-despair state in which the lateral tegmental norepinephrine inhibitory loop dominates orbitofrontal centers for social cognition. These insecure-avoidant children have a bias toward withdrawal and become incapable of seeking support when they are stressed.

Mothers of insecure-resistant (ambivalent) infants are inconsistent in their attachment behaviors, sometimes providing contact and comfort and sometimes withholding these responses. In addition, such mothers frequently overstimulate their infants by not discontinuing facial and vocal interaction when the child enters a hyperaroused state. These mothers may also provide deficient shaming interactions during the late practicing period. The child responds to the mother's unpredictability by a reluctance to leave her and explore her environment. In addition, she may become impulsive and have difficulty coping with stress. Schore (1994) suggests that such children develop an overactive sympathetic ventral tegmental dopamine excitatory loop and an underdeveloped parasympathetic lateral tegmental norepinephrine inhibitory loop. Thus, insecure-resistant children have under-regulated emotion and are susceptible to angry, hostile, and aggressive interactional styles.

The hypothesis that follows from the argumentation above is that the SSC, the heart of which is the orbitofrontal cortex, would have deficiencies in insecure-avoidant and insecure-resistant children. The overdevelopment of the parasympathetic norepinephrine system in the former and the overdeveloped sympathetic dopamine system in the latter would result in deficits in social and personal reasoning leading to inhibition in avoidant children and impulsiveness in resistant children. We would expect the inhibition and impulsiveness to affect the pragmatics of their verbal interaction; that is, we would predict anomalies in what they say, how much they say, and how they say it.

In fact, there is some indirect evidence for this claim. Main (1993) reports the development of and research done on the Adult Attachment Interview (AAI). This instrument assesses the participant's early attachment experiences and their later effects. The interviews are subject to rigorous discourse analyses, and the results of these analyses have been found to correlate with the kind of attachment behavior children of these parents demonstrate in a procedure called the Strange Situation (SS). In this experimental situation, the mother and child are placed in an unfamiliar room.

The mother sits quietly while the child explores the new environment. A stranger enters. In the ensuing interaction there are two mother-child separations. In the first, the mother leaves and the child is alone with the stranger. The mother then returns. Then she and the stranger both leave and the child is entirely alone. Then the stranger returns and tries to comfort the child if she is distressed. Finally, the mother returns. The researcher observes the child's attachment behavior during the reunions.

Correlating the AAI with the SS, the investigators have found that "the parent's response to the interview task strongly resembles the infant's response to that parent in the Strange Situation" (Main, 1993, pp. 224–225). The dismissing adults tend to have children who are characterized as insecure-avoidant and preoccupied adults tend to have children who are classified as insecure-resistant/ambivalent.

The discourse of adults classified as dismissing on the AAI has the following characteristics:

1. The participants tend to dismiss the significance of their attachment experiences.
2. At some point in the interview the participants describe their parents positively and at other times negatively; they do not appear to notice the contradiction.
3. They exhibit difficulty in remembering childhood experiences.
4. They appear to answer the interview questions without linking them to memories of the situations or events elicited.

Adults classified as preoccupied have the following discourse characteristics on the AAI:

1. Participants demonstrate an angry, passive, or sometimes fearful orientation to their former attachment figures.
2. They often get stuck on a particular topic and provide grammatically cumbersome utterances.
3. They use psychological jargon, nonsense words, childlike speech, and phrases that are vague and repetitive.
4. When reporting a childhood incident, they may address the parent as if he/she were present.
5. Their responses to the interview questions are often lengthy and irrelevant.

In other research, the investigators have found that when the interview is administered to pregnant mothers three months before the birth of their children, the classification on the AAI predicts the child's attachment behavior with the mother when the child is one year old.

The correlation between the AAI and the child's attachment behavior indicates an affective influence of the parent on the child. Since classification on the AAI also indicates that the adults' attachment experiences influence their discourse concerning those experiences, we might expect that children with particular Strange Situation behavioral classifications will also have characteristic discourse features if, as adults, they are asked to recount their attachment experiences. In fact, we might expect them to evidence these discourse characteristics when they are stressed in general.

The theoretical perspective presented above suggests that the role of affect in first language acquisition is on the acquisition of pragmatics because attachment and pragmatics seem to be subserved by the same neural system that underlies stimulus appraisal, affect regulation, and social reasoning. This system, at the very least, involves the amygdala at the limbic level and the orbitofrontal cortex at the cortical level. We might predict then that damage to this system either through insults to brain tissue, developmental anomalies resulting from inadequate attachment interaction, or other causes, would affect discourse pragmatics. The prediction also goes in the other direction. Individuals with pragmatic deficits might be expected to have deficits in the neural systems for attachment, stimulus appraisal, affect regulation, and social reasoning.

Additional indirect evidence for the hypothesis that inadequate parent-child interaction during the critical period for the development of the orbitofrontal specialization for social cognition would come from the discourse and conversational analysis of the verbal interaction of patients such as Elliot (Damasio, 1994) who has been clearly identified as having orbitofrontal damage. We would assume that these patients would fail to generate somatic markers (bodily states) in response to the intentions they form about what conversational interaction to undertake. They would also fail to generate somatic markers with regard to their actual contribution to the discourse or to the contributions of their interlocutors. That, we would predict, would lead to interactional anomalies, particularly under stress. In fact, the discourse of Patient *A* presented in Chapter 2 is consistent with this hypothesis.

A similar source of data might also come from individuals diagnosed as psychopaths. LaPierre, Braun, and Hodgins (1995) tested prisoners who had been diagnosed as having psychopathic personalities and discovered that they showed significant correspondence with the response profile of orbitofrontal patients. Therefore, we would assume that such individuals would have difficulties in reasoning about personal and social issues, and might evidence those difficulties in the moment-to-moment personal and social decision making that is required in conversational interaction. This would be particularly likely to occur under stress.

The perspective presented in this chapter leads also to the prediction that aspects of language that are specifically designed to express affect would be particularly vulnerable to damage to the prefrontal–limbic–body proper systems that support attachment, stimulus appraisal, affect regulation, and social cognition.

Autism

Autism is an impairment that appears in inflicted children prior to 30 months of age and affects their ability to relate socially to others, their ability to communicate, and their ability to conceive of and understand the intentions and dispositions of others. Trevarthen, Aitken, Papoudi, and Robarts (1996) offer the following characterization of the syndrome:

> Autism is a defect in psychological development that directly affects the way the expressions and actions of others are perceived. This is associated with problems in expressive communication, in understanding other persons' thoughts, and in comprehending the ordinary use of language and the meanings others give by convention to actions and objects. The causal brain fault also affects basic functions of perception, motor coordination, thinking and learning to varying degrees. (p. 23)

Trevarthen et al. (1996) indicate that the prevalence of autism is approximately 4.5 to 6 cases in a population of 10,000.

Hobson (1989) sees autism as resulting from a core deficit in person relatedness. In the beginning of this chapter, we described the visual, vocal, and bodily interaction and attunement that exists between infant and caretaker from the earliest stages. This relatedness was argued to be a product of innately programmed sociostatic value. Hobson (1989) takes the same view, and also supports the notion that "a normal infant is 'prewired' to manifest particular patterns of behavior, and to be sensitive to the body configurations, sounds, rhythms, actions, and movements of his caretakers" (p. 24). Via this innate propensity to feel in their bodies the bodily expression of another, an intersubjectivity and affective relatedness is established between infant and caregiver. Hobson sees the primary deficit in autism as an impairment in this biological basis for affective and social relations.

According to Hobson (1989), the ability to abstract and to symbolize derives from intersubjective affective relatedness with others. In learning to abstract, the child extracts qualities of agents, events, and objects according to their affective value, which is partially determined by the child's coreferencing the entity during interaction with the caretaker. Entities with shared affective values, that is, qualities relevant to the child's intentions, desires, and purposes, become categories. A category becomes further established if the child perceives that other individuals also view it as an abstract concept. Thus, abstractions emerge through affective contemplation of percepts and through social intercourse about the concept and its concrete instantiations.

Hobson (1989) suggests that the ability to symbolize derives from the ability to shift points of view and that this perspective taking is interpersonal in nature. In interaction with others, the child learns to recognize the various mental orientations she has toward an object and the various orientations others take toward the same object. These mental perspectives are generally affective in nature, involving gaze, facial expressions, gesture, and body orientation. The child experiences her own orientation in interaction with a caregiver whose perspective toward the same object (or agent or event) may vary in affective tone as signaled by bodily expression. The interindividual affective coreferencing of elements in the environment by the child and the adult may coincide or diverge, and the child notices and experiences these perspectives. Thus, by mutually attuned interaction in an event, meaning is negotiated, and the child learns how the other's mind is oriented toward elements in the surrounding environment and whether that orientation is the same as or different from hers.

Concomitant with this development and deriving from it, the child can learn to relate to others as they relate to other things. In other words, the child can "make the discovery that a sound, or a conventional gesture, or a physical object can point to, reference, or stand for another" (p. 31), and having recognized

> that a person is a being whose experiences are "about" things, he may then see how one object or event can also be "about" another. An individual who understands symbols is able to orient himself to a symbol in a way that encompasses the symbol's orientation to its referent. So just as the young child relates to the caretaker's relation to the world, he now comes to relate to one thing's symbolic relation to another. This ushers in a new phase of development, for the caretaker can now introduce novel symbolic meanings into the child's relations with his world. In addition, the primitive forms of taking one thing as another can undergo a formal transformation, so that affective modes of symbolism can continue to operate even when the objective properties of things are understood as such. (p. 31)

For Hobson, then, the problems autistics have in cognition, communication, and imagination derive from a basic deficit in person relatedness. He believes that their difficulties in social reasoning or in the development of a theory of mind, involving the ability to determine the intentions and dispositions of others, results from this primary deficit in relating to others.

Baron-Cohen (1995) focuses on the theory of mind problem in autism. He argues that all normal humans have the ability to impute mental states to themselves and others. In other words, we attribute intentional states such as beliefs, desires, thoughts, intentions, hopes, memories, fears, promises, and so on to others (and ourselves) in order to predict and explain behavior. This attribution process allows us to make decisions about how to respond to the physical and verbal behavior of conspecifics. Baron-Cohen (1995) argues that such "mindreading is good for a number of important things, including social understanding, behavioral prediction, social interaction, and communication" (p. 30).

Baron-Cohen (1995) presents a theory of mindreading, which consists of a set of four mechanisms: an intentionality detector (ID), an eye direction detector (EDD), a shared attention mechanism (SAM), and a theory of mind mechanism (ToMM). See Figure 6.2.

The ID (Intentionality Detector) is an innate mechanism that interprets moving objects as agents with goals and desires. The movement may be perceived through any sensory modality (usually vision, touch, or audition). When the mechanism determines that the movement is not self-caused, it changes its interpretation and assumes that a prior intentional agency generated the movement.

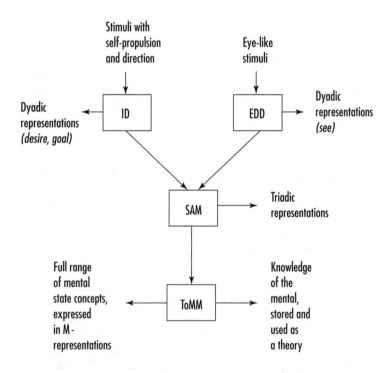

Figure 6.2. The Four Components of Baron-Cohen's Mindreading System (from Baron-Cohen, 1995, p.32).

The second mindreading mechanism is the EDD (Eye Direction Detector) which, like the ID, is an inherited system. It performs three functions. First, it detects and recognizes eyes. Baron-Cohen (1995) reports research that indicates that infants show a preference for eyes over other parts of the face and this is demonstrated by the fact they look longer at eyes than any other facial feature. The EDD also determines the direction of eye gaze. Thus it assesses whether the eyes it perceives are looking at it or at something else. An infant will look longer at a face that is looking at it than at a face which is looking in another direction. Also, as we saw in Schore's (1994) work, when an infant perceives eyes directed at her, it may cause brain stem catecholamines to innervate the forebrain, generating arousal of the automatic nervous system. Finally, the EDD interprets eye gaze as seeing. The infant innately assumes that eyes can see, and she distinguishes seeing from not seeing. The infant also interprets eye contact as evidence that an agent sees her and she sees the agent. Whereas the ID can use any sensory modality, the EDD is, of course, limited to vision.

The third mindreading system, the SAM (Shared Attention Mechanism), determines when and if the agent and self are both looking at a third object (or agent). This knowledge is generated when the EDD of the self, by visually referencing the agent, observes that it and the agent are gazing at the same thing. The SAM relies heavily on the EDD, but can operate with input only from the ID, as is the case with blind children who generate shared attention by touching an object and feeling the agent touch the same object. Baron-Cohen (1995) cites evidence for a SAM from research (Butterworth, 1991; Scaife & Bruner, 1975) that shows that infants beginning at about nine months will turn their gaze in the same direction as that of an agent and then check back and forth between the agent and the object to see that the agent's and the self's joint gaze is in the same direction and on the same object. He also reports research indicating that, at about the same time, children will point at an object of interest to foster shared attention to it (Bates, Benigni, Bretherton, Camaioni, & Volterra, 1979).

The final component in Baron-Cohen's theory of mindreading is the ToMM (Theory of Mind Mechanism). This system, which is at the apex of the mindreading mechanisms, takes the information on intentional mental states (goals and desires) and perceptual mental states (seeing) as they are coordinated in shared attention and forms representations of an agent's epistemic mental states. Baron-Cohen (1995), citing Leslie and Thaiss (1992) and Leslie and Roth (1993), suggests that the representations have the following form:

	believes	
	desires	
	thinks	
	intends	
Agent	hopes	something.
	remembers	
	fears	
	promises	
	etc.	

Here, of course, the agent may also be the self. The "something" is a proposition such as, "it is cold" or "the car is in the garage."

Baron-Cohen (1995), citing Leslie (1987) and Dunn and Dale (1984) suggests that a child's ability to pretend is evidence for the operation of the ToMM and that the epistemic state "pretend" is probably the first to be represented. He also notes that between three and four years of age, children show an understanding that knowledge results from perception (Pratt & Bryant, 1990), that people sometimes have true beliefs and sometimes false beliefs (Perner, 1991; Wellman, 1990), and that people can be deceived (Sodian, 1991; Sodian & Firth, 1992). Autistic children (Baron-Cohen, 1995) are believed to have deficits in their mindreading systems. They typically show "lack of normal eye contact, lack of normal social awareness or appropriate social behavior, 'aloneness,' one-sidedness in interaction, and inability to join a social group" (Baron-Cohen, 1995, pp. 62–63). Baron-Cohen argues that failures in autistics' development of mindreading abilities produce abnormalities in social development, in communication development, and in pretend play. It appears that autistics have intact ID's. They seem to be able to recognize desires and goals. They understand that someone may *want* ice cream or *intend* to go swimming. They also recognize animacy, a quality which

Baron-Cohen points out is very close to agency. Finally, autistics understand that desires lead to emotions. When a person gets what he wants, he feels happy, and when he fails to get what he wants, he feels sad. It also appears that autistics have functioning EDDs. Baron-Cohen (1995) reports that they know when someone is looking at them; they infer that an agent's eye direction indicates he or she is seeing something, and they can figure out what someone is looking at.

With regard to the SAM, Baron-Cohen argues that autistics have severe impairments in joint attention. They do not evidence gaze monitoring and they do not use pointing gestures to direct the visual attention of others. In addition, they lack the showing gesture that normal children use to display something of interest to others. Baron-Cohen (1995) argues that "by and large, . . . [autistics] bring an object over to someone, or point an object out, or lead someone to an object and place the person's hand on it, only when they want the person to operate that object or to get it for them. This is not shared attention in any sense; these behaviors are primarily instrumental, and do not indicate a desire to share interest with another person for its own sake" (p. 69).

According to Baron-Cohen (1995), autistics have dysfunctional ToMMs. They fail various tests of false belief. For example, if an autistic observes child *A* put an object in one place, and while *A* is absent, child *B* puts the object in another location, when asked, the autistic will respond that when child *A* returns she will believe that the object is in the new location. In other words, the autistic responds by considering only her own knowledge, not that of the other person. Autistic children also have difficulty in understanding "knowing." For example, in an experiment conducted by Leslie and Firth (1988), an autistic "child was shown an actor watching the experimenter hiding a 'counter' (a plastic token). When the actor left, the experimenter asked the child to put a second counter in a second hiding place. The child was then asked where the actor would look for the counter on her return" (Baron-Cohen, 1995, p. 76). The autistic children tended to indicate the location about which the actor was ignorant. Finally, children with autism tend to have either great difficulty with pretend play or lack it completely.

Baron-Cohen (1995), in exploring the neural substrate for mindreading, suggests that the superior temporal sulcus (STS), the

amygdala, and orbitofrontal cortex are the brain areas that subserve this function. While the location of the SAM is unclear,
Baron-Cohen believes that the EDD is located in a circuit that
includes the STS and the amygdala. He bases this finding on
research (Bruce, Desimore, & Gross, 1981; Perrett, Rolls, & Cann,
1982) that shows certain cells in the temporal lobe, which contains
both the STS and the amygdala, fire more frequently when an animal is looking at a face than do neighboring cells and more than
when the animal is looking at other stimuli. The researchers also
found very specific cells that fire when the animal has its gaze
directed at the eyes of another animal. Baron-Cohen (1995) also
cites research showing that some animals and humans with damage to the STS have difficulty determining gaze direction (Campbell, Heywood, Cowey, Regard, & Landis, 1990; Heywood & Cowey,
1991; Perrett, Hietanen, Oram, & Benson, 1991). In addition, he
notes that there are face-responsive cells and cells responsive to
eye direction in the medial and lateral amygdala (Brothers, Ring,
& Kling, 1990; Leonard, Rolls, Wilson, & Bayliss, 1985; Nakamura, Mikami, & Kubota, 1992) and that neuroanatomical
research has shown that damage to the connection between the
STS and the lateral amygdala causes problems in social perception (Kling & Brothers, 1992).

Baron-Cohen (1995) suggests that the ToMM is largely
instantiated in the orbitofrontal cortex (OFC). One body of evidence he offers in support of this suggestion is the deficits in
social and personal reasoning evidenced by patients with orbitofrontal damage such as Elliot, who was described in Chapter 2.
He also reports research from a neuroimaging study (Baron-
Cohen, Ring, Moriarty, Schmitz, Costa, & Ell, 1994), which
showed increased neural activity in the OFC (particularly the
right OFC) when subjects were asked to pick out mental state
terms (e.g., think, know, pretend, imagine, hope, fear, remember,
plan, intend, want, dream) from a list of words. Baron-Cohen
(1995) states, "although this test taps only one aspect of the
ToMM, it is again consistent with the earlier evidence suggesting
that ToMM is located in the OFC" (p. 93).

Baron-Cohen also suggests that the ID may be associated
with the STS because research (Perrett et al., 1991) indicates
that certain cells in that region fire more frequently when an animal is watching an agent doing something. In addition, other

STS cells respond to self-propelled motion, as when an animal reaches for an object. Both these aspects of movement indicate goals and desires of the moving agent.

It would appear to be a fairly straightforward task, particularly with modern neuroimaging techniques, to see whether autistics have damage to the amygdala, the STS, or the OFC. Some studies have indicated frontal lobe damage, temporal lobe damage, or amygdala damage. These areas fit nicely with Baron-Cohen's predictions, but as he points out, the studies are usually not specific about where in the temporal lobe, or frontal lobe, the lesion may be. Both the amygdala and the STS are in the temporal lobe, and the frontal lobe has many areas with different functions. In addition, some studies report that autistics have brain damage in areas other than in the amygdala-STS-OFC circuit. However, as Baron-Cohen indicates, future research may be facilitated by the specific hypotheses generated in his theory of mind-reading.

Baron-Cohen (1988) indicates that the following pragmatic deficits have been reported in the literature on autistics' speech:

1. the use of speech in which relevant information is not shared and meaning is not communicated;
2. asking questions obsessively about a particular area of interest;
3. ego-centric speech characterized by
    a. echolalia
    b. the articulation of private thoughts
    c. making remarks which are irrelevant to the context
    d. self-repetition;
4. confusion betwen roles as speaker (providing information) and as hearer (receiving information);
5. violations of politeness due to a lack of understanding of the appropriate social rules;
6. the use of a limited set of speech acts and the noncommunicative use of gestures;
7. impaired knowledge of discourse rules;
8. the use of excessively formal or pedantic speech styles by higher functioning autistics;
9. the use of inappropriate strategies to get the attention of interlocutors in order to speak with them;

10. the inability to take into account that the listener was not present at the event the autistic is describing;

11. the inability to maintain a conversation unless the interlocutor frequently asks questions;

12. asking questions the answers to which they already know;

13. compulsively maintaining a topic;

14. failure to understand questions as requests for information;

15. deficits in the understanding and use of appropriate turn taking behavior;

16. impairments in the ability to use and understand appropriate facial expressions;

17. difficulty in appropriate turn taking (i.e., inappropriately interrupting the speaker).

Baron-Cohen (1995) in a discussion of Pinker's (1994) book, *The Language Instinct,* points out that the language faculty would be hopelessly inadequate without the ability to mindread. Here, I would suggest that Baron-Cohen is implicitly making the same distinction that Locke (1995) makes, a distinction between a specialization for social cognition (SSC), which subserves intentionality detection, shared attention, and a theory of mind, and a grammatical analysis module (GAM), which constrains the form of utterances. Baron-Cohen suggests that a person with an intact GAM but with deficits in mindreading (i.e., a damaged SSC) would speak in perfectly grammatical sentences but would have difficulties with the social dialog of normal communication. He argues that the

> drive to inform, to exchange information, to persuade, or to find out about the other person's thoughts is principally based on mindreading, and that mindreading is enabled by the language faculty. But by itself, unless it is linked up to the mindreading system, the language faculty may hardly be used—at least, not socially. (Baron-Cohen, 1995, p. 131)

It would seem that Pinker, in his excellent book, has described only one component of language (the GAM) and therefore, only treats the "grammatical instinct" and does not treat the specialization for social cognition—mindreading capacities that govern language pragmatics—discourse and conversation. Baron-Cohen (1995) concludes, "The limitation of the language faculty without an accompanying mindreading system suggests that mindreading may have preceded language in evolution. However, that mindreading may have benefited from the existence of a language faculty, both phylogenetically and ontogenetically, is also quite plausible. Studies of the relationship have hardly begun" (p. 132).

Developmental Language Disability

Stivers' (1995) reviews several studies of children who generally have appropriate grammar but whose discourse is abnormal (Blank, Gessner, & Esposito, 1979; Brook & Bowler, 1992; Byram, Morgan, & colleagues, 1994; Conti-Ramsden & Gunn, 1986; Fey & Leonard, 1993; Fujiki & Brinton, 1991; Greenlee, 1981; McTear, 1985b). Stivers notes that there has been difficulty settling on a label for such difficulties in communicative interaction. It has sometimes been called semantic-pragmatic syndrome or developmental language disability, but the characteristic problems in verbal discourse also correspond to those seen in autism. Another problem identified by Stivers is that, although the children all have communicative impairments, because of apparent pragmatic difficulties, the specific symptoms vary from child to child. Some of the discourse problems reported in Stivers' review are:

1. poor eye contact (Conti-Ramsden & Gunn, 1986);
2. lack of spontaneous initiative in conversation (Conti-Ramsden & Gunn, 1986);
3. failure to respond to conversational initiatives (Conti-Ramsden & Gunn, 1986);
4. failure to seek conversational interaction (Conti-Ramsden & Gunn, 1986);
5. difficulties in making inferences and predicting sequential and causal relationships (Conti-Ramsden & Gunn, 1986);
6. restricting communication to certain individuals such as parents (Blank et al., 1979);
7. irrelevant and inappropriate responses (Blank et al., 1979; Greenlee, 1981);
8. lack of attention to responses made by interlocutors (Blank et al., 1979);

9. frequent topic switching (Blank et al., 1979);
10. failure to use gestures and difficulty in comprehending them (Blank et al., 1979);
11. confusion in the use of personal pronouns (e.g., using *I* for *you* and vice versa) (Greenlee, 1981);
12. introducing unidentified referents into the discourse (Greenlee, 1981);
13. overly assertive (i.e., efforts to dominate talk, retain speaker position, and to assert topic control) (Fujuki & Brinton, 1991).

McTear (1985a, 1985b) notes that the methodology used to study subjects with pragmatic disorders has frequently been inappropriate for the task. He recommends the use of procedures developed for discourse and conversational analysis, where naturalistic interaction between the patient and interlocutors is recorded and transcribed to generate in-depth case studies. In his own research (McTear, 1985b), he used conversational analysis to identify problems in the speech of a 10-year-old boy who displayed deficiencies in conversational ability. McTear found that the patient had difficulties in both the interactional and transactional aspects of discourse. The "interactional aspects of conversation are the ability to take and assign turns with a minimum of gap and overlap at turn boundaries, and the ability to respond appropriately to preceding utterances" (McTear, 1985b, p. 132). "The transactional component involves the propositional content of discourse, including notions such as relevance, conversational maxims, pragmatic appropriacy, cohesion and coherence" (McTear, 1985b, p. 132).

Among the interactional difficulties, the boy sometimes provided literal responses to the researcher's questions instead of responding to the intended meaning.

> A: can you tell me about it (i.e. TV programme)
> C: yes
> (1.0)
> A: well tell me about it
> what's it like?
> C: the man always fights the bad men . . .
> (Note: A = adult; C = child; 1.0 = gap measured in
>   seconds)

(McTear, 1985b, p. 132)

In the next example, the patient took an appropriate turn, but the content of the turn was inappropriate because it commented on something he should not have known.

> A: now do you want to see if you can play some games with me?
> C: yes
> A: they're very easy games um (1.0)
> C: they are indeed
> A: well we'll see

(McTear, 1985b, p. 133)

The patient also failed to use ellipsis appropriately and thus provided more information than required in normal conversation.

> A: are they friends of yours?
> C: they are friends of mine

(McTear, 1985b, p. 133)

With regard to the transactional aspects of discourse, it was frequently difficult to determine the factual accuracy of the boy's speech because of contradictions and inaccuracies in his utterances. This problem is illustrated in the following example in which he discussed a sports day that was to take place at school.

> A: which race would you like to be in?
> C: I like to be in X at the Sports Day
> (Note: X is a town several miles from the school)
> A: in X?
> C: yes
> A: what do you mean?
> C: I mean something
> A: is there a Sports Day in X?
> C: there is not, there is a Sports Day in Y
> (Note: Y is the name of the child's school)
> A: then what's X got to do with it?
> C: nothing
> A: then why did you mention it?
> C: indeed I did mention it
> A: why did you mention it?
> C: I don't know

(McTear, 1985b, pp. 135–136)

The hypothesis that would follow from the argumentation presented in this section is that children with developmental language disability may have problems with attachment relations, affect regulation, social cognition, or stimulus appraisal that have either generated or result from anomalies in the orbitofrontal-amygdala-body proper neural circuits, which also seem to govern language pragmatics.

Right-Hemisphere Damage

There is a substantial amount of literature indicating that patients with right-hemisphere damage have difficulties in the pragmatic aspects of language. In this regard, it is interesting to note that Schore (1994) argues that the attachment interactions between caretaker and child are mediated right hemisphere to right hemisphere. In other words, the facial and vocal affective communication between the mother and child during the practicing period with regard to stimulus appraisal, affect regulation, and social cognition involves predominantly right-hemisphere activity on the part of both parties. In may be for this reason that right-hemisphere damage results in pragmatic deficits while grammar, a left-hemisphere capacity, is undisturbed.

Joanette, Goulet, and Hannequin (1990) have synthesized the literature on the role of the right hemisphere in verbal communication and show that right-hemisphere damage results in pragmatic deficits involving organizational difficulties, interpretation difficulties, and prosodic difficulties. These pragmatic deficits are summarized below:

I. Organizational difficulties
   a. problems in organizing utterances into coherent sequences
   b. introduction of extraneous material
   c. a tendency to confabulate
   d. difficulties elaborating a story or reconstructing it from its parts
   e. a paucity of information in narratives
II. Interpretation difficulties
   a. difficulties in relating context to discourse
   b. difficulty using context to reject incongruous events

    c. difficulty in rejecting an initial interpretation when contradictory information has been presented

    d. difficulties dealing with texts that contain two possible explanations

    e. difficulty in dealing with metaphor (i.e., difficulty rejecting a literal interpretation when offered)

    f. difficulty in understanding indirect speech acts

    g. difficulty extracting implicit information from an oral or written text

III. Prosodic difficulties

    a. difficulty in the expression of emotional prosody (i.e., flat, monotonous speech)

    b. difficulty in the comprehension of emotional prosody (i.e., difficulties with the perception or categorization of emotional intonation)

    c. difficulty with the comprehension of linguistic prosody when it involves emphatic stress (e.g., *Joe* plays the trumpet vs. Joe plays the *trumpet*) or intonation based modality (e.g., declarative: Bill likes pasta. vs. interrogative: Bill likes pasta?)

    d. some difficulty in the production of linguistic prosody

It should be noted that not all right-hemisphere patients have difficulties with pragmatics and not all pragmatic problems are found in every patient with right-hemisphere damage. In addition, although language deficits following right-hemisphere damage frequently affect pragmatics, these deficits seem to resist precise anatomical localization within that hemisphere. Alexander, Benson, and Stuss (1989) report, "as yet, no compelling evidence exists that proves that any one of these deficits reflects damage to any one region of the right hemisphere; they have been most commonly described following central (simultaneous frontal and parietal) damage or frontal damage" (Weylman et al., 1988, p. 680).

However, Damasio (1994) has indicated that there are two areas, one in the right anterior parietal lobe and another in the frontal lobe, which when damaged, cause problems in personal and social reasoning. Therefore, we might suspect that damage affecting these areas could possibly disturb personal and social decision making in discourse pragmatics.

In both the left and right hemispheres, just posterior to the central sulcus, is the somatosensory area, which processes bodily sensations such as pain, temperature, and touch as well as the position and movement of various parts of the body. There is also a secondary somatosensory region located inside the sylvian fissure both anterior and posterior to the somatosensory strip, extending to the insula. See Figure 6.3.

When this secondary area, also known as S2, is damaged on the right side of the brain, it produces paralysis on the left side of the body and a condition known as anosognosia. Quite remarkably, such patients behave as though the paralysis did not exist and insist that they have no impairment. When told about their condition, they are unconcerned and make light of the situation. Damasio (1994) reports,

> Emotion and feeling are nowhere to be found in anosognosic patients, and perhaps this is the only felicitous aspect of their otherwise tragic condition. Per-

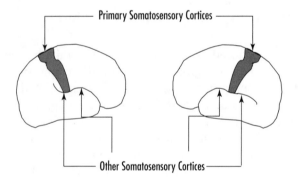

Diagram of a human brain showing the right and left hemispheres seen from the outside. The shaded areas cover the primary somatosensory cortices. Other somatosensory areas, respectively the second sensory area (S2) and the insula, are buried inside the sylvian fissure immediately anterior and posterior to the bottom of the primary somatosensory cortex. They are thus not visible in a surface rendering. Their approximate location in the depth is identified by the arrows.

Figure 6.3. The Location of the Secondary Sensory Area (S2) (From Damasio, 1994, p.65).

haps it is no surprise that these patients' planning for the future, their personal and social decision-making, is profoundly impaired. Paralysis is perhaps the least of their troubles. (p. 64)

Damasio also argues that interconnections among areas of the right hemisphere produce "the most comprehensive and integrated map of the current body state available to the brain" (p. 66). He indicates that this hemisphere is dominant for body sense in the same way that the left hemisphere is dominant for language. Highly coordinated maps for visceral states and maps for musculoskeletal states of the limbs, trunk, and head are found in this hemisphere. As explained earlier, emotions are generated by bodily states (somatic markers) and are interpreted by the brain as feelings. These somatic representations make the right hemisphere also dominant for affect and emotion. Damage to this hemisphere then is likely to interfere with the feelings that help guide social reasoning and thus undermine pragmatic decisions, which guide the social use of language. In other words, while extensive damage to S2 and the insula results in full blown anosognosia, lesser lesions in various parts of the right hemisphere may disrupt the somatosensory maps such that social reasoning is impaired resulting in pragmatic anomalies in social discourse.

Damasio (1994) also reports that damage to another area in the frontal lobes, which is involved in movement, emotion, and attention, leads to a nearly total lack of motion and speech. This area consists of the anterior cingulate, the supplementary motor area (SMA) and a region known as M3, which is at the inferior part of the SMA within the cingulate sulcus. See Figure 6.4. Damasio (1994) describes a patient with damage to this area who became largely motionless and speechless. Except for a few words, consisting of her name and the names of members of her immediate family, she said nothing. Movements were limited to actions such as adjusting bed covers, but generally she was still. After several months, when she began to recover, Damasio (1994) reports:

Contrary to what one might have thought, her mind had not been imprisoned in the jail of her immobility. Instead it appeared that there had not been much mind at all, no real thinking or reasoning. The passivity in her face and

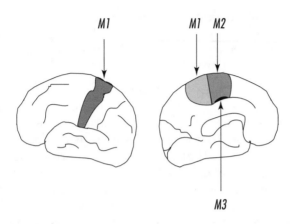

Diagram of a human brain representing the left cerebral hemisphere seen from the outside (left panel) and the inside (right panel). The location of the three main cortical motor regions: M1, M2, M3. M1 includes the so-called "motor strip" which shows up in every cartoon of the brain. An ugly human figure ("Penfield's homunculus") is often drawn on top of it. The less well known M2 is the supplementary motor area, the internal part of area 6. Even less known is M3 which is buried in the depth of the cingulate sulcus.

Figure 6.4. The Location of Motor Areas M2 and M3 (From Damasio, 1994, p.72).

body was the appropriate reflection of her lack of mental animation. At this later date she was certain about not having felt anguished by the absence of communication. Nothing had forced her not to speak her mind. Rather, as she recalled, "I really had nothing to say." (p. 73)

In another report on damage to this area, Damasio and Van Hosen (1983) state that the recovering patient had a general reduction in speech output. In addition, there were gaps in her discourse in which the patient said nothing when the social circumstance would lead to the expectation of some verbal interaction. For example, on one occasion she stood up and left a session without saying anything. Later she indicated that on that occasion, she had experienced a sudden inhibition of speech. The authors speculate that she may have had a disturbance in the drive to speak. They summarize her condition in the following way:

> In short, the results of damage to the cingulate and nearby SMA seem to have been a profound disturbance of behavior which prevented both the normal *expression* and normal *experience* of affect. The patient had a "neutral" facial expression and reported a "neutralized" will to move or communicate. The outer manifestation of these disturbances could best be described as akinesia and mutism, but they might as well be designated as a state of aspontaneity and nonlateralized neglect of most stimuli. At no point did the patient show evidence of impaired social judgment or facetiousness, two signs often associated with disturbances of frontal lobe origin. (p. 100)

Joanette et al. (1990) indicate that patients with right hemisphere damage often have an attitude of emotional indifference, and they speculate that this attitude may contribute to the reduced information in these patients' speech and their difficulties with the organization of discourse. Damasio and Van Hosen (1983) indicate that lesions of M3 in either the right or left hemisphere can produce the clinical picture described above. Once again we might speculate that right-hemisphere damage that affects circuits related to the M3 region, but that might even be some distance from it, could contribute to the patient's general attitude of indifference to issues of pragmatic appropriateness, without producing the akinesia and mutism that results when M3 is damaged directly.

Affect Markers in Language

At the beginning of this chapter, we made the distinction between a neural specialization for social cognition (SSC) and a module for grammatical analysis (GAM). In our discussion so far, we have treated nongrammatical aspects of language and have shown how the neural substrate for these aspects of pragmatics is the same as that for attachment, affect regulation, stimulus appraisal, and social cognition. However, some languages have specific grammatical markers for affect and emotion and for related social factors such as deference or entitlement. It is in these areas of language that the SSC and the GAM come together.

Ochs and Schieffelin (1989) demonstrate how pervasive affective expression is in language and how it is marked by both discourse and grammatical structures. Speakers use certain features of language to express affect to others; recipients of this speech use these features to construct their own feelings, moods, and attitudes toward their interlocutor's speech.

> To state this in other words, we propose that beyond the function of communicating referential information, languages are responsive to the fundamental need of speakers to convey and assess feelings, moods, dispositions and attitudes. This need is as critical and as human as that of describing events. Interlocutors need to know not only what predication a speaker is making; they need to know as well the affective orientation the speaker is presenting with regard to that particular predication. The affective orientation provides critical cues to the interlocutor as to how that interlocutor should interpret and respond to the predication communicated. For example, interlocutors will respond differently if a speaker couches the predication in a positive or negative affective frame. Indeed, in some cases, the interlocutor will take the affective orientation as the point of departure for the subsequent topic. This happens, for example, when someone makes a statement in a flippant or sarcastic manner and the response centers on the attitude presented rather than the propositional content of the response. (Ochs and Schieffelin, 1989, pp. 9–10)

Ochs and Schieffelin, following Klinnert, Campos, Sorce, Emde, and Svejda (1983), argue that reading an interlocutor's affective keys in verbal interaction is a natural development of the social referencing done by infants in relation to the visual and vocal responses of their mothers during the infant's exploration of the environment. "Affective features in language are members of a set of signs that regulate human behavior. They are crucial to the process of social referencing in which affective information is sought out and used to assess how one might construct a next interactional move" (p. 10).

Ochs and Schieffelin (1989) indicate that there are two kinds of affect markers in language, affective intensifiers and affective specifiers. The former modulate the affective intensity of utterances and the latter indicate the affective orientation (e.g., surprise, pity, irritation, etc.) of particular utterances. The features listed below are examples provided by Ochs and Schieffelin (1989, pp. 12–14) of various ways language can be used to intensify or specify affect. Intensifiers appear to be more numerous than specifiers.

PRONOUNS
First person:
> **Kaluli:** *nelo:* 'to me'–appeal, *niba* 'I not you'–assertive
> **Samoan**: *ita* 'poor me', *sina* 'poor my'—sympathy
> **Hawaiian**: ku'u 'my'—affectionate
> **Japanese**: male and female pronouns vary in intimacy

Second person:
> **Spanish, French, Italian** etc.: t/v pronouns—intimacy/distance, respect/disrespect
> **Japanese**: pronouns used by male speakers vary in affect
> **Samoan**: *ise*—anger

Third person:
> **Italian**: *questo, quello, questa, quella*—can be used for negative affect towards humans, *lui, lei*—can be used for positive affect towards objects.
> **English**: *she, her, he, him*—in presence of referent can express negative affect

Reflexive:
> **Spanish**: *se*—intensification e.g. *se le comió todo* 'she ate it all up'
> **Italian**: *se*—intensification e.g. *se lo mangia tutto* 'she eats it all up'

Determiners:
> **Samoan**: *si* 'the dear' (sing.), *nai* 'the dear' (pl.)—sympathy determiner

Mood:
> **Dyjirbal**: *-bila*—possible event has unpleasant or undesirable consequences
> **Japanese:** conditional *ba*—speaker hopes it will be true vs *to/tara*—negative attitude/warnings
> **English**: *if only*—speaker has positive attitude

Tense/aspect:
  English: -*ing* progressive stative—increase dynamism, vividness e.g. 'I am missing you terribly'
Verb voice:
  Thai, Japanese: adversative passive
  English: 'get' passive, e.g. 'he got stabbed'
  Malagasy: active voice–confrontative, passive and circumstantial voice–polite
Casemarking:
  Spanish: dative—intensify involvement, affect e.g. *mi hijo no me come nada* 'my son won't eat anything for me'
  Italian: dative—intensify involvement, affect e.g. *non mi mangia niente* 'He doesn't eat anything for me'
Number/gender/animacy marking:
  Russian, Polish: plural inflection for single referent—emphasis
  Russian: feminine gender of NP—more incriminatory, more emotional weight, e.g. (speaking to man) *dura* 'fool'
  Russian: animate marking for an inanimate referent—humor, affection, negative or sarcastic effects
Other particles/affixes
  Japanese: sentence-final particles emphasize strength, *zo, ze* or softness associated with male/female demeanor *wa, no*
  Samoan: *mai, atu*—deictic particles, intensifier *a, ia, fo'i*—intensifiers *e*–intensifier, negative affect
  Kinyarwanda: diminutive/augmentative noun affixes to convey positive or negative affect, e.g. -*gi*- in *i-gi-kobwa* 'my beloved girl' *we, ye, yehe, he*—intensifying particles.
  Wolof: *de, daal, waay, kat, kay*—intensifiers
  Kaluli: suffixes on verbs, sentence particles: e.g. -*lodo* 'sadness' -*life*—intensifiers of negative directives
  a:, -a:ya:, -bala:,-bale, -sa:la:—emphasis, intensity
  -*a* -*o* intimacy marker added to personal names, kinterms
  Classical Greek: *me*—clause initial or after initial item, emotional tone, also anticipatory adversative
  Italian (Roman): *ao*—negative affect e.g. *ao ma che sei matto?!* 'hey are you crazy?!*
  -*etto, -etta* 'sweet little'
  -*ino, -ina* 'young, small'
  -*accio, -accia* 'bad, nasty'

-uccio, -uccia 'somewhat positive but not too much, e.g. *caruccia* 'somewhat pretty' (f)
otto, -otta 'jolly' can be affectionate
-one augmentative, e.g. *professorone* 'very good medical doctor'
Spanish (regional): *in, -ino, -ico, -illo, -uco*—diminutives, positive affect
-on, -aco, -azo—augmentatives, derogatory
-ucho,-uelo, -zuelo—diminutives, derogatory
-uzo, -acho—derogatory
re (que) (te), super-, -isimo, -isisimo—adjectival intensifiers
Nahuatl: honorific affixes on nouns, e.g. *tzin*—diminutive, affectionate, not on 1st person pronouns
Reduplication
    Wolof: *lu bari* 'a lot' vs. *lu bari-bari* 'a lot'
PHONOLOGY
Intonation
    English: e.g. stylized low-rise as in I'm   ing
                                         com
Voice quality
    Tuvaluan: choppy speech—excited, used to report others' speech monotone—planned, calm, used to report own speech
    Samoan: loudness, lengthening, stress, glottal stop—intensifier
    Kinyarwanda: vowel lengthening—intensify feeling
Sound repetition
    alliteration
Sound symbolism
    English: /fl/, /sn/ e.g., *flip, flap, sniff* etc.
    Italian:/sh/can be intensifier/deintensifier e.g., *shtupido* 'stupid', *ti shpaka la testa* 'I crack your head,' *ti dishtruggo* 'I'll destroy you', *shciafi* 'slaps'
    Samoan: fronting—refinement, backing—earthiness
Lexicon
    interjections
    response cries; threat startles, revulsion sounds, strain grunts, pain cries, sexual moans, floor cues, etc.
    descriptive terms vs personal names for humans:
        Tuvaluan: descriptive terms—sarcasm, treated like object
        Malagasy: personal names—wishing evil, nomen omen archaic terms—solemn tones or irony

respect vocabulary
praise names, e.g., *'the one who does not hesitate to act'*
nicknames, truncated names, gossip names, deviant forms of
kinterms
Verb variants
Spanish: *ser* vs. *estar* e.g., *es bonito* 'it's pretty' vs *está bonito* 'how pretty it is'
Graded sets
Samoan: *aua* 'don't . . .' *soia* 'cut it out!'
Wolof: *dara, darra, tuus, gatt* 'nothing' . . . 'absolutely nothing'
Word order
Hawaiian: preposed demonstrative conveys either positive or negative affect e.g., postposed demonstrative *nei* 'affection'
DISCOURSE STRUCTURE
Code-switching
  taboo words
  dialects to intensify, e.g., use Prague dialect in literary Czech
  baby talk register to pets and lovers in certain societies
  couplets
  repetition of own/other's utterances
Affective speech acts/activities
  teasing, begging, apologizing, oaths, praises, insults, compliments, assessments, complaints, accusations, blessings, joking, shaming, ridiculing, hortatives, laments, placations, etc.

There are languages such as Kaluli, spoken in New Guinea, that have elaborate morphology to express annoyance, sadness, surprise, and support. Samoan has determiners that mark sympathy, and in Japanese and Dyirbal there are affixes that indicate a positive or negative attitude toward a future event. However, affect markers usually cover a range of positive or negative affect such as happiness, love, and sympathy or sadness, anger, and worry. In addition, affect is usually expressed simultaneously by speech, gesture, and facial expression.

Ochs and Schieffelin (1989) also indicate that language is characterized by particular affect keys that intensify or specify the affect intended for a referent, a proposition, or a sequence of propositions. Such affect keys can appear before (an initiator), after (a terminator), or simultaneously with (a concurrent key) the referent, proposition, or sequence. Concurrent keys can be expressed via phonology, morphology, syntax, or lexicon and are frequently carried by intonation and voice quality. Ochs and Schieffelin (1989) offer the following examples:

Initiator: from Kaluli
Heyo! Ge ga andoma
sorry you woman none
'SORRY! You have no woman!' (p. 19)
Terminator: from Yiddish
Mayn shver, a krenk zol im arayn in di yeasles . . .
'My father-in-law, may a disease enter his gums . . .' (p. 16).

On the basis of Ochs and Schieffelin's survey, it might be reasonable to assume that no utterance in verbal interaction is affectively unmarked. Even the attempt to produce a purely objective referential utterance is probably motivated by the desire to key that neutral affect, and the form of the utterances may index that stance by the very absence of intensifiers or specifiers. Finally, since the neural systems we have described for pragmatics (the orbitofrontal cortex, the amygdala and related limbic areas, and the autonomic, hormonal, and musculoskeletal system) also subserve affect and emotion, we would predict that developmental anomalies in or damage to this system would also affect the appropriate use of grammaticalized affect markers.

Another element of affect (or more specifically socioaffect) in language involves what are called *honorifics*. These are particular grammaticalized forms, on the one hand, which Agha (1993, 1994) shows are used to index social status or deference-entitlements. Agha distinguishes between social status, which accrues to an individual on the basis of his role in society resulting from birth, breeding, age, profession, wealth, and on the other hand deference-entitlements (or simply deference), which is the way one person refers to another establishing a deferential relationship, not necessarily according to preordained social categories, but according to levels of respect that are relevant to the social information being generated in the ongoing discourse. Deference can be made to the addressee, a bystander, or to another referent.

What is important to our discussion here is that decisions have to be made in discourse about when to use an honorific and which honorific to use. These decisions involve social cognition, stimulus appraisal, and affect regulation and, therefore, would be governed by the tripartite neural system (orbitofrontal cortex, limbic system, and body proper), which we have argued is the neural basis for pragmatic choices in language use. With regard to honorific markers of defined categories of social status, the speaker must decide to honor them or not; with regard to more relative categories of deference, the speaker must decide what deference she wants indexed for an addressee, a bystander, or another referent. We would predict that individuals with damage to the neural systems underlying language pragmatics would exhibit deficits in the use of honorifics.

Methodological Considerations

Building on the theory and data presented earlier in this chapter, I have suggested that the orbitofrontal cortex, the amygdala, and the body proper may subserve processes of social cognition, stimulus appraisal, attachment, and affect regulation and that these processes may be relevant to language pragmatics. In concluding this chapter, I would like to consider some methodological issues involved in research designed to explore this perspective.

1. *Parent-child affective misattunement.* Several important considerations must be made in conducting research to test the hypothesis that deficient parent-child interactions during the practicing period can result in pragmatic difficulties. First, sophisticated, ethnographic data-gathering techniques and conversational analysis transcription protocols are necessary. It is only methodology of this kind that is sensitive enough to detect the deficits in pragmatics. Typical clinical assessments of language, which consist of number repetitions, sentence completion and construction, sentence-structure analysis, and comprehension analysis (Novoa & Ardilla, 1987), are inadequate for several reasons. First, most of these probes focus on grammar, in which difficulties would not be expected. Second, even more discourse-focused probes such as oral descriptions, open-ended questions, and picture description (Novoa & Ardilla, 1987) are probably too constrained to reflect adequately the predicted discourse difficulties.

In addition, in order to demonstrate that the pragmatic deficit is caused by deficient caregiver-child interaction during the practicing period, longitudinal case studies must be made of children who are clinically identified as insecure-avoidant or insecure-resistant. Assessment of such individuals' language would have to be made on a regular basis, preferably well into adulthood. Such research is of course difficult, but it is what would be required for empirical verification of the hypothesis that these verbal interaction patterns are the product of a defective neurobiological SSC.

In detecting pragmatic deficits, it will also be important to know where to look. Because the human brain is highly plastic, particularly in the late phylogenetically and ontogenetically developing prefrontal areas, we would expect that avoidant and resistant children would develop ancillary systems for affect regulation and social cognition such that they would not always exhibit the predicted pragmatic difficulties. However, under stress, the ancillary systems would be vulnerable to failure and verbal interaction would revert to the maldeveloped dopamine and norepinephrine loops. Under these conditions, pragmatic problems would be expected to appear.

There is another issue that must be considered in both the research that generated the pragmatic deficit hypothesis and research that might result from it. The empirical work on mother-infant interaction, on which Schore's (1994) dual-component, affect-regulation system is based, has largely been carried out in industrialized countries where nuclear or near-nuclear family structure is the norm. In these contexts, mothers spend substantial time interacting on a one-to-one basis with their infants. However, researchers have noted that in other cultures interaction patterns may be different. Ochs and Schieffelin (1995) state:

> In other communities, members do not generally set the goal of communicating intentions to children (i.e. wanting children to understand and respond) at quite such an early point in their lives. In a number of societies, infants are not engaged as addressees until they evidence that they can produce recognizable words in the language. (p.77)

In societies such as these, infants are not singled out as preferred addressees. Rather, they tend to participate in communicative interactions in the role of *overhears* of non-simplified conversations between others. This assumes that small children are being socialized in the context of multiparty interactions, the unmarked condition in traditional and many other societies. (p. 78)

Ochs (personal communication) has noted, however, that in her work in Samoa, she did not closely study infants as young as 10–18 months and therefore, cannot say precisely what kinds of interactions mothers and children engage in at that age. One would have to study the practicing period specifically in these cultures to determine whether equivalent attuned and misattuned (shaming) interactions occur in caregiver-infant interaction. It also has been observed that in many traditional cultures infants are socialized by older siblings. One would want to observe whether interaction, which may be equivalent to those in industrialized cultures, occur in these dyads.

It is also possible that patterns such as those described by Ochs and Schieffelin (1995) may be adequate for socializing affect regulation in the cultures in which they occur. On the other hand, in modern industrialized societies, in which the child is not raised by siblings or by "the village," the mother-infant facial and vocal interactions described by Locke (1993), Schore (1994), Trevarthen (1974, 1993), and others may be cultural adaptations that are absolutely essential for the development of appropriate affect regulation and hence social cognition. In this case, it could be argued that in cultures in which nuclear families are the norm, the mother-infant attunement interactions in the early practicing period and misattunement-reattunement interactions in the late practicing period are indeed necessary for the appropriate development of the dopamine and norepinephrine neural circuits, and if such interactions are inadequate, affect regulation and social cognition will suffer and pragmatic deficits will result.

2. *Research on normal discourse.* For interaction to be pragmatically appropriate, it requires:

1. that the interlocutor be able to make hypotheses about the intentionality of the speaker. That is, the interlocutor must be able to attribute to the speaker beliefs, desires, emotions,

feelings, and perhaps even cognitions. She may do this correctly or incorrectly;

2. the interlocutor must then appraise the speaker's intentions and the on-going interaction according to pleasantness, novelty, goal/need significance, coping demands, self/social image;

3. this appraisal will generate bodily states in the autonomic nervous system, the endocrine system and the musculoskeletal system. These somatic markers constitute emotions, which are interpreted by the brain as feelings. These feelings will influence the interlocutor's decisions about the pragmatic form of her speech when she takes a turn; therefore, the feelings must be appropriately regulated;

4. this cycle of pragmatic decision making will continue throughout the discourse interaction, and therefore, should be traceable with measures of autonomic, endocrine, and musculoskeletal activity.

Research indicates several ways in which the autonomic nervous system, the endocrine system, and the musculoskeletal system might be assessed during discourse so that evidence can be brought to bear on the notion that information from the body is involved in making decisions about language pragmatics. Levenson and Gottman (1983) studied 30 married couples during two types of interactions: discussing the events of the day (low conflict) and discussing marital problems (high-conflict). The researchers measured the couples' interbeat interval (IBI), which measures the time between heartbeats, pulse transmission time to the finger (PTT), which measures the force of cardiac contractions and the distensibility of the arteries between the heart and the finger, skin conductance level (SCL), which measures sweat gland activity, and general somatic activity (ACT), which provides a global measure of somatic muscle activity via an electromechanical transducer attached to a platform under the participant's chair. The researchers found that the peripheral measures were greater for the high-conflict interactions (discussion of marital problems) than for low-conflict interactions (discussion of the events of the day).

While IBI, PTT, SCL, and ACT are largely measures of activity in the sympathetic nervous system, assessment of parasympathetic activity is also possible by measuring an individual's vagal tone through quantification of an interlocutor's respiratory sinus arrhythmia (RSA) (Porges, Doussard-Roosevelt, & Maiti, 1994). RSA is characterized by a rhythmic increase in heart rate related to inspiration and a decrease in heart rate associated with expiration. This measurement is made by using the R-wave of an electrocardiogram to detect the heartbeat and then timing between heartbeats.

As indicated in Figure 6.5, sensory information at the level of the cortex is passed to the amygdala where it is assessed for emotional significance and motivational relevance. The amygdala projects to the nucleus ambiguus in the rostral medulla. This nucleus contains the cell bodies of origin of the vagal nerve. The vagus innervates the soft palate, pharynx, larynx, esophagus, bronchi, and heart. This connectivity allows the vagus to regulate autonomic activity related to "the expression of motion, emotion, and communication by regulating metabolic output (i.e., shifts in heart rate) and organs involved in the production of vocalizations" (Porges et al., 1994, p. 172).

Wittling and Schweiger (1993) assessed parasympathetic activity by determining levels of salivary cortisol. They measured subjects' baseline values and then determined values after the subjects had viewed an emotionally adverse film. The subjects kept a cotton swab in their mouths for five minutes. The saliva was then released during a centrifugation, stored at −20°C, and later analyzed for cortisol level.

Kagan (1994) reports research on temperament in children in which seven sympathetically influenced reactions were measured: heart rate, heart-rate variability, heart-rate acceleration, blood pressure, pupillary dilation, muscle tension in the vocal folds, and urinary norepinephrine. Individuals may vary in how their autonomic, endocrine, and musculoskeletal systems signal the personal and social decision-making mechanisms in the brain. In addition, stimuli generated in the on-line verbal interaction may target different aspects of the peripheral nervous system. Therefore, it would appear that in order to appropriately associate somatic markers with ongoing discourse, multiple measures of the periphery must be taken.

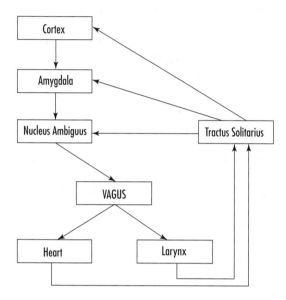

Figure 6.5. Schematization of the Vagal Circuit of Emotion Regulation (from Porges et al., 1994, p. 177).

Summary of the Role of Affect in Primary Language Acquisition and Use

1. Affective facial and vocal interaction between infant and mother fosters the development of the neural systems for attachment, affect regulation, stimulus appraisal, social cognition, and language pragmatics.

2. One account for autism is that the pragmatic difficulties these patients have result from an inadequate theory of mind due to damage to the orbitofrontal cortex or to temporal lobe areas related to the limbic system.

3. Pragmatic deficits may result from damage to the right hemisphere's highly integrated maps for bodily states. These

maps may be centered around the frontal area M3 and parietal areas involving S2 and the insula.

4. The largely right-hemisphere frontolimbic circuits for social and personal reasoning link up to areas of the brain specialized for syntactic processing where affect and social designations may receive specific grammatical marking.

5. Thus, affect plays an essential role in primary language acquisition and use in the area of pragmatic knowledge and decision making by virtue of the fact that pragmatics, as a socioaffective aspect of language, is encoded as part of the neural system responsible for attachment, affect regulation, stimulus appraisal and social cognition.

6. To explore the hypothesis that the neural substrate for language pragmatics involves the same areas of the brain (orbitofrontal cortex, amygdala, related limbic areas, and the body proper) that subserve attachment, affect regulation, stimulus appraisal, and social cognition, researchers might study the discourse of children who have had avoidant and resistant attachments and might also examine the autonomic, endocrine, and musculoskeletal reactions of normal individuals in various discourse contexts.

As Baron-Cohen (1988) notes, "it is reasonable to assume, then, that whatever underlies the deficit in social skills is also likely to underlie the deficit in pragmatic skills" (p. 380). In language then, it is reasonable that pragmatics will be subserved by a neural system that is involved in social cognition and its concomitant processes of attachment, affect regulation, and stimulus appraisal. This neural system consists of the orbitofrontal cortex, the amygdala, the connections between them, and their mutual connections to the brain stem and hypothalamus which, in turn, control the automatic nervous system, the endocrine system, and motor systems. These networks are also augmented by face-recognition cells in the amygdala, the orbitofrontal cortex, and the superior temporal sulcus. Although it has not been discussed here, these neural areas also operate in conjunction with the anterior cingulate (Brothers, 1995; Devinsky, Morrell, & Voget, 1995). Through the Specialization for Social Cognition (SSC), speakers make social decisions about what to say and how to say it, and about what to hear and how to understand it. The system can be disturbed by damage to the relevant neural tissue or by its failure to develop normally due to inadequate interaction with caregivers during the critical period of experience-dependent growth. The pragmatic deficit may exist without any deficit in grammar because grammar is subserved by a different neural system, the Grammatical Analysis Module (GAM), in a different part of the brain. Therefore, affect does indeed influence first language acquisition through its role in the pragmatic aspects of language.

7

The Role of Affect in Cognition

In this book I have shown how a single neural system might be responsible for several diverse but related processes—attachment, affect regulation, social cognition, and stimulus appraisal. The neural system consists of the amygdala, the orbitofrontal cortex, and the body proper via the hypothalamus and the brain stem. In the future it is likely that related areas will also be seen to play a role. Potential candidates are the septum, the anterior cingulate, and the temporal pole. But what emerges is the notion that processes that may be seen as separate and independent at the psychological level may be united or at least highly integrated at the neural level. For example, at the psychological level, stimulus appraisal and motivation are studied separately, but motivation may simply consist of patterns of stimulus appraisal. Attachment and stimulus appraisal are usually studied separately, but as Schore (1994) suggests, attachment interactions may function to teach the child how to appraise actions, agents, and objects in the world. Motivation to learn a second language is studied separately from pragmatic decision making in one's native language, but both may result from how we appraise agents and events in terms of our sense of novelty, familiarity, and pleasantness and in terms of our goals, coping ability, and self and social image.

All the processes examined in this book have centrally involved affect/emotion/feeling phenomena that are generally studied independently of cognition, but which seem to interact with cognition in the processes of sustained deep learning and pragmatic decision making. So from a neural perspective, not only are various affective processes interrelated, but affect and cognition are also intimately intertwined.

In the last few years, three books (Damasio, 1994; Goleman, 1995; LeDoux, 1996) have appeared that, in effect, challenge prevailing ideas about cognition. Each of these works shows how affect and emotion profoundly influence thought. There are two dominant models of the mind—the computer and the brain. The computer metaphor was introduced with the cognitive revolution in the 1950s. But because computers have no emotion, this aspect of mental life was generally ignored. In a related area, cognitive neuroscience, the brain was the model of the mind, and when studying the brain there is no way to avoid emotion. The neurotransmitter centers in the brain stem, the hormone and peptide sources in the hypothalamus, the appraisal areas in the limbic system, and the autonomic and musculosketal responses in the body are recognized by cognitive neuroscientists as important in initiating and modulating our thought, our cognition, and our rationality.

After reading an earlier draft of this book a colleague asked why I didn't call it "The Role of Affect in Cognition." I said I felt the book was far too narrow to warrant such a title, but the book does indeed argue that affect, in the form of stimulus appraisals, is important in second language acquisition and in all sustained deep learning. It also argues that affect is essential in the acquisition and use of pragmatics in one's native language. Therefore, in this final section of the book, I would like to make some speculations about the role of affect in cognition in general, to again attempt to bring together areas that have frequently been treated separately at the psychological level. This section is unquestionably speculative, but such speculation may be warranted. With the recognition that the brain executes both affect and cognition and has evolved over time, it may be helpful to distinguish among different kinds of cognition, some of which may be more closely related to affect than others. Cognitive scientists sometimes tend to view cognition as a single process, but, in fact, there are probably several forms of cognition. First, there is canalized cognition (discussed in Chapter 1) that involves inherited and therefore, innate neural mechanisms, which function automatically to produce learning in a highly restricted domain, on the basis of minimal environmental input. Second, there is the affectively driven cognition involved in sustained deep learning (discussed in Chapter 1), which consists of action tendencies generated by stimulus appraisals. Third, there is social cognition (discussed in Chapter 6) by which people attempt to determine the intentions and dispositions of others. Finally, there is abstract cognition. This is the cognition that is involved in mathematics, logic, and chess, and that is frequently regarded by cognitive scientists as the canonical form of mental activity. In this section I will argue that abstract cognition may have evolved from social cognition. I will then show how affect is important to the process of framing problems in abstract cognition, and finally I will speculate about how the body may be used to facilitate thinking.

Social Cognition

As we have seen, the neural system that we have discussed in relation to stimulus appraisal, attachment, affect regulation, and discourse pragmatics is also the neural substrate for social cognition. Social cognition has already been examined in terms of Damasio's (1994) ideas about the role of somatic markers in personal and social reasoning. In this section, I will attempt to expand this notion in order to explore possible socio-affective roots of rational, logical, and abstract cognition. Brothers (1990) defines social cognition as *"the processing of any information which culminates in the accurate perception of the dispositions and intentions of other individuals"* (p. 28). Because any cognitive act can lead to correct or incorrect results, I would suggest that perhaps the definition need not include the notion of accuracy. For many reasons, we may misinterpret the intentions and dispositions of others. In addition, we might also include in the notion of social cognition the ability to identify our own dispositions and intentions in relation to others.

As mentioned at the beginning of Chapter 6, the position taken in this book is that humans have a neural specialization for social cognition. This specialization is also present in other animals and is particularly evident in nonhuman primates. In both human and nonhuman primates, mental information about intentions and dispositions is conveyed by face, voice, body posture, and gestures (Brothers, 1990).

We saw in Chapter 1 and Chapter 6 that the basic aspects of social cognition come in the form of inherited sociostats—the innate dispositions to interact with conspecifics. Infants attend to facial and vocal communication from caregivers in order to get information about caregivers, affective states. The infants, in turn, use facial expressions, vocalizations, and body movements to index their own affective disposition. We also saw that some aspects of social cognition may not be acquired by autistics. Baron-Cohen (1995) presented arguments that autistic children have impairments in their mechanisms for shared attention (SAM) and for their theory of mind (ToMM).

Brothers (1992) has shown that macaque monkeys have neurons in the superior temporal sulcus (STS) that are responsive to the identity of faces. The STS projects to the amygdala, where face-selective neurons have been found in the basal accessory nucleus in macaques. As we have already discussed, the amygdala projects to the hypothalamus and brain stem, allowing it to influence autonomic, endocrine, and musculoskeletal systems. Part of social cognition is the ability to assess the significance of interactants' movements and gestures. Brothers (1992) reported that, in the medial amygdala of the macaque, there are neurons that are selective for open mouths, yawns, threatening facial movements, frontal eye contact, approach behavior, vocalizing mouth movements, and alternating limb movements characteristic of locomotion. She also reviewed evidence that neurons in the macaque STS code facial expression and unanticipated touch. All of this information is used by the monkeys to make inferences about the mental states of their interactants.

Provinelli and Preuss (1995) have reported that human children at four years of age understand many aspects of how belief and knowledge may be acquired. They know that perception of an event will provide knowledge to the perceiver that someone who has not perceived the event will not have. The authors indicate that tests with chimps and macaques have not provided clear evidence that these primates comprehend the perception-knowledge relationship. There are observational reports that chimpanzees will attempt to deceive, for example, by giving predator calls to distract conspecifics, allowing the deceiving chimp to consume some food without competition from the others. The authors indicate that very little research has been done to see whether nonhuman primates understand false belief, but they reason that if these animals do not understand the perception-knowledge connection from which belief arises, it would be unlikely that they would distinguish false from true beliefs. Provinelli and Preuss (1995) also report that 3-year-old children know that people act on the basis of their desires and that there is some evidence that chimpanzees may also have this ability.

So there is evidence that both human and nonhuman primates have a neural basis for social cognition, but the increasingly complex social interaction of hominids may have fostered a specialization in humans that provides them with an especially well- developed ability to use cognition about the mental states of themselves and others to regulate their behavior (Provinelli & Preuss, 1995).

Nonhuman and human primates live in profoundly social environments. It would appear that the primary task to which we put our mental abilities is in interacting with others. We have to know whom to respect and from whom to expect respect. We have to be able to deceive, and we have to be able to detect deception. We have to know how to curry favor and how to bestow favor. We have to remember to whom we owe a favor and who owes a favor to us. We have to be able to form, maintain, break, and reestablish alliances. We have to be able to recognize and remember who is allied to whom; who is related to whom. We have to compete with conspecifics to establish economic and social status; at the same time, we have to know how to cooperate with them to accomplish the same thing. We have to know when to assert and when to concede; when to challenge and when to submit; and when to express emotion and when to suppress it.

It is interesting to reflect on how much time we spend planning and reviewing social interactions. When we plan a meeting, we think not only about the content as might be indicated by the agenda. We also think about who will attend, how they will react to various issues, who might be an ally, who might be an opponent; how might participant X be converted to my position, how I can control my emotion when I get the anticipated unfavorable reaction from participant Y; how I can maintain my alliance with participant Z when what I propose might threaten him. After the meeting, we review the interactions and try to understand what effect they may have had on the dispositions and intentions of the other participants. We may also try to determine what relationships may have been bruised and therefore may need repair and what support we may have to provide a participant who can now be expected to offer support to us in return.

It has been jokingly suggested that the human brain evolved under adaptive pressure to give dinner parties (Allman, 1994a). A dinner party engages numerous aspects of social intelligence. One must consider reciprocity—to whom do you owe an invitation, whom would you want to indebt with an invitation, which potential guests might not be appropriate invitees, either because another invitation might be excessive or because they have not reciprocated and you have taken offense? Which potential invitees would interact well together? Considering the social and work obligations of potential invitees, what would be a good date and time for the party. Taking into consideration the ethnic, religious, and dietary preferences of your guests, what should be served? Who should be seated next to whom? What sort of topics might be avoided (shop talk, politics, bilingual education, capital gains tax cut)? What sort of topics might be encouraged (the academy awards, flavored coffee, population control, the role of emotion in cognition)?

Allman (1994a) aptly summarizes the pervasive social dimension of our social cognition: "Our lives are a constant making, unmaking, and redefining of relationships with others, weaving a vast fabric of relations between brother and sister, parent and child, husband and wife, coworkers, neighbors, communities, leaders, and nations" (p. 22).

Baron-Cohen (1995) cites Humphrey's (1984) characterization of our social nature:

> Thus social primates are required by the very nature of the system they create and maintain to be calculating beings; they must be able to calculate the consequences of their own behavior, to calculate the likely behavior of others, to calculate the balance of advantage and loss—and all this in a context where the evidence on which their calculations are based is ephemeral, ambiguous, and likely to change, not least as a consequence of their own actions. In such a situation, "social skill" goes hand in hand with intellect, and here at last the intellectual faculties required are of the highest order. The game of social plot and counter-plot cannot be played merely on the basis of accumulated knowledge, any more than can a game of chess. (p. 18)

It has been suggested that the human brain evolved to its current size and complexity in order to handle the social cognition we have just described. The brain had achieved its present architecture before the onset of technology, the development of formal logic, and the emergence of scientific reasoning. Is it possible then that rational, logical, scientific thought is dependent upon and derived from social intelligence. Is it an abstraction from the personal and social reasoning carried out by the orbitofrontal cortex, amygdala, and peripheral nervous system? Evidence to support this speculation comes from the observation that humans reason more easily and effectively when a problem is cast in social terms than when it is formulated abstractly.

Allman (1994a, 1994b) cites the work of Cosmides and Tooby (Cosmides, 1989; Cosmides & Tooby, 1989), who experimentally demonstrated that humans perform better on logic problems that are embedded in a context of social interaction. This is illustrated in the following two problems from Allman (1994b). In the first, only about 25% of the people tested were able to generate the correct solution; in the second, which is socially contextualized, 75% chose the correct answer.

> 1. Part of your new clerical job at the local high school is to make sure that student documents have been processed correctly. Your job is to make sure the documents conform to the following alphanumeric rule: "If a person had a D rating, then his documents must be marked code 3."
>
> You suspect the secretary you replaced did not categorize the students' documents correctly. The cards below have information about the documents of four people who are enrolled at this high school. One side of a card tells a person's letter rating and the other side of the card tells that person's number code. Indicate only the card(s) you definitely need to turn over to see if the documents of any of these people violate this rule.

> 2. In its crackdown against drunk drivers, Massachusetts law enforcement officials are revoking liquor licenses left and right. You are a bouncer in a Boston bar, and you'll lose your job unless you enforce the following law:

"If a person is drinking beer, then he or she must be over 20 years old."

The cards below have information about four people sitting at a table in your bar. Each card represents one person. One side of a card tells what a person is drinking and the other side of the card tells that person's age. Indicate only the card(s) you definitely need to turn over to see if any of these people are breaking the law.

| DRINKING BEER | DRINKING COKE | 25 yrs old | 16 yrs old |

Answers: *First problem: the D and 7 cards. Fewer than 25 percent of people got this right. On the "social" problem, about 75 percent correctly chose "drinking beer" and "16 years old" cards.* (p. 78)

Even reasoning processes such as transitive inference may have been based on social knowledge. The inference that A is larger than C if A is larger than B and B is larger that C could have been derived from the social knowledge that animal A is stronger than animal B and B is stronger than C (Cheney and Seyfarth, 1990).

Cheney and Seyfarth (1990) note that vervet monkeys are good primatologists, but not good naturalists. They only seem to be interested in those aspects of their environment that are relevant to their survival. Humans, on the other hand, are interested in many things about their environment that are unrelated to issues of survival. Monkey cognition seems to be domain specific, and they don't seem to generalize knowledge across domains. Apes, who are able to handle symbols to some extent, are somewhat better at generalizing knowledge across domains. Humans seem to make such transfers with facility; it may have been the development of language and the consequent ability to manipulate symbols that facilitated the transfer of social knowledge to the domains of abstract logical thinking.

Framing

De Sousa (1987) in his book, *The Rationality of Emotion*, points out that emotion allows us to deal with the "frame problem." When attempting to solve a problem, we are potentially faced with a wide range of hypotheses and a wide range of information relevant to these hypotheses. Emotion biases us to focus on a subset of the hypotheses and helps us to limit the range of information that we will see as relevant to them. Emotions thus tell us where to look for a solution, but in doing so, they, of course, can be either right or wrong.

For example, in attempting to understand a complex problem such as second language acquisition, a vast array of approaches and explanations are possible. Researchers have suggested, as crucial, such diverse explanations as access to Universal Grammar, form of the input, type of interaction, affective and motivational variables, influence of the native language, types of cognitive strategies employed, and type of instruction provided. Where one decides to focus is essentially an emotional decision in which alternatives are appraised by schematic emotional memory (as described in Chapter 1), according to the dimensions of stimulus appraisal (novelty, pleasantness, goal/need significance, coping ability, and self and social image). De Sousa (1987) uses the term "paradigm scenarios" to refer to the stimulus appraisals made by schematic emotional memory. He characterizes paradigm scenarios in the following way:

> My hypothesis is this: We are made familiar with the vocabulary of emotion by association with *paradigm scenarios*. These are drawn first from our daily life as small children and later reinforced by the stories, art, and culture to which we are exposed. Later still, in literate cultures, they are supplemented and refined by literature. Paradigm scenarios involve two aspects: first, a situation type providing the characteristic *objects* of the specific emotion-type . . . and second, a set of characteristic or "normal" *responses* to the situation, where normality is first a biological matter and then very quickly becomes a cultural one. It is in large part in virtue of the response component of the scenarios that emotions are commonly held to *motivate*. But this is, in a way, back-to-front: for the emotion often takes its name from the response disposition and is only afterward assumed to cause it. (p. 182)

An illustration of how emotion helps frame a problem is provided in a recent article by Eubank and Gregg (1995). They argue that explanation in SLA should be guided by the current theory of Universal Grammar. Their rationale is that this theory is *"the only one there is"* (p. 51). This claim is clearly a case of emotion framing a problem by limiting alternatives. Current generative grammar is not the only theory there is. Other grammatical perspectives exist. I think it is unlikely that Eubank and Gregg have systematically examined all alternatives and have a rational basis for eliminating them. They indicate that the theory of Universal Grammar is the most complete grammatical theory available. One, of course, is not bound to use completeness as the criterion for choice of a theoretical framework, but evidently their affectively based stimulus-appraisal systems and their knowledge of this particular paradigm lead them to choose this perspective to examine SLA, but it is an emotional framing that provides them with their theory. My own choice is to focus on variable success in SLA and to do so by adopting an affective/motivational perspective. This is also an emotional framing of the problem.

Several years ago at UCLA, there were two linguists who had adopted diametrically opposed approaches to grammar. One was a generativist, who viewed grammar as a neurally instantiated set of constraints on the form of languages. The other was a functionalist, who viewed grammar as an emergent property of discourse. Anyone who knew these linguists would agree that both were extremely intelligent and eminently reasonable. In addition, they each had access to the linguistic knowledge that informed the other's perspective. Clearly in this case, each individual's schematic emotional memory (value-category memory, paradigm scenario) had framed the "grammar problem" differently and led them to adopt opposing hypotheses. It remains to be seen which is correct.

So far we have been discussing the role of emotionally based framing on the issue of theory selection or theory adoption. But once one has adopted a theoretical orientation, additional framing problems exist. One must use some research procedures and not others, but which procedures to choose constitutes a second-order framing problem. Rationality involves the logical, systematic, and appropriate application of sequences of steps to problem solving. Once a sequence has been chosen, it can continue with emotion only providing the motivation to continue. But which sequence to choose initially and which alternate sequence to apply if the first choice doesn't work may require emotional feedback from somatic markers and brain-based feelings. These emotions and feelings may also be required to know when to stop a procedure and how to recognize a solution, that is, to choose the best solution among those that several sequences have produced.

Schwarz (1990) discusses the role of affective states in cognition. He argues that we frequently use feelings as information. In other words, when faced with a situation about which we have to make a judgment, we often ask ourselves how we feel about it. This recourse to feelings may lead us to choose one procedure over another, one set of data rather than another, or one solution instead of another.

Such reasoning by feeling is quite automatic when one is asked to make an affective judgment, for example, when asked whether one likes a particular person, movie, food, and so on. It is also employed when so little data are available that feelings constitute one's only source of information. A person may also reason by feeling as a shortcut when she judges that the issue is not crucial and would not have significant consequences.

Processing demands also influence when we use feelings as information. If a situation is so complex and cumbersome that bottom-up reasoning based on large amounts of data would be difficult or impossible, we may reason on the basis of feelings. We may also employ feelings when time constraints and competing tasks limit our cognitive capacities.

Using experimental evidence and some speculation, Schwarz (1990) also argues that "negative affective states . . . foster the use of effortful, detail-oriented, analytical processing strategies, whereas positive affective states foster the use of less effortful heuristic strategies" (p. 527). In negative affective states, a person may be threatened or concerned about unfavorable outcomes and therefore may want to alter the current situation. To do so she may:

1. carefully assess the features of the current situation;
2. analyze the causes of the current situation;
3. analyze the various ways the situation might be changed;
4. analyze the potential outcomes of the various changes;
5. anticipate risk and, therefore, avoid novel situations;

6. generate a narrower focus of attention;
7. seek detailed information that would bear on the issue;
8. make effortful attempts to avoid logical inconsistencies.

In a positive state, a person may feel safe and unthreatened and, therefore, may:

1. be willing to take risks, generate novel approaches, and pursue creative associations;
2. rely less on detailed-oriented judgment strategies;
3. maintain a wider focus of attention;
4. draw upon more diverse sources of knowledge;
5. use broad rather than narrow strategies.

From the foregoing, we see that affect influences cognition by helping us frame the problem and by influencing our processing strategies.

Musculoskeletal Reasoning

As I have already argued on the basis of Damasio's (1994) work, social reasoning has its basis in emotional states, which are generated in the body and interpreted by the brain as feelings. Therefore abstract, logical, scientific thinking, which may be derived from social cognition, may also be rooted in affective states generated in the body. In this section, we will examine some ways in which physicists and congenitally blind children may use their bodies to think about inanimate matter.

Ochs and colleagues at UCLA (Ochs, Gonzalez, & Jacoby, 1996) have studied the discussions of physicists in laboratory meetings. The interactional patterns that emerged suggest an emotional basis for the physicists' reasoning. In one example, a graduate student, Miguel, has conducted some experiments on phase transitions in disordered magnets, the results of which are at variance with a computer simulation done by another investigator, an experiment conducted by a third research group, and measurements from two experimental procedures used in his own lab. These discrepancies could mean that his results are correct, that they are wrong, or that there is some experimental anomaly responsible for these results. The experimenter, Miguel, and the principal investigator, Ron, who discuss the results, must attempt to resolve these discrepancies by working through the various findings.

In the laboratory, there is a diagram on the blackboard that depicts a diluted antiferromagnetic system consisting of three phase states and transitions between them. Ron is attempting to understand Miguel's results. In doing so, with reference to the diagram on the blackboard, Ron uses utterances such as

When I approach a phase transition line in different directions.

Why don't I go to the long range ordered phase in the Klee-man experiment.

I go here.

If I come in this way and go here.

When I come down I'm in the domain state.

I go here and there's still a decay present . . . if I come in this way and go here there's no decay.

Miguel uses utterances such as,

Here when you reach this point here . . . we are in the domain state.

And as–when you cut the field, you reach the long range order state.

Ron is using the pronoun "I" and Miguel is using the pronoun "you" and "we" when referring to the inanimate physical entities such as subatomic particles or random magnets. The authors suggest that Ron and Miguel are manifesting "an extreme form of subjectivity by stepping into the universe of physical processes to take the perspective of physical constructs (i.e., to symbolically live their experiences)" (p. 349). In addition, the physicists refer extensively to the graph and, using gestures, they point to and trace the movement of the inanimate physical entities with which they have identified. Ochs et al. (1996) state that

indexical gestures are so much a part of the physicists' dis-course practices, it appears that physicists come to their understandings and interpretations of physics partly through such sensori-motor and symbolic re-enactments of physical events and that the collaborative thinking-through process requires that this sensori-motor involv-ment be witnessed and evaluated by others present. (pp. 352–353)

I would further suggest that by "becoming" the physical enti-ties they are studying and by using gestures to move through the phase transitions indicated in the graph, the physicists create in themselves bodily states or somatic markers. As discussed ear-lier, these bodily states involving the musculoskeletal system, the autonomic nervous system, and the endocrine system consti-tute, in Damasio's terms, emotions that are interpreted by the brain as feelings which may help the physicists in thinking through their problem and choosing among various possible explanations for their results. In essence, they are using emo-tions to organize their cognition; they are thinking with their bodies in order to generate affect on which to cognize.

Another example of the role of musculoskeletal activity in thinking may be provided by the observation (Iverson & Golden-Meadow, 1997) that congenitally blind children gesture when they speak. The researchers examined the gestures of congenitally blind and sighted children on several conservation tasks:

The experimenter presented the eight conservation tasks to all subjects in the following fixed order: two continuous quantity tasks, two length tasks, two number tasks, and two mass tasks. Each task consisted of three phases (a) initial equality, (b) transformation, and (c) final equality. For example, in the initial equality phase of the first con-tinuous quantity task, two identical tall, round containers filled with salt were placed in front of the child, and the child was asked to verify that the two containers held the same amount of salt. In the transformation phase, salt was poured from one of the tall containers to a short con-tainer placed in front of the child. Blind . . . children were asked to keep their hands over the experimenter's hands during this transformation and all subsequent transfor-mation phases. The child was then asked two questions: (a) the judgement question, "Do the two containers have the same or different amounts of salt in them?" and (b) the explanation question, "How can you tell?" or "How do you know?" In the final equality phase, salt from the short container was poured back into the original tall container and the child was again asked if the two containers had the same or different amounts of salt. A similar procedure was followed for the remaining seven tasks, which involved different transformations. (p. 455)

The researchers report that in spite of the fact that the blind children had never been exposed to the communicative function of gestures (i.e., they had never seen anyone use them) they did indeed gesture during the conservation task, and their gestures were very similar in both the form they took and the content they expressed to those of the sighted children.

The authors suggest that the blind children used gestures to help them think through the cognitive problems posed in the conservation tasks. In a similar vein, it had also been observed that people gesture when talking on the telephone. Here the gesture would not have any communicative value, but the musculoskeletal activity, as in the blind children, may facilitate the speaker's thinking through conceptual issues in his discourse or it may contribute to the formulation of grammatical and pragmatic aspects of his speech.

I have argued in this book that musculoskeletal activity in the body is one aspect of emotion and that it generates somatic markers that are communicated to the brain to facilitate social and personal reasoning. The hypothesis proposed here is that the musculoskeletal activity may facilitate cognitive reasoning as well as social and personal reasoning, and that the former may be phylogenetically derived from the latter.

Summary

In this chapter the argument was made that abstract logical cognition may be derived from the affective nature of social cognition. In addition, it was suggested that affect may influence cognition through its role in framing a problem and in adopting processing strategies. I also examined how physicists and congenitally blind children may use bodily states or somatic markers, which contain affective information in the form of musculoskeletal position and movement, to reason about the physical world.

One might ask whether these speculations about the possible affective underpinnings of cognition in general are appropriate. Do they take us away from language acquisition, which is the focus of the book? Language acquisition is a branch of applied linguistics, and applied linguistics is the application of various fields (anthroplology, psychology, sociology, neuroscience, education, and linguistics among others) to the study of language acquisition and use. In Chapters 1–6, I applied information from psychology and neurobiology to problems of first and second language acquisition. That application showed that both forms of language acquisition have important affective components. To conclude the book, I moved in the other direction, that is, I applied the perspective on affect generated in a study of language to broader aspects of cognition, in the hope that if the dialog worked in one direction (from affective perspectives in psychology and neurobiology to language), it would also be fruitful in the other direction (from an affective perspective on language to issues of cognition in psychology and in neuroscience).

References

Adolphs, R., Tranel, D., Damasio, H., & Damasio, A. (1994). Impaired recognition of emotion in facial expressions following bilateral damage to the human amygdala. *Nature, 372*, 669–672.

Aggleton, J.P. & Mishkin, M. (1986). The amygdala: Sensory gateway to the emotions. In R. Plutchik & H. Kellerman (Eds.), *Emotion: Theory, research, and experience*. Vol. 3 of Biological foundations of emotion (281–300). New York: Academic Press.

Agha, A. (1993). Grammatical and indexical convention in honorific discourse. *Journal of Linguistic Anthropology, 3,* 131–163.

Agha, A. (1994). Honorification. *Annual Review of Anthropology, 23,* 277–302.

Ainsworth, M.D.S. (1985). Patterns of infant–mother attachments: Antecedents and effects on development. *Bulletin of the New York Academy of Medicine, 61,* 771–791.

Alexander, M.P., Benson, D.F., & Stuss, D.T. (1989). Frontal lobes and language. *Brain and Language, 37,* 656–691.

Allen, R.E. & Oliver, J.M. (1982). The effects of child maltreatment on language development. *Child Abuse and Neglect, 6,* 299-305.

Allman, W.F. (1994a). *The Stone Age present*. NY: Simon & Schuster.

Allman, W.F. (1994b). Why IQ isn't destiny. *U.S. News & World Report, 117,* 73–80.

Allman, J. & Brothers, L. (1994). Faces, fear and the amygdala. *Nature, 372,* 613–614.

Amaral, D.G., Price, J.L., Pitkänen, A., & Carmichael, S.T. (1992). Anatomical organization of the primate amygdaloid complex. In J.A. Aggleton (Ed.), *The Amygdala: Neurobiological aspects of emotion, memory, and mental dysfunction* (pp. 1-66). New York: Wiley–Liss.

Bailey, K.M. (1983). Competitiveness and anxiety in adult second language learning: Looking *at* and *through* the diary studies. In H.D. Seliger & M.H. Long (Eds.), *Classroom oriented research in second language acquisition* (67–103). Rowley, MA: Newbury House.

Bailey, K.M. (1985). Classroom-centered research on language teaching and learning. In M. Celce-Murcia (Ed.), *Beyond basics: Issues and research in TESOL* (pp. 96–121). Rowley, MA: Newbury House.

Bailey, K.M. (1991). Diary studies of classroom language learning: The doubting game and the believing game. In E. Sadtons (Ed.), *Language acquisition and the second/foreign language classroom.* Singapore: SEAMEO Reigonal Language Centre.

Bailey, K.M., & Ochsner, R. (1983). A methodological review of the diary studies: Windmill tilting or social science? In K.M. Bailey, M.H. Long, & S.Peck (Eds.), *Second Language Acquisition Studies,* (pp. 188–198). Rowley, MA: Newbury House.

Bandura, A. (1991). Self-regulation of motivation through anticipatory and self-reactive mechanisms. In R.A. Dienstbier (Ed.), *Nebraska Symposium on Motivation 1990: Perspectives on Motivation* (pp.69–164). Lincoln: University of Nebraska Press.

Barbas, H. (1995). Anatomic basis of cognitive-emotional interactions in the primate preforntal cortex. *Neuroscience and Biobehavioral Reviews, 19,* 499–510.

Baron-Cohen, S. (1988). Social and pragmatic deficits in autism: Cognitive or affective? *Journal of Autism and Developmental Disorders, 18,* 379–402.

Baron-Cohen, S. (1995). *Mindblindness: An essay on autism and theory of mind.* Cambridge, MA: The MIT Press.

Baron-Cohen, S., Ring, H., Moriarty, J., Schmitz, P., Costa, D., & Ell, P. (1994). Recognition of mental state terms: Clinical findings in children with autism, and a functional neuroimaging study of normal adults. *British Journal of Psychiatry, 165,* 640–649.

Bates, E., Benigni, L., Bretherton, I., Camaioni, L., & Volterra, V. (1979). Cognition and communication from 9–13 months: Correlational findings. In E. Bates (Ed.), *The emergence of symbols: Cognition and communication in infancy.* New York: Academic Press.

Bernbrock, C. (1977). *An introspective study of second language learning.* Unpublished manuscript, English Department (ESL Section), University of California, Los Angeles.

Bernstein, D.A., Roy, E.J., Srull, T.K., & Wickens, C.D. (1991). *Psychology* (2nd ed.) (p. 473). Boston: Houghton Mifflin.

Blank, M., Gessner, M., & Esposito, A. (1979). Language without communication: A case study. *Journal of Child Language, 6,* 329–352.

Bornstein, R.F. (1992). Subliminal mere exposure effects. In R.F. Bornstein & T.S. Pittman (Eds.), *Perception without awareness: Cognitive, clinical, and social perspectives* (pp.191–210). New York: Guilford.

Brickner, R.M. (1936). *The intellectual functions of the frontal lobes: Study based upon observation of a man after partial bilateral frontal lobectomy.* New York: Macmillan.

Brook, S.L., & Bowler, D.M. (1992). Autism by another name? Semantic and pragmatic impairments in children. *Journal of Autism and Developmental Disorders, 22*, 61–81.

Brothers, L. (1990). The social brain: A project for integrating primate behavior and neurophysiology in a new domain. *Concepts in Neuroscience, 1*, 27–51.

Brothers, L. (1992). Perception of social acts in primates: Cognition and neurobiology. *The Neurosciences, 4*, 409–414.

Brothers, L. (1995). Neurophysiology of the perception of intentions by primates. In M.S. Gazzaniga (Ed.), *The Cognitive Neurosciences* (pp. 1107–1115). Cambridge, MA: The MIT Press.

Brothers, L., & Ring, B. (1993). Mesial temporal neurons in the macaque monkey with responses selective for aspects of social stimuli. *Behavioural Brain Research 57*, 53–61.

Brothers, L., Ring, B., & Kling, A. (1990). Response of neurons in the macaque amygdala to complex social stimuli. *Behavioural Brain Research, 41*, 199–213.

Bruce, C., Desimore, R., & Gross, C. (1981). Visual properties of neurons in a polysensory area in superior temporal sulcus of the macaque. *Journal of Neurophysiology, 46*, 369–384.

Butterworth, G. (1991). The ontogeny and phylogeny of joint visual attention. In A. Whiten (Ed.), *Natural theories of mind*. Oxford: Blackwell.

Byram, M., Morgan, C., & colleagues. (1994). *Teaching–and–learning language–and–culture*. Clevedon, England: Multilingual Matters Ltd.

Campbell, R., Heywood, C., Cowey, A., Regard, M., & Landis, T. (1990). Sensitivity to eye-gaze in prosopognosic patients and monkeys with superior temporal sulcus ablation. *Neuropsychologia, 28*, 1123–1142.

Carroll, J.B. (1965). The prediction of success in foreign language training. In R. Glaser (Ed.), *Training, Research, and Education*. New York: Wiley.

Carroll, J.B. (1981). Twenty–five years of research on foreign language aptitude. In K. Diller (Ed.), *Individual differences and universals in language learning aptitude* (pp. 83–118). Rowley, MA: Newbury House.

Carrol J.B. & Sapon, S. (1959) *Modern Language Aptitude Test*—From A. New York. The Psychological Corporation.

Cartwright, R., & Lamberg, L. (1992). *Crisis dreaming: Using your dreams to solve your problems*. New York: Harper Collins.

Cheney, D.L., & Seyfarth, R.M. (1990). *How monkeys see the world*. Chicago: University of Chicago Press.

Clément, R., Dörnyei, Z., & Noels, K.A. (1994). Motivation, self-confidence, and group cohesion in the foreign language classroom. *Language Learning, 44*, 417–448.

Conti-Ramsden, G., & Gunn, M. (1986). The development of conversational disability: A case study. *British Journal of Disorders of Communication, 21*, 339–351.

Cosmides, L. (1989). The logic of social exchange: Has natural selection shaped how humans reason? Studies with the Wason selection task. *Cognition, 31*, 187–276.

Cosmides, L., & Tooby, J. (1989). Evolutionary psychology and the generation of culture, Part II. Case study: A computational theory of social exchange. *Ethology and Sociobiology, 10*, 51–97.

Coster, W., & Cicchetti, D. (1983). Research on the communicative development of maltreated children: Clinical implications. *Topics in Language Disorders, 13*, 25–38.

Crick, F., & Mitchison, G. (1983). The function of dream sleep. *Nature, 304*, 111–114.

Crookes, G. & Schmidt, R.W. (1991). Motivation: Reopening the research agenda. *Language Learning, 41*, 469–512.

Csikszentmihalyi, M., & Larson, R. (1987). Validity and reliability of the experience-sampling method. *The Journal of Nervous and Mental Disease, 175*, 526–536.

Csikszentmihalyi, M., & Nakamura, J. (1989). The dynamics of intrinsic motivation: A study of adolescents. In C. Ames & R. Ames (Eds.), *Research on motivation in education*, Vol. 3: *Goals and cognitions* (pp.44–71). San Diego: Academic Press.

Damasio, A.R. (1994). *Descartes' error: Emotion, reason, and the human brain*. New York: G.P. Putnam's Sons.

Damasio, A.R. (1995). Toward a neurobiology of emotion and feeling: Operational concepts and hypotheses. *The Neuroscientist, 1*, 19–25.

Damasio, H., Grabowski, T., Frank, R., Galaburda, A.M., & Damasio, A.R. (1994). The return of Phineas Gage: Clues about the brain from the skull of a famous patient. *Science, 264*, 1102–1105.

Damasio, A.R. & Van Hosen, G.W. (1983). Emotional disturbances associated with focal lesions of the limbic frontal lobe. In K.M. Heilman & P. Satz (Eds.), *The Neuropsychology of human emotions: Recent Advances* NewYork: The Guilford Press.

de Sousa, R. (1987). *The rationality of emotion*. Cambridge, MA: The MIT Press.

Devinsky, O., Morrell, M.J., & Voget, B.A. (1995). Contributions of anterior cingulate cortex to behavior. *Brain, 118*, 279–306.

Dörnyei, Z. (1994). Motivation and motivating in the foreign language classroom. *The Modern Language Journal, 78*, 273–283.

Dörnyei, Z. (1996). *Ten commandments for motivating language learners.* Paper presented at TESOL, Chicago, March.

Dunn, J. & Dale, N. (1984). I a daddy: 2 year olds' collaboration in joint pretence with sibling and with mother. In L. Bretherton (Ed.), *Symbolic play: The development of social understanding.* New York: Academic Press.

Edelman, G.M. (1989). *The remembered present.* New York: Basic Books

Edelman, G.M. (1992). *Bright air brillant fire: On the matter of the mind.* New York : Basic Books.

Ellsworth, P.C. (1991). Some implications of cognitive appraisal theories of emotion. In K.T. Strongman (Ed.), *International review of studies on emotion.* New York: Wiley Press.

Erhman, M. (1996). *Understanding second language learning difficulties.* Thousand Oaks, CA: Sage Publications.

Eubank, L., & Gregg, K.R. (1995). "Et in amygdala ego"? UG, (S)LA, and neurobiology. *Studies in Second Language Acquisition, 17,* 35–57.

Fey, M .E., & Leanord, L.B. (1983). Pragmatic skills of children with specific language impairment. In T.M. Gallagher & C.A. Prutting (Eds.), *Pragmatic assessment and interaction issues in language* (pp. 65–82). San Diego: College-Hill.

Frijda, N.H. (1986). *The emotions.* Cambridge, England: Cambridge University Press.

Frijda, N.H. (1987). Emotion, cognitive structures and action tendency. *Cognition & Emotion, 1,* 115–144.

Frijda, N.H. (1993a). Appraisal and beyond. *Cognition & Emotion, 7,* 225–231.

Frijda, N.H. (1993b) The place of appraisal in emotion. *Cognition & Emotion 7,* 357–387.

Frijda, N.H., Knipers, P., & ter Schure, E. (1989). Relations among emotion, appraisal, and emotional action readiness. *Journal of Personality and Social Psychology, 57,* 212–228.

Frisch, K.V. (1967). *The dance-langugage and orientation of bees.* Cambridge, MA: Harvard University Press.

Fujiki, M. & Brinton, B. (1991). The verbal noncommunicator: A case study. *Language, Speech, and Hearing Services in Schools, 22,* 322–333.

Gaffan, D. (1992). Amygdala and memory of reward. In J.P. Aggleton (Ed.), *The Amygdala: Neurobiological aspects of emotion, memory, and mental dysfunction.* New York: Wiley-Liss.

Gallistel, C.R., (1995). The replacement of general-purpose theories with adaptive specializations. In M.S. Gazzaniga (Ed.), *The cognitive neurosciences.* Cambridge, MA: The MIT Press.

Gardner, R. (1985). *Social psychology and second language learning: The role of attitudes and motivation.* London: Edward Arnold.

Gardner, R.C. & MacIntyre, P.D. (1993). A student's contribution to second language learning. Part II: Affective variables. *Language Teaching, 26,* 1–11.

Gehm, T., & Scherer, K.R. (1988). Relating situation evaluation to emotion differentiation: Nonmetric analysis of cross-cultural questionnaire data. In K.R. Scherer (Ed.), *Facets of emotion: Recent research* (pp. 61–77). Hillsdale, NJ: Lawrence Erlbaum.

Goleman, D. (1995). *Emotional intelligence: Why it can matter more than I.Q.* New York: Bantam Books.

Grafman, J. (1995). Similarities and distinctions among current models of prefrontal cortical functions. In J. Grafman, K. J. Holyoak, & F. Boller (Eds.), *Structure and functions of the human prefrontal cortex. Annals of the New York Academy of Sciences,* Vol. 769. NewYork: The New York Academy of Sciences.

Greenlee, M. (1981). Learning to tell the forest through the trees: Unravelling discourse features of a psychotic child. *First Language, 2,* 83–102.

Halgren, E. (1981). The amygdala's contribution to emotions and memory: Current studies in humans. In Y. Ben-Ari (Ed.), *The Amygdaloid Complex,* (pp. 395–408) Amsterdam: Elsevier.

Heywood, C.A., & Cowey, A. (1992). The role of the "face-cell" area in the discrimination and recognition of faces by monkeys. *Philosophical Transactions of the Royal Society of London, B 335,* 31–38.

Hobson, J.A. (1990). Sleep and dreaming. *Journal of Neuroscience, 10,* 371–382.

Hobson, P.R. (1989). Beyond cognition: A theory of autism. In G. Dawson (Ed.), *Autism: Nature, diagnosis and treatment.* (pp. 22–48) New York: Guilford Press.

Hoffman, E. (1989). *Lost in translation: A life in a new language.* New York: Penguin Books.

Hornik, R., Risenhoover, N., & Gunnar, M. (1987). The effects of maternal positive, neutral, and negative affective communications on infant responses to new toys. *Child Development, 58,* 937–944.

Humphrey, N. (1984). *Consciousness regained.* New York: Oxford University Press.

Iverson, J.M., & Goldin-Medow, S. (1997). What's communication got to do with it? Gesture in children blind from birth. *Developmental Psychology, 33,* 453–467.

Jacobs, W.J., & Nadel, L. (1985). Stress-induced recovery of fears and phobias. *Psychological Review, 92,* 512–531.

Joanette, Y., Goulet, P., & Hannequin, D. (1990). *The right hemisphere and verbal communication.* New York: Springer-Verlag.

Kagan, J. (1994). *Galen's prophecy: Temperament in human nature.* New York: Basic Books.

Kaplan, A. (1993). *French lessons: A memoir.* Chicago: University of Chicago Press.

Kling, A., & Brothers, L. (1992). The amygdala and social behavior. In J.P. Aggleton (Ed.), *The amygdala: Neurobiological aspects of emotion, memory, and mental dysfunction* (pp. 353–377). New York: Wiley–Liss.

Klinnert, M., Campos, J.J., Sorce, J.F., Emde, R.N., & Svejda, M. (1983). Emotions as behavior regulators: Social referencing in infancy. In R. Plutchik & M. Kellerman (Eds.), *Emotion: Theory, research, and experience* (pp. 257–285). New York: Academic Press.

Klüver, H., & Bucy, P.C. (1939). Preliminary analysis of functions of the temporal lobes in monkeys. *Archives of Neurology and Psychiatry, 42,* 979–1000.

LaPierre, D., Braun, C.M.J, & Hodgins, S. (1995). Ventral frontal deficits in psychopathy: Neuropsychological test findings. *Neuropsychologia, 33,* 139–151.

Larsen, D.A., & Smalley, W.A. (1972). *Becoming bilingual, a guide to language learning.* New Cannan, CT: Practical Anthropology.

Lazarus, R.S. (1982). Thoughts on the relations between emotion and cognition. *American Psychologist, 37,* 1019–1024.

Lazarus, R.S. (1984). On the primacy of cognition. *American Psychologist, 39,* 124–129.

Lazarus, R.S., Averill, J.R., & Opton, E.M. Jr. (1970). Towards a cognitive theory of emotion. In M. Arnold (Ed.), *Feeling and emotion.* New York: Academic Press.

Lazarus, R.S., & Folkman, S. (1984). *Stress, appraisal, and coping.* New York: Springer-Verlag.

Lazarus, R.S., & Smith, C.A. (1988). Knowledge and appraisal in the cognitive-emotion relationship. *Cognition & Emotion, 2,* 281–300.

LeDoux, J.E. (1986). The neurobiology of emotion. In J.E. LeDoux & W. Hirst (Eds.), *Mind and brain: Dialogues in cognitive neuroscience* (pp. 301–354). New York: Cambridge University Press.

LeDoux, J.E. (1993). Cognition versus emotion, again—This time in the brain: A response to Parrott and Schulkin. *Cognition & Emotion, 7,* 61–64

LeDoux, J.E. (1994). Emotion, memory and the brain. *Scientific American 270,* 50–57.

LeDoux, J.E. (1996). *The emotional brain.* New York: Simon and Schuster.

Leichman, H. (1977). *A diary of one person's acquisition of Indonesian.* Unpublished manuscript, English Department (ESL Section), University of California, Los Angeles.

Leonord, C., Rolls, E., Wilson, F., & Bayliss, G. (1985). Neurons in the amygdala of the monkey with responses selective for faces. *Behavior and Brain Research, 15,* 159–176.

Leslie, A., (1987). Pretence and representation: The orgins of "theory of mind." *Psychological Review, 94,* 412–426.

Leslie, A., & Frith, U. (1988). Autistic children's understanding of seeing, knowing, and believing. *British Journal of Developmental Psychology, 6,* 315–324.

Leslie, A., & Roth, D. (1993). What can autism teach us about metarepresentation? In S. Baron-Cohen, H. Tager–Flusberg, & D.J. Cohen (Eds.), *Understanding other minds: Perspectives from autism.* Oxford University Press.

Leslie, A., & Thaiss, L. (1992). Domain specificity in conceptual development: Evidence from autism. *Cognition, 43,* 225–251.

Levenson, R.W., & Gottman, J.M. (1983). Marital interaction: Physiological linkage and affective exchange. *Journal of Personality and Social Psychology, 45,* 587–597.

Leventhal, H. (1979). A perceptual-motor processing model of emotion. In P. Pilner, K. Blankenstein, & I.M. Spiegel (Eds.), *Perception of emotion in self and others, 5* (pp. 1–46). New York: Plenum.

Leventhal, H. (1980). Toward a comprehensive theory of emotion. In L. Berkowitz (Ed.), *Advances in Experimental Social Psychology, 13* (pp. 139–207). New York: Academic Press.

Leventhal, H., (1984). A perceptual-motor theory of emotion. In L. Berkowitz (Ed.), *Advances in Experimental Social Psychology, 17,* 117–182. New York: Academic Press

Leventhal, H., & Scherer, K. (1987). The relationship of emotion to cognition: A functional approach to a semantic controversy. *Cognition & Emotion, 1,* 3–28.

Lewis, M.C. (1996). Self-organizing cognitive appraisals. *Cognition & Emotion, 10,* 1–25.

Lichtenberg, J.D. (1989). *Psychoanalysis and motivation.* Hillsdale, NJ: The Analytic Press.

Locke, J.L. (1992). Neural specializations for language: A developmental perspective. *Seminars in the Neurosciences, 4,* 425–431.

Locke, J.L. (1993a). *The child's path to spoken language.* Cambridge, MA: Harvard University Press.

Locke, J.L. (1993b). Phases in the development of linguistic capacity. In D.C. Gajdusek, & G. M. McKhann, & C.L. Bolis (Eds.), *Evolution and neurology of language. Discussions in neuroscience,* Vol. 10, Geneva: Elsevier.

Locke, J.L. (1995). Development of the capacity for spoken language. In P.F. Fletcher & B. MacWhinney (Eds.). *The handbook of child language* (pp. 278–302). Oxford: Blackwell.

Lynch, B. (1979). *The adult second language learner: An introspective analysis of an individual learning Spanish as a second language.* Unpublished manuscript, California State University, San Jose.

Mahler, M., Pine, F., & Bergman, A. (1975). *The psychological birth of the human infant.* New York: Basic Books.

Main, M. (1993). Discourse, prediction and recent studies in attachment: Implications for psychoanalysis. In T. Shapiro & R.N. Emde (Eds.), *Research in psychoanalysis: Process, development, outcome* (pp. 209–244). CT: International Universities Press.

Main, M., & Solomon, J. (1986). Discovery of a new, insecure-disorganized/disoriented attachment pattern. In T.B. Brazelton & M. Yogman (Eds.), *Affective development in infancy* (pp. 95–124). Norwood, NJ: Ablex.

Mamelak, A.N., & Hobson, J.A. (1989). Dream bizarreness as the cognitive correlate of altered neural behavior in REM sleep. *Journal of Cognitive Neuroscience, 1,* 201–222.

Maquet, P., Peters, J–M., Aerts, J., Delfoire, G., Degueldre, C., Luxen, A., & Franck, G. (1996). Functional neuroanatomy of human rapid–eye–movement sleep and dreaming. *Nature, 383,* 163–166.

Massimini, F., Csikszentmihalyi, M., & Carli, M. (1987). The monotoring of optimal experience: A tool for psychiatric rehabilitation. *Journal of Nervous and Mental Disease, 175,* 545–549.

McLaughlin, B. (1987). *Theories of second language learning.* London: Edward Arnold.

McTear, M. (1985a). Pragmatic disorders: A question of direction. *British Journal of Disorders of Communication, 20,* 119–127.

McTear, M. (1985b). Pragmatic disorders: A case study of conversational disability. *British Journal of Disorders of Communication, 20,* 129–142.

Mishkin, M., & Appenzeller, T. (1987). The anatomy of memory. *Scientific American, 256,* 80–89.

Murphy, S., & Zajonc, R. (1993). Affect, cognition, and awareness: Affective priming with suboptimal and optimal stimuli. *Journal of Personality and Social Psychology, 64,* 723–739.

Nakamura, K., Mikami, A., & Kubota, K. (1992). Activity of single neurons in the monkey amygdala during performance of a visual discrimination task. *Journal of Neurophysiology, 67,* 1447–1463.

Novoa, O.P., & Ardilla, A. (1987). Linguistic abilities in patients with prefrontal damage. *Brain and Language, 30,* 206–225.

Oatley, K., & Johnson-Laird, P.N. (1987). Towards a cognitive theory of emotions. *Cognition and Emotion, 1,* 29–50.

Ochs, E., Gonzales, P., & Jacoby, S. (1996). "When I come down I'm in the domain state": Grammar and graphic representation in the interpretive activity of physicists. In E. Ochs, E. Schegloff, & S. Thompson (Eds.), *Interaction and Grammar* (pp. 328-369). New York: Cambridge University Press.

Ochs, E., & Schieffelin, B. (1989). Language has a heart. *Text, 9,* 7–25.

Ochs, E., & Schieffelin, B. (1995). The impact of language socialization on grammatical development. In P. Fletcher & B. MacWhinney (Eds.), *The handbook of child language* (pp. 73–94).Oxford: Blackwell.

Ortony, A., Clore, G.L., & Collins, A. (1988). *The cognitive structure of emotions.* New York: Cambridge University Press.

Oxford, R., & Shearin, J. (1994). Language learning motivation: Expanding the theoretical framework. *The Modern Language Journal, 78,* 12–28.

Perner, J. (1991). *Understanding the representational mind.* Cambridge, MA: The MIT Press.

Perrett, D., Hietanen, M., Oram, W., & Benson, P. (1992). Organization and function of cells responsive to faces in the temporal cortex. *Philosophical Transactions of the Royal Society of London, B 335,* 23-30.

Perrett, D., Rolls, E., & Cann, W. (1982). Visual neurons responsive to faces in the monkey temporal cortex. *Experimental Brain Research, 47,* 329–342.

Pinker, S. (1994). *The language instinct.* New York: William Morrow.

Porges, W., Doussard-Roosevelt, J.A., & Maiti, A.K. (1994). Vagal tone and the physiological regulation of emotion. In N.A. Fox (Ed.), *The development of emotional regulation: Biological and behavioral considerations* (pp. 167–186). Monographs of the Society for Research in Child Development. Serial No. 240, Vol. 59, Nos. 2–3, 1994. Chicago: University of Chicago Press.

Pratt, C., & Bryant, P. (1990). Young children understand that looking leads to knowing (so long as they are looking into a single barrel). *Child Development, 61,* 973–983.

Prigogine, I., & Stengers, I. (1984). *Order out of chaos.* New York: Bantam.

Provinelli, D.J., & Preuss, T.M. (1995). Theory of mind: Evolutionary history of a cognitive specialization. *Trends in Neuroscience, 18,* 418–424.

Robbins, T.W., & Everitt, B.J. (1996). Neurobehavioral mechanisms of reward and motivation. *Current Opinion in Neurobiology, 6,* 228–236.

Roseman, I.J. (1984). Cognitive determinants of emotion: A structural theory. In P. Shaver (Ed.), *Review of personality and social psychology: Vol. 5. Emotions, relationships, and health* (pp. 11–36). Beverly Hills, CA: Sage.

Roseman, I.J. (1991). Appraisal determinants of discrete emotions. *Cognition & Emotion, 5,* 161–200.

Roseman, I.J., Anotniou, A.A., Jose, P.E. (1996). Appraisal determinants of emotions: Constructing a more accurate and comprehensive theory. *Cognition & Emotion, 10,* 241–277.

Scaife, M., & Bruner, J. (1975). The capacity for joint visual attention in the infant. *Nature, 253,* 265–266.

Scherer, K.R. (1984). Emotion as a multi-component process: A model and some cross-cultural data. In P. Shaver (Ed.), *Review of personality and social psychology: Vol. 5. Emotions, relationships and health* (pp. 37–63). Beverly Hills, CA: Sage.

Scherer, K.R. (1988). Criteria for emotion-antecedent appraisal: A review. In V. Hamilton, G.H. Bower, & N.H. Frijda (Eds.), *Cognitive perspectives on emotion and motivation* (pp. 89–126). Dordrecht, the Netherlands: Kluwer.

Scherer, K.R. (1993). Studying the emotion-antecedent process: An expert system approach. *Cognition & Emotion, 7,* 325–355.

Schmidt, R., Boraie D., & Kassabgy, O. (1996). Foreign language motivation: Internal structure and external connections. In R.L. Oxford (Ed.), *Language learning motivation: Pathways to the new century* (pp. 13–87). University of Hawaii at Manoa: Second Language Teaching & Curriculum Center.

Schmidt, R., & Savage, W. (1992). Challenge, skill, and motivation. *PASAA, 22,* 14–28.

Schore, A.N. (1994). *Affect regulation and the orgin of the self: The neurobiology of emotional development.* Hillsdale, NJ: Lawrence Erlbaum.

Schumann, F.E., & Schumann, J.H. (1977). Diary of a language learner: An introspective study of second language learning. In H.D. Brown, R.H. Crymes, & C.A. Yorio (Eds.), *Teaching and learning: Trends in research and practice* (pp. 241–249). Washington, DC: TESOL.

Schumann, J.H. (1975). Affective factors and the problem of age in second language acquisition. *Language Learning, 25,* 209–235.

Schumann, J.H. (1976). Social distance as a factor in second language acquisition. *Language Learning, 26,* 135–144.

Schumann, J.H. (1978a). *The pidginization process: A model for second language acquisition*. Rowley, MA: Newbury House.

Schumann, J.H. (1978b). The relationship of pidginization, creolization and decreolization to second language acquisition. *Language Learning, 28,* 367–380.

Schumann, J.H. (1978c). The acculturation model for second language acquisition. In R. Gingras (Ed.), *Second language acquisition and foreign language teaching* (pp. 27–50). Arlington, VA: Center for Applied Linguistics.

Schumann, J.H. (1978d). Social and psychological factors in second language acquisition. In J. Richards (Ed.), *Understanding second and foreign language learning* (pp. 163–178). Rowley, MA: Newbury House.

Schumann, J.H. (1986). Research on the acculturation model for second language acquisition. *Journal of Multilingual and Multicultural Development, 7,* 379–392.

Schumann, J.H. (1994) Where is cognition? Emotion and cognition in second language acquisition. *Studies in Second Language Acquisition, 16,* 231–242.

Schwarz, N. (1990). Feelings as information: Informational and motivational functions of affective states. In R.M. Sorrentino & E.T. Higgens (Eds.), *Handbook of motivation and cognition: Foundations of social behavior: Vol. 2* (pp. 527–561). New York: The Guilford Press.

Skehan, P. (1989). *Individual differences in second-language learning*. New York: Edward Arnold.

Smith, C.A. & Ellsworth, P.C. (1985). Patterns of cognitive appraisal in emotion. *Journal of Personality and Social Psychology, 48,* 813–838.

Smith, C.A. & Ellsworth, P.C. (1987). Patterns of appraisal and emotion related to taking an exam. *Journal of Personality and Social Psychology, 52,* 475–488.

Smith, C.A. & Lazarus, R.S. (1993). Appraisal components, core relational themes, and emotions. *Cognition & Emotion, 7,* 233–269.

Snyder, F. (1970). The phenomenology of dreaming. In L. Madow & L. Snow (Eds.), *The psychodynamic implications of the physiological studies on dreams* (pp. 124–151). Springfield, IL: Charles C. Thomas.

Sodian, B., (1991). The development of deception in young children. *British Journal of Developmental Psychology, 9,* 173–188.

Sodian, B. J & Frith, U. (1992). Deception and sabotage in autistic, retarded, and normal children. *Journal of Child Psychology and Psychiatry, 33,* 591–606.

Solomon, R.C. (1976). *The passions, the myth and nature of human emotion*. Garden City, NY: Doubleday.

Spolsky, B. (1969). Attitudinal aspects of second language learning. *Language Learning, 19,* 271–283.

Stengal, E. (1939). On learning a new language. *International Journal of Psychoanalysis, 20,* 471–479.

Stivers, T. (1995). *Fitting pragmatics into the puzzle: A look at second language acquisition and pragmatic disorders.* Unpublished manuscript. Applied Linguistics Program, University of California, Los Angeles.

Tremblay, P.F., & Gardner, R.C. (1995). Expanding the motivation construct in language learning. *The Modern Language Journal, 79,* 505–520.

Trevarthen, C. (1974). Conversations with a two-month old. *New Scientist, 62,* 230–235.

Trevarthen, C. (1993). The self born in intersubjectivity: The psychology of an infant communicating. In U. Neisser (Ed.), *The perceived self: Ecological and interpersonal sources of self-knowledge* (pp. 121–173). New York: Cambridge University Press.

Trevarthen, C., Aitken, K., Papoudi, D., & Robarts, J. (1996). *Children with autism: Diagnosis and interventions to meet their needs.* London: Jessica Kingsley.

Van Lancker, D. (1991). Personal relevance and the human right hemisphere. *Brain and Cognition, 17,* 64–92.

Waddington, C.H. (1975). *The evolution of an evolutionist.* Ithaca, NY: Cornell University Press.

Walsleben, M. (1976). *Cognitive and affective factors influencing a learner of Persian (Farsi) including a journal of second language acquisition.* Unpublished manuscript. English Department (ESL Section), University of California, Los Angleles.

Watson, R. (1995). *The philosopher's demise: Learning French.* Columbia, MO: University of Missouri Press.

Weiner, B. (1982). The emotional consequences of casual attribution. In M.S. Clark & S.T. Fiske (Eds.), *Affect and cognition: The 17th Annual Carnegie Symposium on Cognition.* Hillsdale, NJ: Erlbaum.

Weiner, B. (1985). An attribution theory of achievement motivation and emotion. *Psychological Review, 92,* 548–573.

Weiner, B. (1986). *An attribution theory of motivation and emotion.* New York: Springer–Verlag.

Wellman, H. (1990). *Children's theories of mind.* Cambridge, MA: The MIT Press.

Weylman, S.T., Brownell, H.H., & Gardner, H. (1988). "It's what you mean, not what you say": Pragmatic language use and brain-damaged patients. In F. Plum (Ed.), *Language, communication, and the brain* (pp. 229–244). New York: Raven Press.

Winson, J. (1990). The meaning of dreams. *Scientific American, 263,* 86–96.

Wittling, W., & Schweiger, E. (1993). Neuroendocrine brain asymmetry and physical complaints. *Neuropsychologia, 31,* 591–608.

Young, A.W., Aggleton, J.P., Hellawell, D.J., Johnson, M., Broks, P., & Hanley, J.R. (1995). Face processing impairments after amygdalotomy. *Brain, 118,* 15–24.

Zajonc, R.B. (1980). Feeling and thinking: Preferences need no inferences. *American Psychologist, 35,* 151–175.

Zajonc, R.B. (1984). On the primacy of affect. *American Psychologist, 39,* 117–123.

Appendix

Language Learning Biographies

Chizu Kanada I

My first experience of the English language came as I was entering junior high school. I was twelve. My mother had bought us, my two little brothers and me, a set of Britannica English learning materials designed for children. I remember them vividly. They consisted of several picture plays, three volumes of adventure stories, a set of folding pictures with accompanying short stories, simulated classroom exercises, songs, and quizzes, and two dozen illustrated story books. Everything came with tapes, and the idea was for us to look at the pictures or read the texts while listening to the tapes.

Except for the illustrated books, most of the material was prepared in Japanese and incorporated English phrases. The stories were set in environments where the characters needed to speak English to survive a variety of adventures. We liked them so much—I remember listening to some of the tapes every day for two months.

With the tapes, listening and speaking skills were emphasized. I recall there being pauses after the English sentences, allowing us to repeat what the recording had just said. My brothers and I often exaggerated the curious sounds (some simply did not exist in Japanese) and would tease each other's clumsy imitations. When I think back on it, these acts of parodying English may well have been our attempt to cover the embarrassment we felt over not speaking the language exactly right. Certainly I was aware that there were some sounds I could not readily reproduce. But I plugged along anyway, and especially enjoyed singing along with the English songs.

I had known from an early age that a language called English existed. This is probably due to the fact that before I was born my mother taught English at a junior high school. To this day she speaks fondly of this experience. I am sure that she had spoken highly of the language and those who learned it, for by the time I entered junior high I was a very enthusiastic young English learner.

I remember being especially fascinated by the way English sounded. This language was pretty; listening to it was for me a musical experience.

My second year at junior high school was an important time (by then I had had about 125 hours of classroom instruction). My English teacher was a real inspiration. For one, his pronunciation was remarkable. He was Japanese, but his English sounded native to my ear, just like the speakers on our Britannica tapes. He told us that as a child he used to go to play at a nearby station of the U.S. Occupation Army. That experience made his language skills all the more fascinating.

The teacher also introduced me to the world of written English. He organized a Pen-pal Club and matched American teenagers with us. I became a member and had a pen-pal in Illinois. (Since then I have seen her twice while in the States, and we still write to each other.) Exchanging letters with her, at an average rate of one a month, was great fun and a wonderful, inspiring way to learn the language. As my list of pen-pals grew (including two in Indonesia), I found it especially fulfilling to use new words and expressions borrowed from the letters of one in writing to another.

During these years, the classroom remained my primary place of contact with the English language. We had four hours of English class a week. We usually went through mechanical vocabulary drills at the beginning of each session, then were asked to translate our textbook sentence by sentence into Japanese, and finally were called on to answer questions from the end of each chapter. We rarely used a language lab. Frankly, I did not find classroom activities particularly engaging, but through hard work I was successful. I also received much encouragement from both teachers and family members.

At senior high school I continued to do well in English class. Since most of this instruction was geared toward university entrance exams, we had to memorize phrases and patterns deemed important (such as "It was not until— that —, "I cannot help — ing," etc.). At the beginning of each session, students were randomly asked to recite the memorized sentences in front of the entire class. I actually found this exercise quite useful because I learned to expand on the assigned sentence patterns by replacing the original words with words of my own choosing. To this day I remember—and use!—many of those patterns.

As with junior high, I continued to supplement my classroom learning at senior high school. At the age of sixteen I began listening to a twenty-minute English conversation lesson on radio. The programme was broadcast every day except Sunday. Keeping up with the routine turned out to be very helpful, for it gave me a chance to listen to native speakers and to learn idiomatic phrases and colloquial expressions. I found that listening to the same skit many times over helped me remember the words and sentence patterns well. I also found that it was easier for me to orally reproduce them once I was used to listening to them. Inspired by the success of this approach, I tried listening to English tapes as I fell asleep at night. This method was advertised as enhancing one's memory of the content. But I did not sustain my commitment long enough to see any advantages.

When I think back on my efforts during these early years of English learning, I realize how few opportunities I had to reinforce what I had learned. I had no need to use English for my daily routine. Although I was performing well in what the junior and senior high school English curriculum demanded of me, I believe the amount and quality of what I actually acquired were minimal given the time I put into learning it. Had my experience with the language remained at this level, my enthusiasm would have eventually waned.

My first opportunity to interact with non-Japanese people came when I was seventeen. The local city office hosted a youth group from what was then West Germany, and my family volunteered to provide a week's room and board for two boys. They were seventeen and eighteen. I was extremely excited. I do not remember how well I communicated with them, but I do remember their English (their second or third language) was much better than mine. But I managed to establish friendships with them. Both the boys and my family enjoyed each other's company.

There was one boy in the group I especially liked. He did not stay with us, but I met and talked with him when all the participants in the program got together to socialize. He played European handball, a game I played passionately every day while in high school. I was excited to know that this completely different-looking young man played the same sport I did. I was eager to talk to him about handball and other things. I found him to be very gentle and thoughtful and I was very much attracted to him. After he left, I started to write to him, and our correspondence lasted for many years.

I feel that, from this point on, the motivation for my language learning moved decisively out of the classroom context and became centered around people. Certainly the prospect of becoming able to communicate with people like my German friend appealed to me immensely. It was at this time that I entered a college in Tokyo. In addition to taking intensive English courses (one of the areas my college specialized in was English), I studiously participated in a number of international functions for youths where I met many non-Japanese, all of whom I recall as being wonderful people.

I spent about seven hours a week in English class at college. Required courses included Text Reading A, Text Reading B, English Composition, English Conversation, and Lab (aural comprehension and pronunciation practices). As well as I did in my courses, however, nothing kept me motivated as much as the prospect of spending my junior year abroad. I had been thinking of this since my first term, and I eventually realized my dream with a fruitful year at an American college. But my first opportunity to use English outside Japan came quite unexpectedly and before my year in the U.S.

At the age of twenty-one I went to Australia with a British organization. We stayed in Australia's Northern Territory for two and a half months and were engaged in excavation projects, the survey and protection of natural and historic resources, providing community services, and the like. It was the first opportunity for me to be immersed in English and to use it quite literally as a survival tool. Here, too, as always, amidst the breathtaking landscapes and thrilling canoe trips, it was the people I met that made the most enduring impression on me. The many friendships I formed convinced me how precious a life tool my English could be.

This experience in Australia dramatically expanded my conception of English and its speakers. It made me see that the United States of America was not the only place where English was spoken. (I had internalized the quick and easy connection so commonly made in Japan between the English language and Americans.) The people I was with were predominantly British, but there were also local Australians including Caucasians, Asian-Australians, and aborigines. They all spoke "English," but differently. This was most striking in their phonological variations. The reality of differences within English was an exciting discovery for me. I wanted to explore the linguistic and cultural forces that might account for such variety.

As soon as I came back from Australia, I was off to the United States. I spent a full academic year there as a visiting student and took courses that could be transferred to my home college in Tokyo. My experience there was of another order entirely from anything I had experienced hitherto. It was such a struggle, so arduous, with just enough fun and consolation to keep me going. But it was also during this year that a breakthrough occurred for me and my English ability. It was about the eighth month that I finally started to formulate English sentences without first translating them from Japanese. In other words, I no longer had to have an entire sentence down perfectly before I spoke it, but rather, I became able to speak as I thought. It was as if English finally became a part of my thought processes.

Until then, I had been "writing" English sentences in my head. I actually visualized each letter of the alphabet in each word of the sentence I was formulating. I would then check for grammatical errors and, finally, produce it orally. This was not a fast process. The final stage of actually speaking was not easy, either, because it required a lot of care to say what I had "written" while adhering to the rules of pronunciation.

This pre-thinking in Japanese was particularly disadvantageous in the classroom context. I would often find that the discussion had moved on to other subjects by the time I was ready to express my ideas. It was excruciating. My self-esteem was badly hurt because I was used to being an articulate student. I would often go to see a writing specialist who ended up being my counselor as well. One day I burst into tears in his office as I was relating to him my problems with English. It was as if all the repressed frustration, depression, and humiliation surfaced all at once. He asked me if I wanted to go home—to Japan. I remember being surprised at my own reaction because my answer was a defiant "no." I definitely wanted to stay, no question about it. After this incident, I learned to let myself burst open every now and then. I was able to make some good friends, a couple of whom were especially supportive and understanding.

When it came time to return to Tokyo, I felt I was leaving just as I was starting to function "normally" in English. I had a clear sense that I was beginning to reach a stage that was critical to my language development. At the very least, I was convinced that I needed to be in an environment where English was the principal mode of thinking and speaking: an everyday necessity. That was why I immediately started to look for ways that would take me back to an English speaking environment. I entertained the possibility of being a waitress at a Japanese restaurant in Bath, England; of becoming a graduate student in English at a British institution; and of undertaking graduate study in comparative literature at a North American institution. As I look back on myself trying to find my way, I realize that English, my second language, came to be an integral part of not only my career choices but also my life path. My passion for English has had such a strong impact on my life; certainly at that particular point it was the central axis of my decision.

In the end, I chose to pursue a modified form of the third path. My two years at the University of British Columbia expanded my active vocabulary and greatly developed my thought processes in English. Learning patterns and a reasonable vocabulary base were gradually established. I learned mostly through reading books, and through classroom exchanges and conversations with friends. I recognized that I acquire new words most easily when I see them in written form and hear them in use, particularly when each encounter is temporally close to the other. I also learned a great deal, with the help of several editors, by writing academic papers and, later, specifically for the past four years, recommendation letters for students I was teaching Japanese to. The latter experience at Smith College and Northwestern University led me to familiarize myself with a range of new vocabulary, such as that of the classroom teacher, the counselor, and the administrator.

Last summer, in my sixteenth year of learning English, I married a wonderful Canadian man. It made me think of how extraordinary the ramifications have been of my learning this second language. And as I get to know my new family, and begin making plans for one of my own, I am sure this linguistic life journey will continue to be as challenging and rewarding as it has always been.

Chizu Kanada II

In this paper, I look analytically at my experiences in learning the English language. It now appears this process was conditioned by stimulus appraisals I made along the way. What follows is my effort to specify their variety and import in light of our reading on second language acquisition.

In undertaking this analysis, I have found K.R. Scherer's (1984) stimulus evaluation model particularly useful. In it, Scherer identifies five of what he calls stimulus evaluation checks. They are novelty, intrinsic pleasantness, goal/need significance, coping potential, and norm/self compatibility. Below I take several episodes, in more or less chronological fashion, from my English language learning experience, and discuss them using Scherer's model as my guide. The principal assumption I make in the paper is that my degree of enthusiasm and length of commitment to learning English have been dictated by these appraisals, and whatever proficiency I have consequently achieved can be adequately accounted for in reference to them.

My earliest appraisal of English was not, strictly speaking, "mine," in the sense that it was made in the determining context of my relationship with my mother. Even before my direct exposure to English, I already had available a persuasively positive appraisal: my recognition of how fondly my mother spoke of her experience as an English teacher. As a young child, I loved and respected my mother dearly. When she spoke highly of something,

I took notice. Over time, I strived to identify myself with her—to be, as it were, like her—and to do the things that commanded her respect. I believe my enthusiastic preparation to confront English was one such early effort. In Scherer's terms, I evaluated the stimulus of the approaching new language in expectation of the good image my mother would hold of me. It seems I thought this would please my mother, my most significant childhood other. At the same time, however, my powerful identification with her made for a variant motivating force not fully accounted for by the positive connotations of enthusiasm. For, my desire to be like her was intertwined with my fear of failing to please her. Preserving my mother's good image of me was perhaps my strongest early motivation, in language learning as in much else.

When at length I encountered the language at school—at the age of 13 in junior high—I found its sounds and sights exceedingly pleasant. The flow of syllables, with their unfamiliar cadence, was pretty. There was a musical quality to it. And I found written forms no less pleasingly novel. I was struck by the mechanics of English writing, moving horizontally from left to right, and by the shapes of individual letters and the strange topography they formed when brought together as words. I was especially fond of the hand-written style of English, so different from the typically squarish shapes of Japanese. I remember proudly showing my English handwriting to my mother, and receiving further encouragement from her. This in turn satisfied my desire to please her, as well of course as allaying my fear of not being able to do so.

As I made progress in junior high school English, I came to evaluate stimuli increasingly in terms of my self and social image in class. From the outset, I had done well in English, and so thought nothing of attempting to maintain high standards. This required a lot of hard work. A cycle of sustained effort, good performance, and further motivation resulted, with each of the three feeding into the others and collectively sustaining my commitment. In terms of my social image, it meant a good deal to appear "smart" in class. I was reasonably good at every subject, but was especially strong in English. English class became an excellent opportunity for me to maintain a high social profile. My ego was flattered and reassured when I was able to answer my classmates' questions as to the meaning or usage of a word. I would work harder not to disappoint what I perceived to be their high expectations of me. Here again, the flip side of this enthusiasm was, of course, the fear of failure. Only now, in this case and thereafter, the motivating place of my mother was being supplemented by the stimuli of a larger social community.

As in junior high, senior high school English continued to be novel (there was no end to the new material) and pleasant (I still liked the way English sounded). I also continued to rely on my achievements there as a source of good self and social image. In the last year or so, however, a different perspective for evaluating stimuli became important to my English learning experience. This was Scherer's goal-significance of learning. I had decided to apply to several colleges whose specialty was English. In order to pass their entrance exams, I needed to study English even harder than before. So I started to supplement high school English with extracurricular activities. This included listening to a twenty-minute English conversation lesson on radio six days a week. From the first this was instrumentally motivated, but I ended up enjoying it immensely. It turned out to be extremely helpful as well.

Another auditory exercise I attempted was listening to English tapes as I fell asleep at night. This exercise was also goal oriented and instrumentally motivated, but my commitment to it did not last long. I have tried to figure out why, and have concluded that a major tool was played by my parents and my subsequent appraisal of their reaction vis-à-vis my coping potential and social or familial image. One of my brothers and I pleaded with our parents to buy us the apparatus for "sleep learning." It was widely advertised as enhancing one's memory of the content of the tapes provided. My parents opposed the idea, first, because they did not believe one could memorize anything while asleep, second, because they were concerned it would interfere with our sleep, and third, because the apparatus was not cheap. In the end, my brother and I set out instead to make do with what we had—a couple of old English tapes and an even older tape recorder. There were problems from the outset. We had no way of making the tape turn off automatically (the apparatus we had wanted came with a timer). But apart from this and other technical difficulties, we were confronted more significantly with our parents' continuing disbelief and discouragement. Our brief encounter with this method bore few fruits, but I believe our parents' negative feedback was decisive in this regard. We decided that this stimulus (our parents' negative evaluation) was beyond our coping capacity. In order to preserve our good image at home, we abandoned the exercise altogether.

The biggest turning point in my English learning career came while I was in senior high school; and yet, like the radio program and sleep learning it had little to do with school per se. This was the one week myself and my family spent in the company of exchange students from Germany. This was my first real opportunity to use my English with non-Japanese speakers of the language. All I had learned in the past five years would be tested. Although I do not believe I thought of it in quite these terms, I was being given the opportunity to assess the results of my efforts to date. My appraisal during and after my performance would determine my subsequent relationship with the English language.

It turned out that I had a wonderful time with our visitors, and, equally important, I realized I could not have done so without my English. It was a revelation to me that I could actually communicate and even establish meaningful friendships in this language. My self-esteem was reassured and my efforts richly rewarded. There was even an unexpected bonus. I met a boy I especially liked and was able to become close friends with him, which reinforced the pleasantness of the experience even more. My appraisal of this stimulus also clarified the goal-significance of becoming a better speaker of English.

At the age of eighteen, I was successful in entering the university of my dreams—Tsuda Juku, an all women's college in Tokyo and a school which promised the most rigorous of English programs. Some comment on the relation between Japanese women and learning English bears mention here, for by entering this school I was distinguishing myself in a very particular way.

English is the foreign language of choice among many Japanese, in terms of general prestige and acceptability. This is held to be especially true for young Japanese women who aspire to a professional life. Somehow the deviation this signals from the traditional-ideal track of becoming "a good wife and wise mother" can be compensated for by the cultivation of special skills such as English. As a young woman studying English at a prestigious Tokyo college, I took advantage of this cultural expectation. I was able to justify my aspiration to obtain a skilled, full-time job by demonstrating excellence in English. In this way I was able to keep my self and social image in high profile, while insuring that the goal-significance of learning the language was legitimated by my community.

While at Tsuda, I spent my junior year abroad at an American college, an experience that was, in important ways, without precedent for me. With the benefit of hindsight, these eight months spent away from mother, family, home school, and home-land amounted to a textbook example of the very first stages of acculturation. I certainly experienced all the classic forms of disorientation, as identified, for example, by Erwin Stengal (1939) and Larsen and Smalley (1972)—namely, language shock, culture shock, and culture stress (see Schumann, 1975). As I contended with the attendant anxiety, frustration, and questioning of identity, I had no choice but to negotiate everyday stimuli as best I could, by making evaluations of them. At one point, in the throes of a crisis so acute an acquaintance suggested I might like to return to Japan early, I had my coping capacity sorely tested. I believed stimuli that brought on crises were nonetheless manageable within the limits of my capacity to cope. Ultimately, that was why I did not pack up and go home, though I also wanted a chance to restore my self-image, and to do so within the context in which it had been damaged.

Fortunately, in the second half of my stay at the college, I came to see more clearly the positive goal-significance of the stimuli, no matter how adverse they felt at times. By then I had gotten a firmer grip on the language, and felt I would be able to ride out the rough parts in order to slowly but measurably approach my goals. With my improved proficiency in English I could also justify feeling better about myself. And so thus emboldened with a restored sense of self-image and an intensified aspiration toward my goals, I was ready from the moment I eventually returned to Japan to go straight back to an English speaking environment. What had begun as a difficult, alienating experience had become something I wanted passionately to extend.

My second phase of acculturation began seventeen months after my return from the U.S. and has lasted six years in all, extending up to the present. I spent the first two of these years at the University of British Columbia where I received an MA in literature from the Asian Studies Department. It was imperative for me to improve my English in order to complete my program satisfactorily. Accordingly, all the stimuli were significant to achieve my goal. Due to this overriding orientation toward the goal, and backed up as always by my fear of failure, I believe I was able to overcome the occasional adversities within my coping capacity. It was also important for me to prove to myself, and to my family and friends, that I was capable of meeting this challenge. In the end, I was successful. By the time I finished my program, I believe my interlanguage had moved significantly closer to my target language.

I spent the next two years of this second phase at Smith College, where I taught Japanese to young American women. The stimuli there concerning English were mostly related to acquiring vocabulary and discourse patterns appropriate to the roles of classroom teacher, counselor, and administrator. I assessed these stimuli positively and was willing to learn my way in hitherto unfamiliar areas of English. Meeting the expectations of my students and colleagues was especially important, for I wanted to be recognized as an approved member of their community. My performance would also determine whether I had a job the following year. This was a powerfully effective source of motivation, and made the notion of fearing to fail very real indeed.

I next moved to Northwestern University and taught Japanese there for two years. I feel that my interlanguage fossilized there because I had less opportunity to use English. My teaching load increased and accordingly my administrative duties decreased, duties which were typically carried out in English. My daily professional interaction tended to be limited to my Japanese colleagues. I was able to fulfill my teaching and counseling responsibilities with the English I had already acquired at Smith, so from a utilitarian point of view, I did not need to improve my language skills. This situation presented me with an interesting dilemma. There was a conflict between my own self-image and the image I wanted my students and colleagues to have of me. In order to enhance my self-image, I wanted to keep improving my English by attending workshops and academic courses. In order to preserve my social image as a devoted teacher, I needed to be fully attentive to my teaching responsibilities. The stimulus was that I did not have enough time to do both. In retrospect, I let my social image override my self-image by giving all my time to teaching. During my final quarter there, however, I allowed myself the luxury of sitting in on a course and being an active participant in the discussions. I suppose I finally found a way to minimally accommodate both desires.

Toward the end of my time at Northwestern I was able to evaluate my four years of full-time teaching as a constructive step toward starting my doctoral study. Thus I am back at the University of British Columbia. I will be setting new goals along the way; and so, my appraisals of stimuli will continue to dictate my experience in this new environment.

In the above, I have tried to analyze my experience of learning English according to Scherer's model of stimulus evaluation. The many variations notwithstanding, it seems I tended to appraise stimuli primarily in light of my coping capacity and self/social image. I believe this proclivity is neither peculiar to me nor a universal experience. Rather I suspect it is fundamentally social in its orientation and needs ultimately to be accounted for, first, in terms of what my particular communities have demanded of me, and second, how I have internalized those demands (with the order here reflecting what I feel to be one of appropriate analytic priority). By way of conclusion I would like to briefly speculate on this important contextual field, and in particular its relation to a predominant motivation in the above narrative: my fear of falling short of community-, and thus, self-expectations. For reasons of space I will limit myself to my experience as a young student in Japan.

Within the community I grew up in, it would be fair to say that the dominant mode of learning was that of competition. Intentionally or not, this was encouraged by both my parents and teachers. As a result, I not only took pride in doing well but that pride became bound up with outdoing others, and generated palpable fears of not being able to do so. I did not have to look far for examples of what failure entailed, especially in my elementary and early high school years before tracking had channeled us in one direction (university) or another (vocations).

I learned I must not become a part of the group said to have failed. In Scherer's model, this socially constructed fear of failure can manifest itself in individuals by strengthening their coping mechanisms or by making them always concerned about their internal and external images. I find these two checkpoints especially salient in my case: my capacity to cope is considerable, as is my concern for my self and social image. Furthermore, this extreme self-consciousness has led me to regularly set ambitious goals for myself, a third checkpoint from Scherer's scheme and one, I believe, of particular significance to the process of learning, for the emergence of this latter might be said to mark the moment where community standards have been fully assimilated. More so, perhaps, than the other points on Scherer's list, the setting of and striving toward goals suggests a particularly deliberate, motivated activity that assumes the framework of broader expectations. In my case, this meant the necessity of succeeding so as not to fail, a lesson I had learned well by the time I began studying high school English.

Commentary

In Chizu Kanada's story there seems to be a general pattern of appraisal that directed her language learning. From the beginning she liked English—its sound in the spoken form and its shape in the written form. This initial positive appraisal, reinforced by her mother's love of the language, led Chizu's efforts to study the language. The efforts resulted in successful learning, which provided an enhanced self and social image. These rewards were motivating and led to additional efforts. Finally a fear of failure—a fear of jeopardizing her social image—provided additional motivational support. This cycle seemed to repeat itself over time and sustained English language learning for the many years necessary to achieve a high degree of proficiency.

Another interesting aspect of appraisal emerged in Chizu's study—the conflicting efforts created by self-image versus social-image appraisals. At Northwestern University she was pulled in different directions by two goals. She wanted to be a good Japanese teacher and those efforts limited the amount of time she could spend improving her English. So for a while she let her social-image goals as a Japanese teacher override her self-image goals as a learner of English. Eventually, however, she brought them into balance by taking the time to actively participate in an English-medium university course.

Susan Rowlands Shrimpton I

One of my favorite memories of a high school Canadian literature course was reading Stephen Leacock's *Sunshine Sketches of a Little Town,* a collection of anecdotes of small town Canada set in the early part of the twentieth century. This book's charm was in its characters whose familiar situations made me think of my own family and friends—of how life's problems seem so important at the time but insignificant in retrospect. In the same way, the stand-up comic is able to recreate everyday life in a way that makes one appreciate how common an existence we all lead. No matter what language we speak, no matter what we wear to cover our bodies, no matter what we put into our mouths to satisfy our hunger, no matter where we live, we all share life. In writing this paper, it occurred to me that my language learning memories are sunshine sketches of many little towns and as Stephen Leacock's stories made me smile (or even occasionally roar with laughter), so do my own.

In my early elementary school years I became aware of languages other than English. Although the neighborhood in which I lived was 99.9% W.A.S.P., I played with the kids who did not compose the majority. I suppose my senses were aroused. We were unable to communicate orally at first, so we learned to communicate through food, art, and play. It seems an unfair exchange today but I'm sure I swapped the mysterious homemade lunches of my friends for penny candy (which was equally mysterious to a child from Kenya or Japan). We whiled away many rainy afternoons drawing and working on various craft projects. I can't really ever remember talking.

French as a school subject began in grade eight. I remember Miss Loweryson, a gentle old woman, who made certain that French was a participatory class. By the third year in her class, we were permitted to work on other subjects' homework or any other activity as long as we carried on small talk in French. My friend Carol became quite proficient in describing her knitting projects in French as Miss Loweryson was also fond of the hobby.

French 11 and 12 were intensive. The courses were challenging, yet I received top marks. I also received a scholarship for my achievements. My teachers were both multilingual and had traveled extensively around the world. Not only were they able to bring languages to life through story, but they made the acquisition process feel worthwhile. They had high expectations for their students though, and conducted rigorous programmes.

After graduation from high school, I spent the summer at the Université du Québec à Trois Rivières at a six-week immersion programme. The *monitrice* assigned to my group made us forget that we were learning French because we were so busy completing "projects." Ginette conducted "lessons" at her apartment where she taught us the fine art of salad preparation (she ate like a bird) and we began to learn the lyrics to Quebec's top 40.

My interest in French dwindled rapidly when I entered an advanced section of a first year French course at the University of British Columbia. As the weeks progressed, I took a seat further and further back in the classroom. The major cause of my lack of interest and self-esteem was the number of students whose spoken French was far superior to mine. By the second month of my second-year university course I moved right out of the classroom to the registrar's office to withdraw. In my second year class, it wasn't the other students who intimidated me that drove me to withdraw as much as it was the mundanity of the grammatical exercises.

In 1985 after graduating from UBC I went to Japan to teach English. I spoke not one word of Japanese. At the time of arrival, I had no intention of studying it, either. That notion changed though by the end of my first day in Japan. I knew that I was going to have to learn to communicate in Japanese in order to survive in the small town in which I had been placed. I hadn't been there 12 hours and I had already failed in communicating with the international operator (who spoke English) and with the salesgirl at Baskin and Robbins where the ice cream flavor signs were printed in English. The day after I moved into my own apartment (about a week after I arrived in Japan), I realized that I was also going to have to learn to read Japanese. Never in my worst nightmares did I imagine that a simple task like buying groceries would result in tears, frustration, and a few missed meals. I returned home determined to master hiragana and katakana in a few days.

The next time I returned to the grocery store with my kana flashcards. I wanted to know what I was buying. No more mistaking miso for peanut butter! I remember my first attempt was sounding out the word "hotcake" which was printed in katakana. The process took several minutes. As I stood in the aisle staring at the box of pancake mix and referring to my flashcards, I was the subject of several people's stares and comments. Even when I managed to make out the sounds "ho-t-to-ke-i-ki," I couldn't figure out what it was immediately. Of course, it finally clicked and I purchased the item. I knew then that learning to read Japanese wasn't going to be impossible. However, in my tremendous excitement, I managed to trip over a young child who was sitting on the floor in one of the aisles of the store. The poor kid wailed at the sight of the huge foreigner by whom he had just been kicked. The mother was very calm about the incident but I felt terrible that I couldn't even say that I was sorry to the child.

I met a Japanese woman who volunteered to teach me Japanese in exchange for assistance in comprehending English news magazines. She was very kind and always brought me some home cooking or information on Japan or Japanese. Unfortunately, I didn't learn much Japanese from her. At that point in my Japanese learning I couldn't understand what she was trying to teach me. When I look back however, I see that she was trying to explain how Japanese verb conjugation can be made simpler by using the 50 sound chart (alphabet chart) as a tool. Four years later, I was shown the chart again and found it a very useful tool. I wondered then how often in my own teaching that I had been teaching over my students' heads.

Tomoko insisted on seeing me even though I'd told her that her Japanese lessons were too difficult for me. Instead she took me places and taught me how to navigate my way around the Kansai area. She would often teach me "chunks" of language as I requested it. I would repeat the chunk until I had mastered it. I remember my first chunk very well: "Would you mind taking my picture for me?" Two years later I formally learned that grammatical pattern and was glad that I already "knew" how to use it.

It is surprising that any foreigners learn to speak Japanese well in Japan. Most of the time, even one's mediocre language ability is instantly rewarded with "Your Japanese is very skillfully spoken!" Most foreigners are aware of these tactics that are meant to keep Japanese a language spoken only by the Japanese, but there are others who are satisfied with acceptable skillful foreigner pidgin Japanese. I was fortunate at work in that my students and colleagues recognized my serious attempt at acquiring Japanese. They would answer my questions (as best as a native speaker can) and encourage my participation in their conversations. One of my students, a housewife in her late thirties, came to me one day and asked me if I wanted to speak Japanese like a foreigner or more like a native speaker. She explained to me what made my language sound so un-Japanese. At first, I was rather insulted that my Japanese sounded so poor when I thought that I was doing well. But I took Eriko's pointers very seriously and made a conscious effort to pronounce syllabic n's and to perfect the Japanese 'r.'

Four months after I arrived in Japan, I took my first trip to Tokyo to visit a friend who was also in Japan teaching English. We had met at a university four years earlier. Lori had arrived in Japan about the same time that I had but when I found her, I was surprised to see how she had adapted her lifestyle to match the neighborhood in which she was living. She had purchased Japanese cooking implements and stocked her kitchen with various Japanese condiments. She'd also been to Yokohama a few times and had learned something about Chinese-Japanese food. I still hadn't overcome my trepidation in eating seaweed flakes or cod roe on top of spaghetti. Lori also had many Japanese acquaintances, many of whom she had met outside of her work, on the streets, in the bars and even in the public bath in her neighborhood. Naturally, Lori's Japanese also reflected her efforts at making her home in Japan. I left Tokyo feeling envious and a little disheartened.

An American friend, who was also struggling to learn Japanese, and I decided to study together regularly every morning before work. The previous night we would memorize dialogues and pattern drills from our text, then, in the morning while out for a brisk walk, we could recite the dialogues and test each other in the drills over and over again. We memorized most of a 30 chapter textbook that way.

As my confidence in my Japanese language abilities grew, I began to venture a little further into the countryside on my days off. Transferring train lines at Nagoya is quite a challenge for a novice. Somehow I found myself in the car of a train that had been sold out and the seat number on my ticket corresponded to a seat which was occupied by a very jolly businessman. I was rather flustered but at least I knew that the train was going to my intended destination. It turned out that I was standing amongst a company trip. (Most companies/offices have a social weekend trip once a year.) It was still morning and this rather raucous group was already dipping into the sake and dried squid. They asked me to join them and offered me a seat. It was a long train ride to Takayama but I managed to speak only Japanese to many different people. My enthusiasm toward my studies doubled.

The more my Japanese improved, the more I went out on my own, the more people I met. I even joined a tennis club where I took lessons and joined tournaments.

One day at the immigration office in Osaka I met a young American to whom I took an instant liking. He was about 6'6", very blonde, and very charming. When we parted, after our long wait in line, we didn't exchange addresses or phone numbers. I didn't have many friends at the time and was sorry that I had let him walk away. I decided to test my Japanese. When it was my turn to approach the counter I explained to the officer that I had been speaking with the young American boy who'd just been served by his colleague across the room and that he had left some important personal papers on the counter. Would he be so kind as to give me a contact number for the young man? I never dreamed that they would reveal personal information but they did. It was almost as if the whole scene had been staged because when I called Andy he wasn't surprised in the least. The reason for including this anecdote is that Andy turned out to be one of my best Japanese teachers. His Japanese was far superior to mine and I learned more Japanese from listening to him speak with native speakers that I had from any textbooks.

In the mid-eighties, Bali was still relatively untouched by the wave of tourists which now infest its hamlets. Many roads were still unpaved and most losmen (inns) did not have electricity or running water. It was during that trip to Bali I traveled alone and met some incredible people. One evening, as the sun was setting over the rice fields and I was writing in my diary, a particularly healthy, elderly Frenchman wearing a backpack and carrying a walking stick in one hand and a "guide Michelin" in the other approached me on the porch of my room. He informed me, in French, that, according to his guide book, I had the best room on the whole island. I was so pleased that I had understood what he said to me. I asked him to join me for some ginger tea. We chatted for a few hours in English and French about our travels and his grandson who had been sending him artwork as he traveled around the world. When I arrived back in Japan a month later, I bought a new French text and cassette tapes and began to watch the French lessons in Japanese on the educational television channel.

No matter where I rested my weary bones in Bali, I was awestruck by the view. Whether it was a view of a lush valley, waves crashing on the shore, or a hedge of hibiscus in full bloom, it moved me to write in my diary, to reflect on my life, more than ever before. I had an opportunity during this trip to find some peace. Perhaps it was my peaceful state of mind, or perhaps it was just a trust in mankind that led me to wander off with strangers to their homes for a meal or to visit their families. I felt privileged to be a part of families of an "ancient" culture, even if for only a few hours at a time. It was a privilege to use the few phrases I had learned with them and to make myself understood to the grandparents.

My third year in Japan I decided to formally enroll in language lessons. For eight months I attended classes every other morning before I went to work. I found that after I would leave a lesson I would begin to hear that day's lesson in the conversations of passengers on the subway. Each lesson opened my ears to new forms and, as a result, introduced them to my own vocabulary.

One of the greatest compliments I received in Japan happened in a drycleaning shop. The clerk had her back turned to me when I entered. I greeted her and talked about the weather while she continued to stand facing away from me. When she finally turned around I thought that she would faint. She managed to catch herself on the counter while saying to me that she thought I was Japanese.

Similar incidences have happened to me in taxis in Japan. It is very important that one know how to give clear directions in Japan as there are no street addresses. On more than one occasion I have hopped into the back of a taxi, reeled off what I thought were clear, simple directions (in Japanese) only to have the driver turn to me and say "no speak English."

After returning to Vancouver two years and eight months later, I enrolled in an intensive summer-session credit course at UBC. It turned out to be eight weeks of grammar translation in class and audio-lingual parroting in the language laboratory. Despite the tediousness of the course, I enjoyed attending class because I was one of the few students who was able to respond the professor's questions or rather dry humor.

I returned to Japan in the summers of 1989 and 1992 to participate in an intensive language program at a language institute. Both summers I lived with families and immersed myself in as much Japanese as possible.

Now, in my second year of motherhood, I am a learner of German as spoken by a caretaker. My dear mother-in-law is determined that mother and son learn her native tongue. My husband encourages us as well.

I consider myself a successful learner of Japanese though I am aware of the language skills which I lack. I wouldn't say that my French has fossilized as, given the opportunity, I would enjoy learning more French. German, of course, is very incomplete but I may just surprise my mother-in-law one day.

Language learning has been an integral part of my personal growth. I will continue to study Japanese and French because I know that improved language facility will make me a more empathetic, understanding person. I do have instrumental motivation for continued language development but that I will have to wait to discuss in the next paper.

Susan Rowlands Shrimpton II

Causal factors for success or lack of success in language learning may be attributed to varying degrees of stimulus appraisal. In the time that is required to achieve near native-speaker proficiency in a language, the learner will encounter a vast range of stimuli, which will be appraised across the entire extent of the positive/negative spectrum.

In this paper I attempt to show how experiences as a language learner and teacher can be analyzed in terms of stimulus appraisals. Using Scherer's (1984) taxonomy of stimulus appraisal, I have categorized the following narratives across spectra of novelty, pleasantness, goal/need significance, coping mechanism and norm/self compatibility (the latter also referred to as self and social image). If educators or researchers are to view learning, more specifically language learning, as cumulative products of stimulus appraisal, then the following narratives should serve to illustrate how personal appraisals operate to foster or inhibit learning. However, in organizing the narratives I had difficulty deciding which category best described each anecdote. Admittedly, category selection is entirely subjective. Nonetheless, I selected categories based on appraisal of associated events and emotions as I remember them today.

I interpreted Scherer's (1984) taxonomy as depicted in Figure A.1.

Novelty

Personal experiences, both as a language learner and teacher, would have me believe that familiarity may be closer to the positive end of the spectrum and novelty closer to the negative end. It may be necessary for the learner and/or teacher, using Krashen's metaphor, to have lowered his or her affective filter before novelty can be appraised positively.

After graduation from high school, I spent the summer at the Université du Québec à Trois Rivières at a six-week immersion program. The *monitrice* assigned to my group spent the early days of the program building trust, security, and a willingness to

+   **—**

NOVELTY · FAMILIARITY
PLEASANTNESS · UNPLEASANTNESS
GOAL/NEED SIGNIFICANCE · · · · · · · · · · · · · · · · · · GOAL/NEED INSIGNIFICANCE
ABILITY TO COPE · INABILITY TO COPE
POSITIVE SELF AND/OR SOCIAL IMAGE · · · · · · · · · · · · · · NEGATIVE SELF AND/OR SOCIAL IMAGE

Figure A.1.

take risks among her students. By the time that she described the degree of interaction with native speakers that would be required in order to complete weekly assignments, we were becoming accustomed to our new surroundings. Although a certain degree of anxiety was always with us, we were able to carry out our projects successfully. Thus, it seemed that facilitating anxiety ameliorated self-esteem and resulted in positive appraisal of the novel language tasks.

As a language teacher I have found that being sensitive to my students' learning styles facilitates productivity and progress. If I begin a lesson with an activity that requires a high degree of interaction, then in order for it to be successful, language expectations must be kept reasonable. Perhaps, what plays a greater role in the success of novel or unexpected language class activities are the variables of length of student/teacher relationship and degree of predictability.

To discuss novelty in terms of my experience as a language learner, I recall a course I took in Japan in the summer of 1989. Tanaka sensei looked like a young college boy the way she wore oversize shirts, the unusual way she smoked cigarettes, and the boyish way she had her hair cropped. As unexpected as the way she looked (for a Japanese woman), she surprised us with her down-to-earth views on society. She taught us, though, as advanced language learners, the importance of speaking the language well. As teachers, if we were to receive the respect normally assigned to the profession, then we should learn to speak like teachers, not like foreign language students. Tanaka sensei was an experienced teacher. For me, what was novel about her lessons were her completely comprehensible grammar explanations. I think that I responded favorably to her unfamiliar teaching strategies, because I found her classes entertaining, informative and immediately transferable. (Further discussed in norm/self compatibility section.)

Pleasantness

If I were asked whether or not the majority of my language learning experiences were pleasant or unpleasant, my initial response would have to be "pleasant." However, after reflecting upon various language experiences in terms of their degree of pleasantness, I realize that I have been motivated by extremely unpleasant circumstances as well.

My initial experiences in junior high school French class were pleasant. My teacher was a kind, gentle old woman, who made certain that French was a participatory class. By the third year in her class, we were permitted to work on other subjects' homework or any other activity as long as we carried on small talk in French. As a result of maintaining a high degree of comfort, self-esteem in French class was high (among members of my group). Toward the end of our third year, we went to Montréal for a 10-day homestay experience. Much to my amazement, my French was superior to my billet's English. This level of French was generally the case for most of our class; however, what our teacher managed to create in three years in the classroom was a similar feeling to that of a family capable of having a good chat over a meal.

In September 1985 I began working for a private language school in Japan. The first few months I was overcome with culture shock. One of the most difficult, ongoing challenges was to learn how to cope as a foreigner in a culture where outsiders are easily recognizable and to come to terms with being "on show" whenever stepping out the front door.

One of my students, Mr. Sato, had been taking private lessons for several years before I arrived in Japan. Mr. Sato came once a week, without fail, to his 8:00 p.m. lesson. Our lessons consisted of negotiated discourse around topics of his choice. As he spoke I would make notes and later, we would review problems with his English. He was a very generous man and would often take me somewhere on Sundays—sometimes with his family, sometimes not. At first, his kindness was a relief. It meant I did not have to negotiate train schedules or admission prices. Mr. Sato took care of everything. Later though, as his generosity began to seem excessive, I started to worry about his motives. I often had difficulty saying no and making an excuse not to go out with him. Mrs. Sato was equally generous. She knit me sweaters, taught me about some of the traditional arts and introduced me to the secret world of Japanese womanhood. However, I did not trust Mr. Sato, even after two worrisome overnight excursions, which I had expected to end in disaster, didn't. We stayed in exclusive traditional inns, in separate rooms. When we were at meals together, we would often overhear conversations in which people speculated as to our relationship. I was embarrassed. He found it amusing. Two years later when I moved to Tokyo, it was easier to distance myself from him but still, from time to time he would call and we would go out for dinner. I asked myself many times, why did I persevere through the continuing uncomfortable situations? Firstly, Mr. Sato introduced me to people and places I would never have seen with anyone else because of his social and financial status. Secondly, from these experiences I learned to appreciate Japan deeply, its culture and its traditions.

Other equally unpleasant experiences revealed aspects of Japan to which most foreigners are not privileged. I befriended the owner of a restaurant located near my office. She took me under her wing like an older sister. When I was lonely, I never hesitated to go to visit her at the restaurant. One night though, the restaurant was busy and she didn't have time to talk with me so I began talking to some men who were sitting around the bar. I was comfortable and felt safe because I was in her restaurant. One of the men asked me if I did any teaching on the side and wondered if I could teach his wife and children. I don't recall exactly how it all happened but one of his children began taking private lessons at the school and I began teaching at his home as well. He asked me to meet him at a sushi restaurant near his office so he could take me to meet his family. He was very late for our meeting so I asked the sushi master if he knew Mr. X (I truly can't remember his name.) He said that his office was upstairs next door. At that time, my Japanese language skills were very minimal. I went next door and knocked on the door. There were a number of rough-looking men sitting around the room. I was frightened but explained that I was looking for Mr. X and that he was supposed to have met me at the sushi restaurant an hour earlier. They told me to go back to the restaurant to wait. He finally did arrive. We had something to eat while we negotiated the schedule and fee for the lessons. Then, he phoned his wife to announce our pending arrival. It wasn't until I sat in the back of his luxurious chauffeur-driven car that I realized what I had done. As I sat on the edge of my seat, I wondered if I could open the door and roll out of the car but, by the time I had formulated my plan, we had arrived at his house. His family and house seemed very normal, all of which caused me to reanalyze my ear-

lier assumptions. However, after noticing the missing digit on
Mr. X's left hand, I reaffirmed my fear. How was I going to get out
of the commitment I had made? I went to his house once a week
to teach English to his wife and children. I saw and heard things
I knew could get me into a great deal of trouble. Every week I
dreaded going there. If I had quit though, I didn't know what
would have happened so I was very careful not to reveal any personal information to his family. Unexpectedly, after six months,
his wife phoned me and asked me not to come anymore. I'm
almost certain that her husband had been murdered. I read in
the paper about a shooting at the building behind the sushi restaurant where we had negotiated our lessons. As I struggle to
remember specific lessons with Mr. X's family, I remember how
diligently I studied during those six months in order to plead my
innocence should I ever have found myself in a dangerous situation. I knew that language could literally save me.

Other awkward, unpleasant situations further prompted me
to return to my daily studies. One incident involved a medical
doctor who excessively patronized me during a consultation due
to my gender, race, and lack of language ability. Another involved
a police officer and a locksmith who were amused that someone
had broken into my apartment and hadn't bothered to steal any
undergarments.

The following anecdote lies more to the center of the pleasantness spectrum. After returning to Vancouver, I realized that
emotions are all relative and that I could put up with a tremendous amount of unpleasantness in order to accomplish something. I enrolled in an intensive summer-session credit course in
Japanese at the University of British Columbia. As indicated in
the previous essay, it turned out to be eight weeks of grammar-
translation in class and audio-lingual parroting in the language
laboratory. Despite the tediousness of the course, I enjoyed
attending class because I was one of the few students who was
able to respond to the professor's questions or rather dry humor.
It was a game. The professor would saunter in each morning in
his dark, somber suit and ask one of the students, who he knew
couldn't answer even a simple question, what he had for breakfast or what time he went to bed or some such question. The
three of us who had spent time in Japan and who could have
answered any of his inane questions were never called upon.

That was the extent of conversation in Dr. Mori's class. The remainder of the period was spent writing our Japanese translations on the chalkboard and then analyzing them for grammatical correctness. Near the end of the course, Professor Soga decided that there would be an oral component to the final examination and that we would be asked to respond to questions about one of the chapters in the textbook in a private interview. This development came as quite a surprise to the entire class, as we hadn't been asked to open our mouths except to describe the morning repas. Even we, the three cocky students who had challenged Dr. Mori all summer, felt intimidated. I also felt partially responsible for the sudden shift in plans. Nevertheless, I accepted Dr. Mori challenge and performed very well. I wonder now, if he had made it easy for us, if I would have performed as well or learned as much that summer?

Goal / Need Significance

When I lived in Japan, in rural Japan, I needed to read in order to survive. Shopping for groceries was a task I put off until I had several hours available to tackle it. At the market across from the school where I taught, the vendors even displayed prices in Chinese characters (instead of Arabic numerals, common in most shops). At the train station, destinations were only written in Chinese characters (except for major stations such as Osaka and Kyoto). So, in my free time I studied passionately. I copied letters over and over. Everywhere I went I carried my notebook in which I wrote down all the words I needed to know how to read. I would sit on the train and stare at signs wondering what they meant.

Learning to cope in my neighborhood was an a immediate goal. I wanted to become a member of Nawate-cho. I didn't want to seem mysterious or cause passersby to fall off their bicycles into the ditch as they inattentively rode past me on the street. So I made a concerted effort to familiarize myself with the local shops and shopkeepers. I bathed at the local public bath instead of in my cramped quarters. I watched the neighbors to learn when and how to air my futon, display my laundry, and maintain the entrance area of my apartment. I also strove to identify words in the local dialect. I didn't want to be a spectacle. In itself, that was enough to keep me studying daily.

An anecdote recounted in the first essay illustrates how I was able to satisfy many goals simultaneously: communicating with the immigration office, making a friend, and significantly improving my language skills. One day at the immigration office in Osaka I met a young American to whom I took an instant liking. He was about 6'6", very blonde, and very charming. When we parted, after our long wait in line, we didn't exchange addresses or phone numbers. I didn't have many friends at the time and was sorry that I had let him walk away. I decided to test my Japanese. When it was my turn to approach the counter I explained to the officer that I had been speaking with the young American boy who'd just been served by his colleague across the room and that he had left some important personal papers on the counter. Would he be so kind as to give me a contact number for the young man? I never dreamed that they would reveal personal information but they did. It was almost as if the whole scene had been staged because when I called Andy he wasn't surprised in the least. The reason for including this anecdote is that Andy turned out to be one of my best Japanese teachers. His Japanese was far superior to mine and I learned more Japanese from listening to him speak with native speakers than I had from any textbooks.

In my third year in Japan I decided to enroll formally in language lessons. For eight months I attended classes every other morning before I went to work. I found that after I would leave a lesson I would begin to hear that day's lesson in the conversations of passengers on the subway. Each lesson opened my ears to new forms and, as a result, introduced them to my own vocabulary. For a while, I became obsessed with trying to understand. I carried a tape recorder and notebook everywhere. Later at home or with a Japanese friend, I would analyze my tapes and notes. For me, the rewards of becoming an excellent speaker of Japanese were within my grasp.

Coping Potential

As I examine my history of French instruction, I am disappointed by the tremendous power of my negative appraisal of university French courses. Though I had been successful in junior high French and was able to meet the challenges of senior high French, my interest dwindled rapidly when I entered an advanced section of a first-year French course at the University of British Columbia. As the weeks progressed, I took a seat further and further back in the classroom. The major cause of my lack of interest and self-esteem was the number of students whose spoken French was far superior to mine. Though I was able to complete the daily assignments without much difficulty, when it came time to review the assignments in class I became confused and frustrated amidst my more proficient peers. By the second month of my second year, the frustration was enough to send me to the registrar's office to withdraw. I couldn't cope with the difficult grammatical exercises when we were expected to analyze them orally. Several years later I realized that instead of withdrawing, I could have moved to an easier section. At the time, however, I couldn't leave the course fast enough.

Perhaps it was the culture shock of la classe française that drove me to quit. I wonder what was different four years later that allowed me to persevere through culture shock in Japan. My first day was enough to drive even a moderately experienced traveler back to the airport but unfortunately the story is far too long to include in this paper. I didn't speak one word of Japanese. At the time of arrival, I had no intention of studying it, either. However, that notion changed by the end of my first day. I knew that I would be obliged to learn to communicate in Japanese in order to survive in the small town in which I had been placed. As mentioned in the first essay, I hadn't been there 12 hours and I had already failed in communicating with the international operator (who spoke English) and with the salesgirl at Baskin and Robbin's where the ice cream flavor signs were printed in English. Never in my worst nightmares did I imagine that such simple tasks would result in utter failure. Nonetheless, my inability to cope drove me to start studying Japanese the next day.

I learned to cope in functional situations quite quickly. My next challenge was to learn to cope in social situations. As confidence in my Japanese language ability grew, I began to venture a little further into the countryside (away from other foreigners and contact with English). I even managed to arrange tickets and make reservations at a travel agency quite early in my language experience. When I traveled I made an effort to talk to strangers. When I went on overnight trips, I stayed at Japanese-style inns where I was forced to share a table at meal times. Each interaction, with its varying degree of success, was a positive experience. I was learning that I could cope with the language and the culture.

Learning to cope in Japan as a white person means learning to cope with the appellation "gaijin." Literally, the word means "outside person." Usually it is accompanied by a pointed finger and even sometimes by such phrases as "this is a pen." This is culture shock. Why would anyone point and say such a stupid thing as "this is a pen"? It took me a long time to understand that being called a "gaijin" wasn't derogatory. The process of learning to cope with the appellation, however, took me deeper into understanding the culture and the language.

Norm / Self Compatibility (Self / Social Image)

Negative norm/self compatibility appraisals have often led to extreme responses. Another way to analyze my university French experience is that I had always been an "A" student. Without the oral skills, it wouldn't have been possible for me to obtain an "A" in second year French; therefore, I withdrew. Similarly, when students correct their teachers, it can be appraised as a challenge to the teacher's status. When a student corrected my Japanese pronunciation, it lead to obsessive practice until the sound was mastered. Furthermore, when I recognized that a colleague had begun the acculturation process long before I even realized that acculturation would be necessary to survive in Japan, I jumped feet first into every cultural and language opportunity I could find. In order to combat my temporary inferiority, or lack of self and social image, I did crazy things like memorize pages and pages of dialogues in texts or initiate conversations or arguments which I knew I couldn't entirely manage (just for practice).

Then there is the story of my next door neighbor in Nawatecho who was a high school English teacher. However, I wasn't privy to this information until one of his students approached me one afternoon to ask me how I would evaluate his English teacher's oral ability. I can't say I blamed the teacher for not revealing his profession to me. Had I been in his situation, I probably would have done the same thing. I never attempted to speak to my next door neighbor in English.

As described in my first paper, one of the greatest compliments I received in Japan happened in a drycleaning store. The clerk had her back turned to me when I entered. I greeted her and talked about the weather while she continued to stand facing away from me. (She was ironing.) When she finally turned around I thought that she would faint. She managed to catch herself on the counter while saying to me that she thought I was Japanese. Similar incidences, yet appraised on the opposite end of the spectrum, have happened to me in taxis in Japan. It is very important that one know how to give clear directions in Japan as there are no street addresses. On more than one occasion I have hopped into the back of a taxi, reeled off what I thought were clear, simple directions (in Japanese) only to have the driver turn to me and say "no speak English." I suppose these are examples of "matched guise reality." Nevertheless, both the positive and negative feedback of my language skills were appraised positively by me. If the taxi driver had responded with a simple positive response, it wouldn't have given me the opportunity to interact with the driver.

A sense of eerie bilingualism haunted a bar I frequented in Tokyo. The first time I visited the bar I asked my friends (who were German) why they were the only Germans at the establishment. They weren't. Almost all of the bar's clientele were German professionals who were in Tokyo on business. I was shocked because I couldn't detect any German accent in their English. This level of pronunciation and intonation was positive reinforcement for my encounter with the drycleaning lady. It was possible that I could have sounded like a native speaker of Japanese.

I returned to Japan in the summers of 1989 and 1992 to participate in intensive language programs at a language institute. Both summers I lived with families and immersed myself in as much Japanese as possible. One of my goals while participating in Japanese courses after I had become a Japanese teacher was to master teacher-talk in Japanese. I often silently criticized my colleagues who taught Spanish or French in English. I wanted to be a better teacher. So, during class, I recorded pertinent expressions and speech styles. Tanaka sensei (mentioned in the first section of this paper) is the model I strive to emulate. She spoke to her students (and not all of them were teachers) with tremendous respect. She used honorific forms with ease which made it less difficult for her students to attempt to reply with due respect. Those of us who understood Tanaka sensei also managed to comprehend her tongue-in-cheek attitude about the excessive nature of Japanese honorifics.

Conclusion

Various degrees of completeness and incompleteness in personal language learning experiences can be attributed to positive, not entirely negative and negative appraisals of stimuli in language environments, which, to me, is an unexpected conclusion. Before writing this paper I would have assumed that positive stimulus appraisals resulted in learning and negative stimulus appraisals resulted in avoidance of the stimuli. As a pedagogue, this realization is a relief. It would indicate that it may not be necessary to please all of the students all of the time, which, as any teacher is aware, is impossible. As a language learner, realizing that less than positive appraisals may lead to deeper learning, reinforces my basic system of beliefs. As a researcher, it suggests alternate methods of analyzing subjects' narratives, responses in questionnaires, and interviews.

Commentary

Rowlands Shrimpton's analysis reveals several interesting things. She indicates that novelty may contrast with familiarity and that either response can be positive or negative. Her experience leads her to suggest that a good student-teacher relationship may be required before novel teaching practices will be appraised positively. Novelty in her Japanese class was valued positively when it made classes entertaining, informative, and usable. So, it appears that she valued novelty when it facilitated achieving her goals, when it was compatible with her coping abilities, and when it was enhancing of her self and social image.

In general, positive appraisals generate motivation that produces effort leading to learning. Negative appraisals generally result in withdrawal and diminished learning. Rowlands Shrimpton shows, however, that for her, situations appraised as unpleasant could be tolerated to achieve desired outcomes. In her relationship with Mr. Sato, she risked and worried about undesired sexual advances, but maintained the relationship because it provided access to Japanese culture and furthered her language learning goals. With Mr. X, fear kept her involved and motivated her to study so that she could explain herself if she were to get into trouble because of the situation. Rowlands Shrimpton was able to put up with a tedious Japanese class at UBC when she was one of the best students in the class. However, she dropped a French class when she found it difficult and feared receiving less than an A. Thus, it appears that she could also tolerate unpleasantness when the tasks were within her coping abilities, but she found situations where she had difficulty coping threatening to her self/social image and, in the case of the French, withdrew. Her experience shows that positive does not always mean pleasant. A language learning experience might be appraised negatively in terms of pleasantness but might be assessed positively on any of the other appraisal dimensions.

Donna Mah I

Being of Chinese extraction I was fortunate to have been exposed to two languages since childhood. Perhaps this early exposure of English and Chinese nurtured my love of languages and the desire to pursue them.

My language studies have included French, German, Mandarin, and Cantonese. I have enjoyed studying each and every language that I have attempted. Sadly however, I cannot yet claim advanced oral proficiency in these foreign languages, but it remains as one of my goals to be functionally trilingual at some point. By functionally trilingual I mean that I would like to be able to communicate intelligently in two languages other than English with native speakers, both in countries where the target language (TL) is the official language and also with foreigners that come to Canada. Oral proficiency is my main objective, however, the ability to read TL newspapers is also desired. Genuinely optimistic, this learner feels very strongly that this objective should not be entirely unattainable.

It is my belief that the most powerful language learning occurs when the learner has access, and possibly subsequent membership, to a target language community. My immersion experiences in Beijing, China, were the most effective language learning experiences that I have had to date. The two consecutive summers (July 1991 and July 1992) that I spent studying Mandarin in Beijing saw my level of language competence rise far beyond its then semi-fossilized status.

To give the most complete picture of my profile as language learner, I have included all of my language experiences to date, from early childhood to the present.

As a fourth generation Chinese-Canadian, English is my native language. I do not recall any discussions or negotiations related to a choice of which language would prevail in our home, since my parents were both born and schooled in Vancouver and almost everyone around us spoke English. In addition, Cantonese (Taishan dialect) was spoken by my parents and grandparents from time to time and I understood whatever I heard, but I did not have to produce much Chinese speech myself. The Chinese that I heard spoken in the home consisted mostly of utilitarian phrases and commands instructing me to perform routine tasks or voicing caution from time to time. The nature of the dialogues came to be predictable and fairly standardized.

I never received any formal Chinese language instruction as a child and my attempts to communicate with my grandmothers, when left alone with them, were a form of very poor broken-Chinese on my part that matched their equally poor broken-English. I rarely spoke to them using only English. I respected that their command of English was very limited, so I tried my best to use what little Chinese I could, whenever I was called upon. Our interactions included a lot of laughter and exaggerated gestures, but we were usually able to get the necessary messages across to each other. It goes without saying that I did not attempt to use my personal dialect of spoken Chinese outside the home, but I continued to understand most of what I heard around me at family gatherings and when we went to Chinatown. Chinese language studies did not commence until my third year in university, at which time I studied Mandarin.

My first formal language study began in grade eight. At that time, French was a required subject for grade eight and nine and could be pursued as an elective up to grade twelve. I enjoyed the classes, especially memorizing dialogues and performing them with others. The grammar studied, i.e., verb conjugation and memorizing grammatical rules, was uninteresting but nonetheless achievable by doing regular (and sometimes irregular) homework. Tests were usually of the fill-in-the-blank variety and I recall scoring quite well. Marks attained were often As or Bs and language learning at this juncture was a positive experience.

I continued my French studies up to second-year university where reading literature was the focus. I did not really enjoy this aspect of studying French and as a result (or was this the cause?) did not score as well as in my previous French classes. Subsequently, I decided to end my study of French after my second-year course was over. In retrospect, I think that if I had enrolled in the conversation classes at university I would have been more likely to continue with French or at least, would have gained more confidence to speak French now.

In dropping French as an undergrad program elective, I now had a space in my timetable to fill for the following year. I enrolled in Beginner's German in the summer of 1978, and studied for six weeks, three hours each day. Once again, I recall memorizing new vocabulary and sentence patterns each day with relative success. In fact, I scored second highest (89%) in the class of seventeen students. The instructor later informed me that the person with the highest mark was someone with previous German experience. She encouraged me to continue with my study of German, but to date, I have not chosen to do so.

The following summer, I elected to study my own heritage language, i.e., Chinese. My first choice would have been to study Cantonese, since that was the language that was predominantly spoken by the Chinese community in Vancouver at that time. Unfortunately, only Mandarin, the official language of mainland China, was offered and so began my next language journey. Studying Chinese at the age of nineteen was influenced, in part, by my Chinese ethnicity. Finally learning the language of my ancestors was exciting for me.

The intensive Mandarin course, for double course credit, was nine weeks long, six hours a day, five days a week. It was hard work! Nevertheless, it was obvious that the students who did not appear to have any previous affiliation with anything "Chinese" were much more disadvantaged than students like me. In fact, even students who spoke Cantonese before this course, seemed to struggle much more than me! While practicing the daily tone drills, I remember how happy I felt that my TL pronunciation was pure; without influence or contamination from Cantonese.

I also recall that I struggled to learn twenty to twenty-five new characters each night while Cantonese speakers had to relearn the traditional characters in the new modified form. This was another area of confusion for some of the native Cantonese speakers. Having no previous experience with Chinese characters myself, this aspect of Chinese was mastered only after many grueling hours of dedicated practice.

Some of the basic grammatical aspects of the language were easier for me to understand than my non-Chinese peers as well. I attribute this to the fact that I had possibly stored some sentence and word-order patterns from my early childhood experiences. Composing simple sentences in the beginning stages was not much of a problem for me although it was an area that required a lot of repetition for the other nonnative speakers of Chinese.

I scored 86% in that intensive beginners' Chinese course and once again felt validated by the experience. At that time, I was able to read and write Chinese as well as speak and understand native speakers at an advanced beginners' level. When I traveled to China the following summer, in 1980, I was very pleased with the response that I received. My positive experiences from that encounter, not only with the Chinese language, but with China itself, established a strong desire within me to return to Beijing to further my Mandarin studies.

In Vancouver in the early 1980s, there were very few opportunities to practice speaking Mandarin, and even though I tried to use the language when I went shopping in Chinatown, the responses were usually less than favorable. Most businesses continued to use Cantonese and I felt somewhat discriminated against in more than a few instances, so I decided to try learning Cantonese. After two six-week sessions of night school, I was able to order in a restaurant, be served "in turn" at a bakery without being passed over and was even bold enough to ask for a discount at one particular establishment that favored Cantonese customers over Canadians. With this accomplishment, I chose not to pursue any more Cantonese and did not generally regard my Cantonese study as an important one. The more interesting challenge for me is to continue studying Mandarin.

The government of this province began sponsoring studies of Asia Pacific languages and culture in 1989 and by then I was eager and had time to resume my Mandarin studies. I participated in several language immersion weekends and enrolled in a conversation class at the local university in the summer of 1990. With this refresher course, I was able to regain my advanced beginner's status in the area of spoken Mandarin. The written aspect of the language was not emphasized.

In July of 1991 and in 1992, I pursued my Mandarin studies with other Canadian teachers in Beijing at the Beijing Language Institute. I was ecstatic that my dream to return to China's capital to study Mandarin was realized two years in a row! It was in these two months, particularly in the second year, that I spent in China, that my level of competence increased the most. During that second summer of study, I happily ventured out on my own and was able to negotiate my way around the city with some degree of confidence.

Upon my return to Vancouver, many of my native-speaker acquaintances commented on the noticeable improvement in the fluency of my speech. In the second year of teaching Mandarin to my Canadian students, I was able to include many more immersion-type strategies in my teaching as well.

Presently, as stated at the outset of this paper, I still cannot claim to have achieved the advanced level of oral proficiency in Mandarin that I would like. It remains as one of my goals to be a more fluent (and possibly literate) Mandarin speaker at some point in the future. To achieve this end most efficiently, I feel that an extended period of time (one to two years) living in Beijing would probably be the most effective course of action.

Donna Mah II

Learning languages in addition to my native language, English, has been an ongoing endeavor for most of my life. The degree of success that has been achieved in each language ranges from very minimal to very good. I feel that my Chinese Canadian background has had something to do with the level of proficiency that has been attained in each language that I chose to study. This essay will analyze my language learning experiences in terms of what factors contributed to the positive and negative appraisals of each situation, which, in turn, influenced the eventual outcomes of each foreign language I attempted to learn.

My exposure to two languages in the home may have influenced my attitudes about language learning in general. As listed in the first paper, English was my first language, however, Cantonese was heard as well. The fact that I mastered English as my native language and achieved only listening comprehension of the second would support the notion that English was appraised more positively than Cantonese. English was perceived as the one that would help me have my goals and needs met. In addition, my school and larger community environment, i.e., a suburb of Vancouver, was comprised of mostly native English speakers. My self and social image was very much constructed in an English-speaking world.

I lived and spoke English; however, the fact remains that I was exposed to another language from birth. The point that is puzzling to me is that I never acquired any oral proficiency in Chinese as a youngster. It is possible that I never actually received enough input.

Nonetheless, I believe that this experience of hearing a language in addition to English contributed to my subsequent attitudes about foreign languages and studying them. I was not embarrassed by my grandmothers who spoke Chinese to me in front of my peers; neither did I not wish to speak Chinese with them. In fact, I remember that one of my grandmothers would often sit with me and we would pore over simple Chinese word books. The laughter that accompanied our times together was very much of the sort described by Stengal (1939) when children enjoy the meaning-making aspect of a foreign language likened to playing games and dressing-up. My encounters with Cantonese in this context, were self-appraised as novel and pleasant and, as such, were enjoyed as games. The encounters with this one grandmother in particular, were positive and playful, but not very frequent. She lived with my family several weeks or months at a time and moved around to live with her other sons' and daughters' families throughout the year. My childhood language encounters to age 12 were mostly of this informal and unstructured nature.

Conscious decisions regarding language studies were realized when I decided to pursue a university education. French 12 was one of the prerequisites for admission. However, my second-class standing (C+) in French at the end of my second year of study in university affected my grade point average and ultimately lowered my overall social and self-image. Furthering French studies at that time was appraised as negative. When my attitude toward studying French was no longer positive, less cognition resulted from lowered levels of interest and attention to the language stimuli. It is difficult to ascertain if the lack of progress was due to the negative stimulus appraisals or vice versa. In addition, the study of French no longer appealed to me in that its relevance was no longer perceived to be significant to meet any immediate goals or needs. Further, the chances that I would encounter French speakers in Vancouver or that I would go to a French-speaking country were slim.

When French was dropped, German became my next elective. The possibility of future travel to Europe played only a minor role in my choosing German as my second foreign language choice, but the desire to achieve good grades was uppermost in my mind. To further ensure success, I decided to fulfill my elective requirement in the summer session without the pressure of my regular course-load. By freeing up time and space in my fall timetable, I was able to concentrate on more music courses in the fall. The decision to take German in the summer also served to help me cope with my major music work-load in the regular term and improved the probability that I would be able to attain better grades.

I applied myself diligently to my summer German studies. The high grade that I attained had a positive effect on my grade point average and my positive self-concept for studying languages was restored. The success was probably also the result of primarily cognitive processes. At 19, I was able to analyze the simple language concepts and grammar that were presented. New vocabulary was memorized nightly and conversations were learned through textbook dialogues. Aural and oral skills that had been refined in my previous Cantonese and French experiences seemed to contribute positively to my German success as well.

My success as a language learner may also have been facilitated by my background in music. Ear training that developed auditory skills was one of the components of my music education from the beginning stages (age 8). Because many of the beginning language skills were taught aurally, my ear-training experiences seemed to help me hear the subtleties in languages with relative ease.

Following my summer of German, I chose to complete my next year's elective requirements in the same manner, for the same reasons. Chinese was chosen first and foremost for the simple reason that it was a six-credit course and I needed six credits! As outlined in my earlier paper, Mandarin, instead of Cantonese was the only Chinese language available to me so it was the one I chose. As luck would have it, I was extremely successful once again! The mark that I obtained was high enough to raise my grade point average for my final year and I graduated with a first-class degree in Music.

What we are beginning to see evolving from this analysis is that my study of foreign languages has less to do with integrative orientations toward the people that speak foreign languages, but seems to be a result of how I chose beginning language courses as the means to completing requirements for my undergraduate degree with as little strain as possible. I have to admit that there appears to be no other conclusion to be drawn from these examples but that I had calculated a sophisticated coping system that would meet specific goals while adding to my positive self-concept as well. I was operating from very strong instrumental motivations.

However, I need to reclaim at least a portion of my integrity now with regard to my subsequent language studies, following the attainment of my degree. Setting aside almost everything that was involved with my Bachelor of Music degree, I continued to pursue Mandarin and Cantonese language studies for reasons distinctly unrelated to the previous motivations.

My initial goal in studying Mandarin was to obtain a good mark that would enhance my grade point average. This instrumental motivation to do well was encouraged early in the course as I demonstrated that I had some innate abilities (possibly aptitude) to reproduce the phonetic codes required. My musical ear training may also have contributed to this aural strength.

As my proficiency increased, my performances were appraised by my teachers as good to very good. The initial instrumental motivation began to shift to an integrative orientation. I began to think that some of the success that I was experiencing must have been related somehow to my Chinese background (causal attribution). The more Mandarin success that I achieved, the more I strived to become more "Chinese."

This notion that I might be able to use Mandarin to integrate with other Chinese people was an area that I felt worth exploring. I attached a positive value to this concept. In reality, Mandarin was not the Chinese language of many Canadians at that time (1979), and so I was not actually able to use Mandarin for gaining access to the target language group. Nonetheless, the positive validation that I received in the course, contributed much to my self-image as a Chinese Canadian, and I completed my beginners' course knowing that I would probably continue this language study at another time.

Studying the Mandarin language was also appraised positively by myself and others, for its status in ancient times. Historically, Mandarin was the language reserved for the highest officials in the imperial court. My parents endorsed this aspect of my Mandarin studies. There was an implied "elitist-upper-class" connotation that went with the language.

My pursuits to master a Chinese language have been influenced by a myriad of complex stimulus appraisals as outlined above, since my first Mandarin course in 1979 to the present, as I continue to strive for advanced oral proficiency in Mandarin. From my initial desire to affiliate with Chinese Canadians, I have shifted 180 degrees and no longer desire to master Cantonese, the language used originally in Vancouver: I now pursue Mandarin instead. Here then, is my interpretation of how this shift evolved.

In 1980, I traveled to Hong Kong and China. The language spoken in Hong Kong is Cantonese; in China it is Mandarin. That experience helped me to decide which language would become my Chinese language of choice.

In Hong Kong, I was nothing. I did not feel that my outward appearance identified me easily as a foreigner, but I could not speak Cantonese and therefore could not negotiate a thing in Hong Kong. English, at that time, did not serve my purposes any better. (Fortunately I was traveling with a group of people that did speak Cantonese and so I was able to go out with others that did not have this same difficulty.) I remained an outsider for the duration of my stay there. This feeling of utter helplessness would stay with me for a long time. The barrier that was between me and the Chinese people in Hong Kong was very negative. My self and social concept was appraised so negatively at that time, that to this day, I still do not desire to return to Hong Kong. I do not wish to acculturate with people in Hong Kong that speak Cantonese!

My experience in China was quite a different matter. First of all, I was immediately recognizable as a foreigner and so did not feel the need to "fit" myself into the landscape in the same way. It was a pleasant experience with a certain degree of excitement. I was able to communicate, although only minimally, with more than a few of the natives. This nourished my bruised ego from the Hong Kong experience a few days before. Within the dynamics of the tour group, I was now the one who could communicate with these Chinese people; the others that knew Cantonese were now the ones at a loss in China. Traveling with a group was also beneficial in that there was always someone close at hand to interpret if necessary. There were virtually no risks involved so my experience in China was invigorating to say the least. It was for these very reasons that I was able to sustain my interest, though not my study, for almost ten years before I could resume my Mandarin pursuits.

My return visits to China in 1991 and 1992 continued to be realized in what I thought to be an integrative orientation. I had convinced myself that it was my positive experiences from university and in China that contributed to my attitude to become more Chinese. However, I think that honestly, once again, I was instrumentally motivated.

Previously, I had thought that I would like to be more Chinese, i.e., to think Chinese and to appreciate the Chinese way of thinking that is often very different from the North American way of thinking. I have held firm to the notion that I am both Chinese and Canadian at the same time and feel very strongly that there are concepts in the East that are not a part of life in the West.

I know that to attain the level of oral proficiency and literacy that I desire, I would have to immerse myself in Beijing for an extended period of time (one year at the very least; two to three years would be much better). My excursions in 1991 and 1992 have given me a taste of the accelerated language development that might result if I chose to acculturate to China. However, realistically, I do not wish to live like the Chinese in China, for I am a Canadian; a product of the West! Living the present standard of living in China would be somewhat of a hardship, to be sure.

The conclusion to be drawn from this portrayal would be that I need to learn Mandarin for reasons other than to be like Chinese people in China that speak Mandarin. I need to be better at Mandarin so that I can teach upper level language courses and raise my social and self-image. I would rather retain my Canadian identity that has privileged access to the Chinese culture, in my western world. My Chinese Canadian identity is something different from someone who is Chinese and lives in another country.

With regards to the level of success that I was able to achieve while in China, I have been praised by my language teachers for taking risks with the language in order to be understood. I was not unlike a child language learner, happy to experiment and play with the new language and not worried about how the stumbling is perceived by others. In a foreign country so far from home, I do not have to retain my Canadian school-teacher identity (language ego). I can become a student once again who needs to experiment with language like a juvenile first language learner in order to master it.

My personal language history seems to endorse the Schumannesque concept that learning second languages is strongly influenced by learners' social, psychological, and affective appraisal systems. The eventual successful or unsuccessful acquisition of second languages is all in your head!

Commentary

Donna Mah's account highlights several interesting factors in second language learning. First, Donna is a fourth-generation Chinese-Canadian. English was the primary language of her home, but Donna developed some receptive competence in Cantonese through exposure to that language from her parents and grandparents. She had a positive appraisal of this early experience, and she feels it may have influenced her attitudes about language learning in general.

Second, her study of French, German, and Mandarin were responses to university elective requirements. Her experiences studying French in high school were enjoyable, but her interest began to wane after two years of studying French literature as an elective in the university. The following year she turned to German as an elective and did very well, but was then attracted to Chinese in her third year, and decided to pursue that language instead of German. Here Donna points out that her major motivation for studying these languages was twofold: to fulfill requirements and to get good grades in order to improve her grade point average.

When Donna took up Chinese, it opened the road for an integrative orientation to influence her language learning. But then she faced competition between language varieties—Cantonese and Mandarin. Cantonese linked her to her home community, but Mandarin was the only dialect taught. Mandarin, however, carried prestige value and this attribute led to Donna receiving parental encouragement to study that variety of Chinese.

Later trips to Hong Kong and Beijing resulted in differential appraisals of these two reference groups. Negative appraisals of the Cantonese speakers in Hong Kong and positive appraisals (coupled with successful performance) in Beijing resulted in an integrative orientation toward Mandarin speakers.

Finally, at the end of her account, identity issues seem settled. Donna sees herself as a Chinese-Canadian and her motivation for the continued acquistion of Mandarin is now instrumental—so that she can teach upper-level language courses. This history captures the dynamic nature of appraisal and consequent motivation in SLA. It can sometimes be instrumental and sometimes integrative, sometimes both. The dynamic can only be captured by longitudinal or historical (i.e., autobiographical) research.

Mayumi Noguchi I

English has been my favorite subject ever since I entered junior high school (when most Japanese students start to learn a foreign language). Right before spring break when I was fourteen years old, my father asked me if I wanted to go to the U.S. on a two-week homestay program in order to experience the world outside Japan. At that time, however, his offer did not appeal to me at all. (I was more interested in other things, such as swimming.) Exactly one year later, he asked me the same question with a kind of threat this time. He said, "The world is requiring more and more internationalized people because we live in the time where no one country can live by itself. Japan's economic power cannot continue to grow without a reciprocal relationship with other countries, such as the U.S. It will be a rewarding and educational experience for you to go to the U.S. at this age, but if you say no this time, I will never ever make this sort of offer to you again. This is the last chance." How could I say no? After all, I told myself, I have always been good at English; there should not be a problem.

"Is this your first time to come to America?" "Four days ago." ". . . ?" Contrary to my assumption, this was the first conversation (or communication breakdown, to be more precise) I had with my host sister, Christine, when we first met in Los Angeles. Right after this conversation took place, my host father told his daughter to use an English-Japanese dictionary. It was too late for me to say "Yes, this is my first time to come to America, I arrived in Los Angeles four days ago." When we got home, Christine asked me something I did not understand. But since it was a yes/no question, I took a chance and said yes. (For some psychological reason, it is always easier for us Japanese to say "yes" than "no".) Then she gave me a sandwich. I had a big breakfast that day and there was no room in my stomach for it to fit in. Eating the sandwich, I thought, whenever you do not understand what a person says to you, it is better to ask for clarification than to put yourself in a difficult situation. Following the dreadful lunch was another lesson. Christine said something pointing at the door to her room and left. I was alone in the kitchen for a while, thinking. She went to her room, saying something with the word 'back.' Did she mean, "Let's go 'back' to my room?" As soon as I entered her room and saw her startled, I knew that she did not mean what I thought she might have meant. Then she said, "I said, 'I will be right back'" in a read-my-lips way. To ask is but a moment's shame. After a long day, I went to the bathroom before going to bed and looked in the mirror, asking myself what made it so difficult to communicate with the family. What made it so frustrating, despite the family's great efforts to communicate with me, was that I could neither understand what they were saying, nor could I make myself understood to them. By the end of the first day, I had totally lost confidence in my English.

After a couple of days, however, I became able to understand most of what Christine (but not the others) was saying. She was talking more clearly and slowly than before. When I did not understand what someone else said, she would paraphrase it for me. I had a chance to go to junior high school with her for a week, and she introduced her friends to me. They asked me some questions, such as "Are Japanese houses made of paper?" and "Do you wear *kimono* when you go to school?" These questions shocked me, but there were more to come: "Do you have a boyfriend?"; "Is he cute?"; and the ultimate question was, "What is he like in bed?" I was fifteen years old at that time and those girls were a year younger.

During this short visit to the U.S., I experienced both language shock and culture shock. However, it did not negatively affect my language learning. It was quite the contrary; I considered it as a rewarding and educational experience as my father had wished it to be, and by the end of this two-week homestay, I had made a decision to come back to the U.S., learn more about its culture, become fluent in English, and communicate with the native speakers freely (or at least to become able to describe what my boyfriend is like—regardless of where he is).

Having experienced the difficulty in communication with the native English speakers, I came to realize that English, which I was learning in school, was of no use in real contexts. As soon as I returned home, I told my parents that I wanted to quit high school in Japan and go back to the U.S. Apparently my father thought that he had made a big mistake by sending me to the U.S. After I finally convinced them, however, my grandmother who had always had the most influence on me dissuaded me. She, who had, after finishing higher education in Japan, graduated from university in Alabama over sixty years ago, told me that it would not be too late to go and study in the U.S. after finishing high school and becoming more mature. In the meantime, I had to study the language on my own because I had lost faith in the way English was taught at school. I thought that it was vital to expose myself to English on a daily basis, and since I was keeping a diary at that time, I decided to write it in English in

me of them said sarcastically, "You must be diligent. You are
ifferent from us. You are superior, aren't you?" and "If you can
peak English so well, why don't you go to UVM (University of
Vermont, which was a few minutes away from SMC) instead?"
Although I expected beforehand that I might face some difficul-
ies in associating with American students, I did not anticipate
problems among Japanese students.

Fortunately, after a placement test (Michigan Test), I was
placed in the highest level and was the only Japanese in the
class. During the first week of classes, however, I did not know
how to keep up with the other students who were mostly from
South America, Central America, and some European countries.
I had no problem with grammar and reading and writing classes,
but a big problem arose in the speaking class, which was based
mainly on discussions. As has frequently been noted, English
teaching in Japan stresses grammar and reading and writing,
not speaking or listening. I did not know how to speak up or state
my opinions in class (which might not be due only to the way
English was taught in Japan, though), while the others spoke
like machine guns. Before I said a word, the topic was already
changed. I was too conscious of grammar.

One day the speaking class teacher brought up a topic about
Japan for class discussion and asked me some questions. Because
I was familiar with the topic, I did not have to think too much
about what to say before answering questions. Then the other
students started asking me questions as well. After I answered
their questions and confirmed that they understood what I had
said, I felt that I could finally become a member of the class.
When I was leaving the classroom satisfied with my achievement, the teacher came to me and said, "You guys are from all
over the world, and your languages vary greatly. In order to
exchange opinions with each other, you must use a common language—English. People would not understand you or learn about
your country unless you speak up." Then I realized that he had
chosen the topic of Japan in order to give me a chance to participate in the discussion. I was grateful to him for that and wanted
to show him my appreciation. Since then I became one of the
most noisy students of his without being too grammar-conscious.
In addition, I fully realized that English was not only a language
to learn and master but also a means to learn other things.

order to increase my vocabulary and become able to exp
thoughts in English. In addition, I took advantage of b
TV and forced myself to watch the movies, news, and oth
grams (e.g., Sesame Street) broadcast in English in order
ter my listening comprehension and to learn phrases
frequently in everyday conversation. I gradually became u
the sound of English, and whenever I did not understan
meaning of a chunk of language, I looked it up in the dictio
and wrote it down along with phonetic symbols. (I did not k
until Christine pointed it out that my "thank you" was
nounced "sank you," "I think" was "I sink," and that my "r" and
were indistinguishable.)

Three years later, with my strong desire to become fluent
English and to learn more about American culture, I enter
Kansai Gaidai College (Kansai Junior College of Foreign La
guages), which was famous for its student exchange progra
with over 100 institutions in the U.S. In the first year in college,
participated in a summer program at Kansai Gaidai Hawaii College, but because students there were all Japanese, I always
spoke Japanese outside the classroom and could not improve my
English proficiency. Instead it made my desire to study at an
"American" university grow even stronger. After passing the
screening exam (TOEFL, English general tests, oral interviews
in English and Japanese), I was sent to Saint Michael's College
in Vermont as an exchange student for the academic year of
1988–89. Since my TOEFL score was not high enough to take a
full regular course-load with American students from the first
semester, I was enrolled in an ESL program first. I was nervous
because I was the first exchange student to SMC and was sent
there alone. I felt pressure that I was obliged to do well both academically and socially as a representative of KG.

As soon as I arrived at the SMC campus, I met many Japanese. They were always together in a group, spent weekends
watching Japanese videos, and, needless to say, spoke Japanese
all the time. There was, like in Japanese society, a hierarchy of
group leadership and group standards. The first thing I did was
try not to get close to them, while they were ready to welcome me
as a newcomer. When they found out that I was an exchange student who received a scholarship that covered the tuition and
room and board fees, I saw a sudden hostility on their faces.

Sometimes we criticized our own countries, and sometimes bragged about them. I could see my own culture from a different perspective. The classes were always like a world exposition.

During pre-departure orientation sessions at KG, we were repeatedly warned about the need to study diligently. Should we get less than a 2.7 GPA during the first semester we would be forced to return to Japan immediately and refund the scholarship. However, I did not want to spend all the time studying in the library without interacting with other students. I tried to get through with homework as fast as possible and interact with other students as much as possible. I did not consider beforehand that I would associate with foreign students because my primary motivation to study in the U.S. was to improve my proficiency in English, nor did I plan to waste time talking with non-English speakers. However, it did not take long to find out that I was wrong. As I mentioned before because I was very grammar-conscious, I tended to be shy or nervous when talking to Americans. I was always concerned about what others would think or how they would react when I spoke halting English. But it did not happen when I was talking with other foreign students, for I knew that they had language difficulties as much as I did. We were very understanding of each other and were free from hesitation. We could compare how we felt about Americans and/or America and could criticize what we did not like without being interfered with by Americans. And, most importantly, I could learn so many things about so many countries that broadened my perspective. I was impressed with those students from developing countries who were eager to pursue an education in order to contribute to the development of their countries. Each of those friends made me persevere and willing to put forth whatever effort was necessary to accomplish the task or goal.

Before starting my study at SMC I spent summer holidays with some American friends who formerly studied at KG. They told me not to expect Americans to help me or take good care of me like we Japanese did for foreign students at KG. They advised me to be aggressive, assertive, and act like Americans. The first stereotype of Americans that came to my mind was individualism. To survive in the U.S. I had to be independent and act as an individual, not as a group member. I decided that the way to experience American culture and to improve my English was to become as American as possible, and I judged that nine months in the U.S. was not going to jeopardize my basic identity and system of values. As a result, people said that I was not a typical Japanese, which was favorable to most of the foreign and American students and unacceptable to the aforementioned Japanese student group.

I consider myself lucky to be given an opportunity (thanks to my father) ten years ago to motivate myself to learn English. As can be seen above, my success in language learning seems to be attributed to affective factors. My English learning started with a strong motive to become able to communicate with the native English speakers. Although I was at first integratively motivated, during the study abroad my motivation also became instrumentally oriented. It was because I had to face job hunting immediately after I returned. For me, integrative and instrumental motivations coexisted; I wanted to get a job that would allow me to interact with the native English speakers, and in order to get such a job, I had to have a good command of English (and academic standing). As a result, I could get the kind of job I was interested in. I worked for the Center for International Education, which operated student exchange programs at KG, for two years after graduation from college and student-worked for two years while studying at KG University to earn a BA. My job was to deal with over 300 international students (mostly from the U.S.) in English on matters such as travel, medical concerns, health insurance, and homestay and/or personal problems, and assist with English-language correspondence and admission procedures.

I think that my speaking and writing skills were improved most in the past six years. None of my skills (speaking, reading, or writing) are complete and I do not anticipate they ever will be. My reading skill lags behind the other two; especially when it comes to expository texts, I often feel like it will take me forever to read and understand. Aside from a lack of knowledge in academic terminology, however, it could be attributed to my reading skill in general, not only in English.

Besides motivation, praise, or recognition of my efforts by others was one of the factors to facilitate my learning; when I first received a favorable comment on my English, I was so happy that it made me work even harder in order to be praised again. (I remember that I used to work on learning big words to impress people.) In addition, my personality seemed to help my learning; I like to laugh and make people laugh, and I have found that it seems a universal phenomenon that the more of a sense of humor you have, the more friends you can make and hence the more interaction you have with people than otherwise. (By exploring how to make American friends laugh, I found that the Japanese sense of humor and that of the U.S. differed.) Also, whenever I met someone who spoke English better than I, I always felt that I wanted to be as good as s/he was (envy?), and used to tell myself: if s/he can do it, I can do it.

I am not sure whether it is categorized as an inhibiting factor, but a certain cultural value may have inhibited improving my skills in communication with a certain sector of people. Because of what I think is the Japanese notion of respect for authority, I tended (and still do) to be nervous when communicating with teachers/professors in English. For example, I become extremely cautious not to be rude or imprudent and consequently become stiff. I have studied for nine months in the U.S. and for almost a year at UBC, but when communicating with a higher-status person such as a teacher, I was always and still am not as comfortable as I would be with colleagues, friends, etc. (status equals). (When I was working at the university in Japan, I did not have this problem even when I interacted in English with Western faculty probably because I considered them as colleagues.) After all, I may not be as acculturated as I thought I was. In terms of acculturation, I think that I was more acculturated when I was in the U.S. five years ago for, as I stated above, my top priority then was to acquire English, and thus I tried to become as American as possible.

Mayumi Noguchi II

The first stimulus appraisal concerning my second language learning took place when I entered junior high school and started learning English. I was at first stimulated by the novelty. I was thrilled and determined to challenge this newly introduced subject. Contrary to my determination, however, I only received 70% in the first mid-term exam. Then my English teacher called me aside and asked me why I did so poorly when one of my classmates (and best friend of mine) received 98%. I did not understand why he was concerned about my testscore when most of the students' marks were lower than mine. I was infuriated. I did not like the teacher very much even before that, but this incident could have inhibited me from further learning. But I decided that the poor mark I received was not attributed to my ability (internal locus), but to the teacher (external locus). In terms of controllability, although the teacher was beyond my control, my effort was within my control. My motivation to study English became instrumentally oriented to get the highest mark in class. In addition, I believed that if I could do so, it would ameliorate my self-image, which had apparently been hurt by this teacher. After I attained this goal in the final exam I came to really like English (and the teacher became really nice to me, although I still never liked him). From the time I became a top student in class, however, I started to have a fear of failure and hence became alert to the preservation and enhancement of self-image.

When my father asked me for the first time if I wanted to go to the U.S., the stimulus was appraised in terms of novelty, coping potential, and goal/need significance. I had never been abroad before and was afraid of being cut off from the supportive network of family and friends for the first time (novelty and coping mechanism). In addition, I was more interested in other things, such as swimming, at that moment, and going to the U.S. seemed irrelevant to my needs (need-significance). When he asked me the same question one year later, I was no longer engaged in club activities and had no excuse. Both preservation (rather than enhancement) of self-image and inclination to please my father made me accept his offer.

In the first few days of my homestay, I was constantly wishing I could have made time go faster. If Christine, my host sister, had not accommodated me (speaking more clearly and slowly than before, helping me understand what others were saying, etc.), I would have considered my visit to the U.S. very unpleasant and had a very negative image of its people; I could have withdrawn my efforts from learning the language further. Christine's understanding and acceptance of my inadequacies, anxieties, and insecurities did enable me to cope with the new environment. (She was my "surrogate family" as in Larsen and Smalley, 1972). Probably because of her, my general attitude toward Americans was positive such that I was motivated to come back to the U.S., learn more about its culture, become fluent in English, and communicate freely with English speakers.

When I was given information on a summer session at Hawaii College, the stimulus was evaluated according to whether the participation in it would promote the achievement of my goals and needs. It was appraised positively and I decided to participate in the program. I studied hard, despite its distractive atmosphere and climate, and grades I received were quite satisfactory. After a 54-day session, however, my oral proficiency did not improve as much as I had expected. I concluded that this unsuccessful outcome was attributed to the lack of interaction with the native English speakers. Classes were conducted from nine in the morning to four in the afternoon, five days a week, and I spent most of the time doing homework after school and on weekends. As a result, I was always either at school with other Japanese students or in a hotel room with a Japanese roommate, conversing in Japanese all the time.

Upon arrival at Saint Michael's College, I met more than a dozen Japanese who invited me to join them and have fun. Of course I wanted to make my one-year stay in the U.S. as enjoyable as possible, but when the stimulus was appraised in terms of goal/need significance based on the past experience that I could not improve my English proficiency in Hawaii because I always spoke Japanese with other students, the appraisal was negative. Therefore, I decided to avoid spending time with them as much as possible. They nevertheless exerted pressure to hold me within their group and eventually made me feel aversion to their collectivism. Not long after, I was told by some American and foreign students that American students had a negative image of Japanese students, because they were always hanging around in a group, speaking Japanese to each other all the time, and never making efforts to interact with Americans. When I managed to make some American friends, they told me that I was an atypical Japanese merely because I was trying to communicate with them and that they did not usually talk with Japanese students because, due to lack of effort, the Japanese students' English was very poor. I was mortified and felt anger toward those Japanese students who apparently made non-Japanese students have such an impression of any Japanese students.

This aversion to the Japanese group and my belief that I would not improve my English as long as I kept speaking Japanese resulted in my isolation from other Japanese students.

In order to prove that I was not one of them, and to have as little contact as possible with them, the first thing I did was to study hard. Consequently, I was placed in the highest level in ESL and was the only Japanese in the class, which was based mainly on discussion. This stimulus situation was negatively appraised according to compatibility with my coping mechanisms, and I was inclined to ask my academic advisor to place me in a lower level which was less discussion-oriented. However, the stimulus appraisal according to whether or not it would promote the achievement of my goals and needs (i.e., improvement of English proficiency, especially oral) was positive. Or it could be that my integrative motivation overrode the negative stimulus appraisal evaluated in terms of compatibility with coping mechanisms. In the meantime, I remained silent and grammar-conscious, trying to figure out how I could break the ice and participate in discussion.

Then one day the teacher brought up a topic about Japan for class discussion and asked me for opinions. This stimulus was appraised according to whether it was compatible with my coping mechanisms right away, and the positive appraisal gave me the go-ahead. Since I was familiar with the topic, it did not require me to think too much before opening my mouth. Subsequently, the other students started to show interest in what I had said, and before long I found myself taking part in discussion. It made me feel like I had finally become part of the class. After this event, I was positively stimulated by its pleasantness to partake actively in discussion. The teacher, like Christine, was the "surrogate family," and he had a deep understanding of my inadequacies, anxieties, and insecurities, and helped me overcome the psychological barriers to my learning. Although it did not happen overnight, he played a significant role as a facilitating factor in my learning. After I was convinced that the way he structured the ESL class was to make it more likely that the students would succeed rather than fail, I became less threatened and less grammar-conscious and hence my learning was facilitated.

During pre-departure orientation sessions at my university, we were repeatedly warned about the need to study diligently.

Should we get less than a 2.7 GPA during the first semester we would be forced to return to Japan immediately and refund the scholarship. While in the U.S., each exchange student received a follow-up warning from the university. I appraised this stimulus in terms of need-significance and generated negative evaluation based again on the experience in Hawaii. If I had not ascribed lack of success in the development of my communication skills in Hawaii to the lack of interaction with the English speakers, the appraisal would have been positive and I would have attended to the stimulus, namely, studied all the time without interacting with other students in order to retain good academic standing. (Nonetheless, since my fear of failure was playing a significant role in my learning, I did not spend all my time interacting with them without studying.)

My primary motivation for language learning was integrative (i.e., desire to learn English in order to become fluent in English and communicate with English speakers). Prior to my study at SMC, I was advised by American friends to become aggressive, assertive, and act like Americans in order to survive and complete the study successfully in the U.S. I was not certain whether or not it was required of me to do so at that time and, thus, I assume that this stimulus was not appraised on the spot. When informed of the impressions of Japanese students generally held by American students, however, the stimulus was appraised. In terms of my goal/need significance, the appraisal was positive and hence I attended to the stimulus; I decided the best way to experience American culture and to improve my English proficiency was to become as American as possible and judged that nine months in the U.S. was not going to jeopardize my basic identity and system of values. When there was a large contingent of Japanese students, it was very easy to withdraw into the security of the Japanese group, to spend weekends watching Japanese videos and cooking Japanese food. If I did so, however, American students would think that I was just another one of those Japanese and it would allow me only superficial contact, if any, with Americans, which would not be sufficient to fulfill my goal and need. Therefore, I tried to be independent and act as an individual, not as a group member as was Japanese social norm. In other words, my integratively oriented motivation fostered ego permeability.

My integrative motivation, which consisted of the desire to learn American culture, to become fluent in English, and to communicate with the native English speakers, seems to be the most important factor in my English learning. However, during the study abroad it also became instrumentally oriented. As the academic year at SMC was drawing to an end, I started to think that I wanted to get a job that would allow me to interact with English speakers, and in order to get such a job, I thought that I had to have a good command of English (and good academic standing).

Upon completion of the one-year study abroad, I was offered an administrative staff position by the Center for International Education at my university. This stimulus was appraised according to whether it would promote the achievement of my goals and needs, whether it was compatible with my coping requirements, and whether it would enhance my self-image. The appraisals were all positive and hence I took the job. At the same time, I experienced pride and self-esteem because I understood that my ability and effort in language learning were recognized by the university.

Commentary

Mayumi Noguchi's language biography illustrates the role of other individuals in fostering stimulus appraisals. Her father's near insistence that she go to the United States for a homestay led to an appraisal profile that ultimately resulted in a high degree of proficiency in English. Mayumi was not excited about going to the U.S.; she would have preferred to remain in Japan to pursue her swimming and to enjoy the company of her teenage friends, but her father imposed his value system on her; ultimately, out of respect she conceded, and the acquisition of English became a value for her. This scenario shows how our stimulus-appraisal systems are often socialized by others. Parents push children to try certain things—foods, musical instruments, sports, school subjects, and so forth. Children may resist and never engage in these activities, or they may try them for a while and then abandon them, or they may, as Mayumi did, engage in the activity, appraise it positively and make it a value of their own.

Frequently, one does not have to be pressured to engage in something new, but because of an attraction to another person, one may willingly try things that would previously have been appraised neutrally or negatively. The motivation in such a situation is to be with, or to impress, or perhaps to compete with the other person. So one stimulus appraisal (e.g., for another person) can lead to an array of agents, objects, and events available for further appraisal. I think this once again illustrates that appraisal trajectories are unique.

Garold L. Murray

The Pursuit of a Glorious Life or How I Acquired a Second Language

> I am a part of all that I have met;
> Yet all experience is an arch wherethrough
> Gleams that untravelled world whose margin fades
> Forever and forever when I move.
> (*Ulysses*, A., Lord Tennyson)

I was not born by the sea, but in a green, winding river valley on land my family had farmed for generations in the heart of anglophone New Brunswick. Interestingly, this place of my childhood was only an hour and thirty minute drive from the Acadian Peninsula and the sea. But we never went there. Only my grandfather made the trip in the fall to hire the French-speaking men to work in his lumber camps after the fishing season had ended. Yet, in spite of my land-locked upbringing, it has been by the sea that I've embarked upon adventure, fallen in love, scratched the surface of the mysteries of life, and acquired a second language.

I remember lying on the beach with Michèle, mesmerized by the ever-changing blue of the Mediterranean, my enchantment broken only by the occasional roar of a jumbo-jet as it took off, out, over the sea from Nice-Côte d'Azur airport. Michèle, *pied noire* by birth, was telling me about fleeing Algeria in her childhood with her mother and younger sister. I had a picture in my mind of a small, frightened child clutching her doll as she lay on a mattress in the dank cellar of her uncle's house. As I listened to her tale of refugees, escaping to the homeland only to become unwanted burdens to their families, it suddenly dawned on me that I was understanding this story told in the lilting French of Provence.

I had arrived in France a year before, not unlike Michèle, in exile from my home after becoming an innocent victim of a potential scandal that threatened the otherwise placid waters of the 1974 federal election campaign. Little planning went into my decision to study French. I simply put my finger on the map of France and quietly slipped out of Canada five days later.

But why France and why study French? Over the years I've been asked this question many times, especially by native speakers of the language. Usually the question is preceded by "Is your mother French?" The answer to the last question is a simple no. I have no answer to the first except to say that I always knew that I would live in the south of France and learn to speak French. I remember as a young child ushering my playmates onto the hayrack behind the barn, telling them to buckle their seatbelts in preparation for take-off. "Where are we going?" they would ask. My answer would always be the south of France. I also have a later memory of going to pick up the newspaper for my mother and, as I walked back to the house, reading a small three paragraph article on the front page: French Song Sparrow Dies. I had never heard of Edith Piaf, but was curiously moved by this report of her death. Ironically, the first French book I remember reading with the enjoyment of relative ease was her biography.

I arrived speaking no French in spite of years of classroom instruction, which relied on methods based on the grammar-translation, audio-lingual, and cognitive approaches. What I did possess was a strong foundation in the rudiments of grammar. Upon enrolling in an audio-visual language programme, *Voix et images de France,* in the *Faculté des lettres* of the Université de Nice, I was assigned to Mme. Terrzolo's class for beginners.

Although Mme. Terrzolo was an excellent teacher, she probably fulfilled a more important role as "den mother" to the motley collection of foreigners in her charge. On the second day when air-raid sirens started to wail and panic seized the class—the western world was embroiled in yet another Suez crisis with French and British navy fleets visibly anchored off the coast—Mme. Terrzolo launched into her role as the disseminator of cultural survival information. Her classes provided us a focus, but the real learning took place in the streets.

Our big concern was to make French friends with whom we could converse in the hopes of improving our language skills. Because the essence of friendship is communication and communication with us was particularly painful, especially for the French, our efforts didn't meet with a great deal of success. The danger was to spend all our time with fellow ex-pats commiserating over the trials of living in France and the foibles of the French. Mme. Terrzolo advised us to stick together for the time being and to communicate in our common language, namely French. To our dismay, we clearly had no choice.

My choice was Yoko. I sat across from her in class. She reeked of breeding and wealth, but both were tempered by a soul of Zen. Bashful glances soon became coy eye contact, eventually blossoming into hours in *cafés,* long walks along the *Promenade des anglais,* evenings in *discothèques,* and the occasional weekend in a *château* converted into a hotel. We spent a lot of time studying together. Our classes, conversational in nature, gave us nothing to study so we developed our own programme, which consisted of vocabulary, grammar, and reading. I read Agatha Christie in translation because of the simplicity and quality of the language, slowly graduating to Georges Simenon. How our conversations with each other, halting and ungrammatical, must have amused the French. Our time together was punctuated by long silences, but happily we did not need the French to teach us that love does not need words.

During the first four months, other than with Yoko, I didn't speak much French. Either I lacked the necessary language or the courage to use it. The French are not a patient, endearing lot when it comes to foreigners struggling with their language. Foreigner talk is not their strong suit. My only exception was Mme. Leclair, the maid in the small hotel where I had a studio, who mothered me linguistically and corrected my pronunciation. Madame was from the Loire and spoke a French that could bring tears to my eyes. It was during a Christmas vacation to Spain and Morocco that I decided "damn the French," resolving to speak their language in spite of them, if not to spite them.

The New Year brought many changes. Yoko was summoned back to Tokyo. I spent more time partying with the Brits. I spoke more French. And one day I met Michèle in the student cafeteria. We agreed to tutor each other in our native languages. Before long I was living with her and her lover, Dany, and *le petit pisseur*, a pup Dany had acquired about the same time Michèle had acquired me. We were young, life was play, and each day brought a new adventure.

Soon after that day on the beach with Michèle, I returned to Canada, where I got a temporary job teaching French in a school in my parents' village. Yet, we three were to be together again the next summer. Once more by the sea, but this time in a cottage on the ocean outside a small town on the Acadian Peninsula, where I had enrolled in an immersion programme for French second language teachers. Michèle was amazed by my fluency compared to the summer before. Surprising, if you consider I spent the winter in an English community.

That summer we discovered the joy, the music, the food, and the hospitality of the Acadian people. I made friends with a family who, over the years, have become more like family than friends. Ironically, I had traveled over three continents before I visited this place so close to my home. Our excitement at having uncovered a new world fueled our exuberance.

After another academic year of teaching French in my parents' village, I was ready for a change. However, I did manage to keep my sanity by flying to Montreal once a month to see French movies, etc. Over the years Montreal was to become my city of choice—a place where I could go and "live in French." But summer came and I was off to study French in Grenoble.

On my way I went to stay with Michèle and Dany, who were now living in Aix-en-Provence. During the days Michèle and I would drive through the sundrenched lavender fields of Haute Provence or we'd sunbathe on the rocks of the *Calanque*. In the evenings the three of us would sit in the café of the Cour Mirabeau, or we'd get together with friends. These were days of sunburnt mirth and evening strolls through the magical realm of Roi René.

In Grenoble only two of the classes were memorable. In one, I met Marisa, a teacher from Valencia, who was to become a close friend. Although French was our common language, we often turned to each other and spoke in our native languages without realizing it. At times it was impossible to believe that we came from different cultures a world apart. In the other class, a lecture on the French military, I rushed in late and slid into a seat at the back beside an elegant Polish woman named Maria who possessed an irresistible introverted Slavic charm. After all these years Maria and Marisa are still the best of friends.

On Friday nights, Dany and Michèle tore into the *cité universitaire* on their powerful motorbike. Within their first hour they had met Marisa, Maria, and the other Polish students, whose love of vodka mixed well with our love of fun. Somehow we met up with a student from the Antilles who had a fabulous collection of dance music in his residence room. This combination caused campus security and us no end of grief.

That fall I was once more back by the sea, enrolled at the Université de Moncton to do my B.Ed. They accepted me on the basis of my application and an interview, not suspecting that I couldn't really read in French. The ten months I spent with the 35 students in the programme marked my integration into the Acadian culture. When they spoke derisively about the English, I'd say what about me? They'd always respond, "T'es pas anglais, toé!" We worked hard, we played even harder, and I learned to read. Today, when I meet one of the group, I can see in their eyes a fondness and a tinge of regret for those days of friendship and frivolity.

My story goes on. That summer I went to live in Montreal. Then I moved back to New Brunswick to teach ESL in the French high school in English-speaking Fredericton. After that there were two long-term relationships, both with French Canadians. In all, I have lived and worked in French off and on for twenty years. This summer I head back to Montreal to be reunited with the Québecois "branch of the family" and to attend the wedding of a young man I watched grow up. How I long to be there, to celebrate and joke with them, to walk those streets!

Today I sit beside another sea reflecting on my story as a French language learner. It's really the story of my adult life. I don't think my French has evolved much since those days at the Université de Moncton. I may know more vocabulary but there are still huge gaps in my competence. My accent has regressed. I make all kinds of mistakes, especially when I'm nervous, many of which I can self-correct. I use more and more *anglicismes*. I need a proofreader for my writing. On the down side I find my vocabulary in English limited and I've lost the "natural" ability to know on which syllable I must place the accent when pronouncing an unfamiliar word. Yet, one thing is certain; learning French altered the course of my life.

A year after my first stay in France I received a letter from a friend telling me she had met Mme. Terrzolo. Not only did Mme. Terrzolo remember me but she said I was one of the best students she had ever had, which surprised me considering the mornings I arrived late for class after a sleepless night. They conjectured about what made me a good language learner: my personality? an irrepressible desire to communicate? a speaking style that was slow allowing me the time to focus on form? They missed the point. I did it for love.

Index

CREDITS

Chap. 7: Allman, W. F. (1994). Why IQ isn't destiny. *U.S. News & World Report, 117, 16,* (October 24), 78. © 1994 *U.S. News & World Report.* Reprinted with permission. Also by permission of author. After Cosmides & Tooby (1989), Cosmides (1989) and Griggs, R.A., & Cox, J. R.. (1982); adapted by permission of the publishers. / Chap. 4: Baron-Cohen, S. (1995). *Mindblindness: An essay on autism and theory of mind,* 30-132. © 1995 by MIT Press. Reprinted with permission. / Chap. 3: Clément, R., Dörnyei, Z., & Noels, K.A. (1994). Motivation, selfconfidence and group cohesion in the foreign language classroom. *Language Learning, 44,* 430, 435. © 1994 by *Language Learning.* Reprinted with permission. Also by permission of author. / Chap. 7: Cosmides, L. (1989). The logic of social exchange: Has natural selection shaped how humans reason? Studies with the Wason selection task. *Cognition, 31,* (April), 192. Reprinted with permission of Elsevier Science, Inc. Also by permission of author. Cosmides, L., & Tooby, J. (1989) Evolutionary psychology and the generation of culture, Part II. Case study: A computational theory of social exchange. *Ethology and Sociobiology, 10,* (January), 88. Reprinted with permission of Elsevier Science, Inc. Also by permission of author. / Chap. 3: Csikszentmihalyi, M. and Larsen, R. (1987) Validity and reliability of the experience-sampling method. *Journal of Nervous and Mental Disease, 175,* 535-36. Copyright © 1987 by Williams & Wilkins. Reprinted with permission by Waverly. Also by permission of author. / Chaps. 1, 2, 6: Damasio, A.R (1994). *Descartes' error: Emotion, reason, and the human brain,* 8-125. Copyright © 1994 by Antonio R. Damasio, M.D. Reprinted with permission of Putnam Publishing Group. Also by permission of author. / Chap. 3: Dörnyei, Z. (1994). Motivation and motivating in the foreign language classroom. *The Modern Language Journal, 78, 3,* (Autumn), 280. Reprinted with permission of The University of Wisconsin Press. Also by permission of author. / Chap. 5: Dörnyei, Z. (1996). Ten commandments for motivating language learners. Paper presented at TESOL, (March). Reprinted with permission of author. / Chap. 1: Edelman, G. (1992). *Bright air brilliant fire: On the matter of the mind,* 120, Copyright © 1992 by BasicBooks. Reprinted with permission of Basic Books, a division of HarperCollins Publishers. Also by permission of author. / Chap. 1: Frijda, N.H., Knipers, P., & ter Schure, E. (1989). Relations among emotion, appraisal, and emotional action readiness. *Journal of Personality & Social Psychology, 57,* 214, 215. © 1989 by the APA. Reprinted with permission.

introspective study of second language learning. In Brown, H.D., Crymes, R.H. & Yorio, C.A. (Eds.), *Teaching and learning: Trends in research and practice,* 243-247. Reprinted with permission of TESOL. Also by permission of author. / Chap. 2: Schumann, J.H. (1990). The role of the amygdala as a mediator of affect and cognition in second language acquisition. In Alatis, J. (Ed.) *Proceedings of the Georgetown University Round Table on Languages and Linguistics 1990/Linguistics, language teaching and language acquisition: The interdependence of theory, practice, and research,* 172-175. Portions of the text reprinted here with permission of Georgetown University Press. / Chap. 2: Schumann, J.H. (1994). Where is cognition: Emotion and cognition in second language acquisition. *Studies in Second Language Acquisition, 16,* 236-238. Copyright © 1994 by Cambridge University Press. Figure 2.4 and portions of the text reprinted here with permission of Cambridge University Press. / Chap. 4: Walsleben, M. (1976). Cognitive and affective factors influencing a learner of Persian (Farsi) including a journal of second language acquisition, 86-87. Unpublished manuscript, English Department (ESL Section), University of California, Los Angeles. (c) Marjorie Creswell Walsleben, Ph.D. Reprinted with permission. / Chap. 4: Watson, R. (1995). *The philosopher's demise: Learning French,* 1-133. © 1995 by The Curators of the University of Missouri. Reprinted with permission of the University of Missouri Press.